Copyright©2021 Kar

All rights reserved

The characters and events are as per author's view and purely based on her experience If anyone find it invasive it is not the author's intention.

No part of this book may be reproduced, or stored in a retrieval system, or transmitted in any form or by any means, electronic, mechanical, photo-copying, recording, or otherwise, without express written permission of the author.

Cover design by: Karma J Francomb

ISBN: 9798756743401
Imprint: Independently published

Acknowledgement

First of all, let me thank my two wonderful parents without them I would never have such a fantastic childhood and five beautiful sisters. Unfortunately, mum passed away in 2007 and she is dearly missed.

Then to my two-favourite persons in the world, my husband Jon Francomb and my son Yeshi Francomb. Without my husband this book won't be possible and thank you for your insight in shaping this book. And my son for existing in my life and being there for me during my downs.

To all my five lovely sisters for their support when I was in need especially my second sister Dorji Dolma. And my youngest sister Yeshey Choden and niece Kuenzang Choden for helping me with Dzongkha spelling.

I thank Wikipedia for providing me with online encyclopaedia, Robert Frost for inspiring me with his poem 'Woods are lovely dark and green' It is one of my favourite poems, Johnny Hates Jazz song, 'I wish I could turn back the clock,' which I always thought is a song by Sir Elton John.

John Milton for his insight on postlapsarian and prelapsarian. Shakespeare for inspiring me with quotes. Gardens of Dreams for information about six seasons and Voltaire's Candide for optimism.

The secret mountain by Enid Blyton my childhood favourite book.

To my editor David Taylor. Thank you, David, for your copy edit. You made the process easier than I thought it would be.

I say Kadrinchay La to all of you.

And lastly, to all the characters in my books. If any of you find it invasive it is not my intention. I have written it based on how I felt at that time and is purely based on my experience.

Karma J Francomb

KADRINCHAY
(Thank You)

About Author

Karma is from Bhutan, a small Himalayan kingdom sandwiched between India and China. She was born in Thimphu, Bhutan and brought up with five other sisters. She spent most of her childhood in Namseling.

This is her first book outlining the ups and downs, trials and tribulations of her journey in Bhutan from Child to motherhood and then arrival in the UK.

Now she is married with one child and lives in the High Peak, England immersing herself in the local cultures and taking full advantage of the beautiful Peaks and Dales.

PROLOGUE

'He wanted an Asian girl, a Western life is what she wanted.' A chiasmus!

Jonathan was in Bhutan working on an aircraft at an airport hangar. He had arrived only a few days ago from the UK with a colleague. He spotted a girl who, every now and then, was walking across the hangar floor; there was something about that girl that drew him to her.

Karma had worked at the same airline company for only a few months. One day, she was returning from the hangar stores, when she saw a *Chilip* (the Bhutanese name for a westerner) watching her. She pretended that she hadn't seen him and walked as quickly as she could back to her office.

Later that day, she was instructed to look after the engineer from England. She didn't know how to react to that. She was happy in one way and a bit nervous in another. She had no idea how to look after a *Chilip*. She had to ask a colleague for advice and for some help. Karma was a fast learner. Soon she was making cups of tea for Jonathan. They didn't say much but always nodded and smiled, happy to see each other. However, apart from these occasions, Jonathan didn't see much more of Karma during his first visit to Bhutan.

On his second visit to Bhutan, Jonathan got a chance to spend a whole day with Karma.

She guided him on a day's hike up to Taktsang monastery. They had dinner together that evening; he really liked what he saw in her.

On his third visit, Karma met him on his arrival at the airport. They soon became better acquainted and started talking about books, family and hobbies.

They saw each other here and there but never alone. It wasn't much but something is better than nothing. To quote an English phrase: *Every little helps.*

Part I

Postlapsarian.

Chapter 1

Pregnancy.

I was born in Bhutan, the eldest child with five sisters. We have a saying in my country: "A small family is a happy family and a big family is a royal family." This saying originated because our fourth king and his four wives have eleven children, therefore, the saying, 'big family, royal family' came into existence with the humorous addition of, 'small family, happy family'. My parents wanted a boy so they kept trying for one but instead they begot six daughters. I didn't mind not having a brother as I got along well with my sisters. They are wonderful girls and it is nice to be part of 'a royal family'.

I did not set a good example as the eldest child as I fell pregnant in my early twenties while in full-time education. When I missed my period, I didn't think much of it. However, with severe morning sickness it dawned on me that I could be a few months pregnant and my concentration was slowly deteriorating. All I wanted to do was curl up in my bed and go to sleep. It was awful. Whenever I went to the toilet, I would squat there for a few minutes trying to squeeze and contract as I willed the baby to come out. Then what would I do? It was just a depressing feeling. All I could do was go home and be a burden to my parents so I took a month's sick leave and went home. When the sick leave was nearly over, I didn't feel like going back to college so I tried to injure myself by breaking my foot. I picked up a heavy stone and threw it onto my right foot with as much force as I dared. It hurt like mad but there was nothing to show any injury to my foot. I had no excuse but to go back to college. My parents knew nothing about my pregnancy.

What was this morning sickness? Where did it come from? I wished that God had allowed this sickness to happen to the fathers and not the mothers. There was a time, so a story goes, that when women were pregnant, men got all the illness and pain pertaining to the pregnancy. Don't you think that would be fun? Men bearing all the pain while the women carried the baby. Until God changed it for the better or worse. The story goes like this:

A man was getting ready for labour pains as his wife was ready to deliver their baby. He was covered up with a blanket keeping himself warm, drinking melted butter for strength and preparing for the nasty pains to begin. The baby would be on its way anytime soon and it would need warm water for bathing. The butler was sent for some water, but before he returned the baby had arrived. After the baby's arrival, there was no sign of the father having gone through the labour pains and the butler still hadn't turned up with the warm water. The maid was sent to look for the butler, and when she found him, he was flat on the ground, soaked in sweat and unconscious. "This is no good," thought God, "I should let all women endure everything to do with a pregnancy." So, for convenience, the Almighty decided to bestow everything to do with pregnancy onto women.

As soon as I returned to college, I was summoned to the matron's office. I felt a foreboding and knew that something was not going to be good and I started to hyperventilate. After summoning all my courage, I knocked faintly on her door, filled with trepidation.

"Come in!" I heard her shout and I opened the door quietly and nervously. I stood at the threshold not able to move an inch. "Come in, sit down, don't be nervous," said the matron of my college. I entered and sat down on the sofa rigidly, staring straight ahead, not able to meet her gaze. "What is wrong with you? You have to be very open if you want me to help you, look at me!" she said sternly. I looked up and she was stood there, towering over my small physique. Did I detect a disobliging nature in her? Is it worth talking to her? I just hoped and prayed that a decision to send me away was not a *fait accompli* before we had even talked.

So young and naïve. I was twenty-two years old, a proper adult but still a girl at heart. Age has a way of creeping up on you with lots of surprises, but your mind tends to retaliate and keeps you young at heart. I had the body of a full-grown woman, yet my mind was not fully developed. I was a *tyro* and a novice in this adult world. I lacked savoir-faire, not knowing what to do and how to overcome such a predicament. I was nervous, scared and had never felt so alone in all my life. Although it was a strange feeling because I wasn't crying. Usually, my tears would flow easily like water rushing over a dam. My mum used to say, "This Karma, she can cry at the drop of a hat. She must be careful or fungi may sprout up under her eyes." She would also say, "I don't know why we bother buying vegetable oil, all we have to do is hang two empty, plastic bottles under her eyes and collect them to use." When I reminisce about my younger days, it always puts a smile on my face, but at the time, I did not find it amusing at all!

"I think I am pregnant. I missed the start of my menstruation cycle and I don't know for how long," I confessed in a mortified tone, keeping my tears at bay. I might have sounded pathetic, feeble, and frail but I couldn't help it. I could see my future career disappearing into thin air. I liked my college and I liked studying and this was the last thing I wanted: no career and an unknown future. I could see my world tumbling down in front of my eyes. Suddenly, it dawned on me that I was knee-deep in shit.

"Everything is going to be fine. Don't worry," said the matron, culminating her not so reassuring speech with a pat on my back. I felt like a dog receiving frugal affection; just a pat to keep it happy. I didn't feel any afflatus in her words, it was like an empty promise. I felt like someone begging for sympathy, but whether I was to get it or not was a big question. However, I didn't have long to wait for an answer to that question.

After waiting with much trepidation, I was summoned to her office again the next day. I didn't have a good friend who could lend their shoulder to cry on. You come to this world alone, you face your suffering alone and you die alone. No one can share this kind of suffering. People think they can but that is just people for you.

"I talked with our principal and she has given you two options," said the matron, "either leave the college quietly and come back for the exams after you have given birth or face the consequences of being expelled." Her words were unsympathetic. I had been so accurate when I spoke of a *fait accompli*; they had already made their decision before talking to me. I had no option but to leave immediately. I dragged myself to my room, slumped on my bed and my floodgates opened.

I couldn't believe my ears, she was supposed to be helping me, but asking me to leave quietly as a mouse was not exactly helping, or was it? I was so confused; I didn't know what to do. I had no one to talk to. My mum and dad were far away and, in those days, mobile phones didn't exist. So, I packed my things and left college not knowing what my future held. I felt like I was walking into the darkness of an abyss, where light is unknown.

Bless my parents, they received me with open arms and looked after me throughout my pregnancy. I did have some idea about birth control, but like a gormless teenager I didn't do anything. My desire for sex had obscured my judgement. I thought I could have sex freely without any consequences — how wrong I was. I had fallen into the pregnancy trap like many foolish, irrational, and stupid teenagers do. My brain was 'full of cow dung' like we Bhutanese say. Whether I liked it or not, I had to face the consequences for my foolishness and doltishness. What a joy! I found out later that my so-called 'first love' had been brainwashed by some of his friends. They had told him, "If you let her carry on with her studies, you will be sorry when she dumps you for a qualified man." All he wanted was to get me pregnant and he succeeded. Now I must bear the consequences.

For some reason, I thought my pregnancy was overdue; I don't know why I thought that as I didn't have a clue when my child had been conceived. Strange. Against my sagacity, I was told I was overdue because I might have stepped over a horse's tether in the early days of pregnancy, and stepping over a horse's tether again would solve the problem. Another solution was to cross a bridge. Therefore, I had to go and find a tethered horse. I could not see how I would have crossed a tether as there were not many horses in the village, but according to my mum, even if it was a broken tether, it would affect the pregnancy just as much. I started to wonder, what if I had to go through a horse's pregnancy term of twelve months? I was uncomfortable enough with nine months, imagine if I had to put up with another three!

I went hunting for horses tethered around the village, knocking on every door with not much luck. The houses in the village were spread out in groups of three or four or so, separated by terraced rice fields. It was not easy walking on the edge of terraced fields. Firstly, I was heavily pregnant. Secondly, the edge was narrow to walk on, and lastly, I was wearing flip flops. It was a very hot March day; the sun was beating down on me which didn't help at all. It made me feel dull, lethargic, and thirsty. I had to stop for a drink of water from a stream that was flowing through a bamboo tube; just a mouthful sent me to the glory of heaven.

"Delicious," I said sotto voce, as cool water went down my throat, cooling every inch of my body. I was enjoying my drink of water when I thought about one of my mum's sayings. She would tell me, "You can't say water is delicious. Water cannot be delicious as it has no taste. It is a bad omen to say this." I stopped drinking, got up and went on with my journey.

I searched the village, leaving no stone unturned, but without success. If I could have, I would have avoided visiting the last house but I had no choice. I came here with a mission, and I am not the kind of person who leaves a job half-done. So, I hiked my last bit of the journey to an isolated house at the top of a small hill; a hill that looks down on all the other houses that are surrounded by terraced rice fields. Walking precariously on the thin edge of the field, I continued my journey. Finally, I made it, sweat streaming down my face making my vision blurred. The door of the isolated house opened just as I raised my hand to knock on it. I then recognised the face of the person that had opened the door. It was Pasa, an old schoolfriend.

"Hello," said Pasa.

"I didn't know you lived here. I always wondered who the house belongs to," I replied.

"It belongs to my aunty, she is bedridden, so I visit now and then to keep an eye on her." Pasa looked miserable as he said this.

"Does she have a horse?" I queried. When he nodded, I couldn't believe my luck. "As you can see, I am pregnant and I think I am overdue. No sign of the baby and it is killing me. Some people think that I might have crossed a horse's tether and I have to cross one again to stop the jinx."

"Follow me," he said, so I followed eagerly. Behind the house, a big, black horse was tied to a tree, happily munching away on its lunch of straw.

"Will he let me cross its tether?" I asked nervously.

"Don't worry. Despite his stature he is very gentle. He won't hurt you," replied Pasa.

"I am a bit worried he will either kick me sideways or bite me," I said.

"Why sideways?" asked Pasa with a grin.

"That's what horses tend to do, kick backwards and cows kick sideways," I answered, mimicking the kicks.

"Ha ha!" he laughed. "Be careful. You can't go kicking in that manner with the size of your belly!"

"All right, can you hold him for me please?" I asked. I crossed the tether once. Not satisfied, I crossed again to make sure that I had done it. I then wondered if I had done the right thing crossing twice as once should have been enough—my brain had started to play tricks on me. I crossed again, making it three times. My brain was then telling me that I shouldn't have crossed a third time! After wracking my brain, I came to the decision that I had to make sure I crossed an odd number of times, as odd means undo and even means redo. By the time I'd figured this out, I had lost my count and I had to leave it at that. I thought I was genuinely coming up with a very good theory. After thanking Pasa, I set off back towards home.

My work did not stop there. I had the second task of crossing a bridge to complete; this was also supposed to help me deliver the baby on time. So, the next day, I walked ten kilometres and crossed two bridges, driving myself so hard that by the end of the day I was exhausted.

To get to these bridges, I left my parents' house and walked alongside the road. I then dropped down to the valley near Wang Chu (Wang - river) where I crossed a suspension bridge. As I crossed the bridge, I made sure that I looked ahead of me and not down at the fast velocity of Wang Chu as this would make me shake with fear. I crossed the bridge at an alarming speed for a pregnant woman! By the time I reached an apple orchard on the other side, I was my normal self, enjoying the beauty of nature. The apple blossoms of white and pink were starting to pop out and were on the verge of blossoming fully. I waddled along the path towards my destination, taking in the stunning views of mountains standing majestically on both sides and also the landscapes of green meadows.

I had crossed one bridge, and for good luck, I decided that I would cross another.

As I walked along a well-trodden path on the hillside that runs parallel to the river, I spotted an eagle diving swiftly into the rapid water. Within a few seconds, it came out again with a helpless trout; its talons dug deep into the fish's head. The poor trout was not able to do anything other than flap its tail. I was very lucky to witness this sight twice, once as a child and now as an adult, as you don't often see eagles hunting. I was intrigued so I followed the eagle and luckily it was heading alongside my path. Suddenly, it dived and landed ahead of me, but at a distance where I was too far away to see any details. I was curious to find out why it had landed and so I walked to the part of the river where the eagle had dived. The eagle was nowhere to be seen, there was just a headless trout lying sadly on the riverbank. I didn't understand why this had happened and it is still a mystery to me.

Leaving the fish behind I continued walking until I crossed a second bridge, but this time it was a Bailey bridge. Bailey bridges are very common in Bhutan and are funded by the Canadian government. Two bridges crossed, the task more than completed, off I went, walking alongside a sawmill which was bursting with life. After the sawmill, I went past the paddy fields, through willow trees and then I scrambled up an uneven path that finally led onto a road. Within a few minutes of scrambling up that path, I was home.

That very night I went into labour! Did my belief in crossing the horse's tether and the bridges work – or was it just purely coincidental?

Chapter 2

Accouchement.

My adventure was over and I was severely fatigued as I went to bed. But lo and behold, I went into labour in the evening, and by six o'clock in the morning, I had driven myself to exhaustion. After a 10 km walk and twelve hours of labour, it came as no surprise that I did not have an ounce of strength left to push my baby into the world. My mum gave herself the task of melting butter for me as it is believed to build up the strength.

"Here sip this," my mother said, spoon feeding me. I didn't even have the strength to sit up straight. The very first sip was delicious and I slurped greedily. By the time I finished half a cup, I started to feel a bit queasy, but miraculously I got some strength back. If my parents weren't happy with my situation they never reacted or showed it, rather they gave me one hundred percent support. I could only say, '*Kadrinchay,* thank you,' to such parents.

I was in labour for twelve hours with no proper professional help, but as always, my parents were there to look after me, and my husband was hovering in the background. In those twelve hours I drank melted butter, clear soup made from beef bone marrow, went to sleep umpteen times, and was always woken up in pain. My mind started to wonder…why didn't God leave things as they were, men with the labour pains. It was as painful as getting kicked in the groin, or maybe not, I don't know how painful that is; men like to think that it is worse than giving birth!

"You had better stay away from me," I said looking at my husband.

"Why?" he asked with incredulity.

"Come closer," I said and gestured with my forefinger, and when he was close enough I whispered in his ear, "I may ask you to chop your penis off."

"Ha-ha," he cackled.

"I am not kidding."

"You think you are funny," he added.

"No, I am serious. Please…" but before I could finish saying what I wanted, the pain surged through me like a knife cutting through my lower abdomen. My back started to ache, but luckily the pain did not linger. It disappeared as soon as it had started, not giving me enough time to grit my teeth.

I was being facetious when I said I might ask him to cut off his penis. It is just one of many Bhutanese jokes:

A man was by his wife's side when she was giving birth to their first child, she was going through a painful, prolonged labour. She started abusing her husband: swearing, shouting at him, and trying to scratch his face. As if that could make the pain go away or subside, but in contrast it became worse.

"I don't want to see your dick again in my life if I have to endure this kind of pain at the end of nine months!" she shouted.

"Now calm down and breathe," the husband said soothingly.

"I am serious, get the hell out of here and chop off your dick," she said trying to punch him and throwing a paroxysm of rage.

"All right, all right, calm down. I am going to cut it off." Then, as he popped his head around the door cautiously, just in case she was in the mood to throw things, he added, "Are you sure that you don't want me to leave even a single inch?"

"Get the hell out of here and don't show your face until you have done your job properly!" she cried, at the top of her voice.

"Are you sure, are you sure?" he shouted back to her. There was silence for a few seconds and then there followed a chopping sound: *THUD!*

"There you go, it is chopped off completely," he said, reappearing at the door.

Months later, the wife looked at her husband with dreamy and horny eyes and asked, "Did you really chop it off?"

"Yes, I did, I chopped it off completely."

"Seriously? Not even an inch left?" asked the wife longingly.

"No, not even an inch my love," the man said. I wanted to avoid this kind of situation; that was why my husband's presence was not welcomed.

During the labour, my mum instructed my dad to get behind me and squeeze me gently. The notion of why me sitting upright, with my dad embracing me from behind, would make birthing a lot easier was difficult to comprehend, but I hadn't the energy to argue. I agreed without any protestation. What was he planning to do? Squeeze until the baby came out? I didn't know then and it is still a mystery. I was beyond caring. I wanted to get my baby out as soon as possible.

"Is everything ok here?" said one of our neighbours as she came sauntering in.

"Everything is all right here, and Karma is enjoying her labour, aren't you?" came my dad's sarcastic reply.

I had to tighten my grip on dad's hand when I felt the pain creeping up again. With every passing hour, the pain became fiercer and more unbearable with shorter intervals. An ache in my abdomen was like the ache I used to get when I ate too many raw strawberries with lots of sugar. I was in agony.

"I think I need to pick you up and shake you," said our neighbour, advancing towards me.

"Sto…" but before I could fully protest, she came around behind me, pushed my dad out of the way, picked me up and shook me as roughly as possible from side to side like a rag doll. She lifted my *kira* and peeked.

"Oh shit….the baby is on the way. I can see its head!" she shouted.

I didn't care if the whole world saw my Dolma Ku—the Bhutanese nickname for women's genitals—which literally means the statue of a goddess called *Dolma (Tara)*, the mother of liberation in Mahayana Buddhism. I know it is a very strange way to nickname a woman's private parts, but Dolma Ku became a cliché in Bhutan.

God knows how long the baby was stuck there. I didn't even feel the baby's head between my legs until the neighbour pointed it out. Now come to think of it, I did wonder about the funny sensation of a ball that was stuck in my Dolma Ku, but the excruciating pain distracted me.

"Look, look, the baby's head and that's my doing. I don't think the baby was willing to come out any sooner if I hadn't shaken her," the neighbour was exclaiming proudly, looking at my dad.

"Really?" I said to myself. All I wanted was to give birth so that both of us could have some peace and quiet.

I think it is a universal truth that when it is not their wife, daughter or relative in this situation, people tend to come up with all sorts of clever advice. Do this, don't do that—suddenly out of nowhere they become an expert in that field. It annoys me no end.

Finally, my baby came into the world, screaming and with the longest head shaped like a gherkin. Luckily, he was alive and healthy, weighing 3.5 kilos with jet black hair. I could tell by the look on his father's face that he was disappointed with the shape of the baby's head, my mum noticed his disappointment too.

"Don't worry, he will be fine. I promise in a few weeks' time his head will be as round as it should be," my mum said as she consoled him.

I don't think he even noticed how beautiful our baby was.

I know I didn't plan this pregnancy and I wished I had never become pregnant, but giving birth to a baby changed my perspective of life. My baby boy, with his jet-black hair and his little arms and legs flying all over the place without control, filled me with joy. My mum bundled him into a blanket and passed him to me. I touched my cheek to his and his skin was soft as butter. I wanted to stay like that forever, inhaling his smell.

My mum was right. In a week's time his head was as round as a football, but my health had deteriorated. I was not able to stand, I had lost my grip and I had an appetite for nothing, I was heading towards the darker side of my life. It was like a knot entangled and refusing to undo and I could hear longanimity knocking, as loud as possible.

When you think life couldn't get worse, it can throw unimaginable things at you.

Chapter 3

Losing the dream.

March 1998, I was supposed to sit my college exams. I had six subjects: Maths, Chemistry, Physics, Biology, English, and Dzongkha. After I was kicked out of the college, I was busy being pregnant so I didn't have the time to revise. It surprised me to know that I still wanted to take the exams. I must have been mad!

"I have arranged a lift to take us to college for your exams tomorrow," my husband said.

"OK, how? And with whom?" I asked inquisitively. I had a premonition that it wouldn't go according to plan.

"My friend has a taxi and he is going to give us a lift. We will stay with my sister until you finish your exams, and I will look after our baby."

"It is not a bad idea, hopefully he will turn up," I said.

"He will pick us up at six in the morning, and I think an hour to get there should be enough."

"I would prefer more than an hour, but if you say so that is fine," I said, still not sure how this could work. I can be a bit jittery when I need to go somewhere, and I like to be there well in advance. The presentiment I was having didn't go away, but I had to tell myself time and time again that it would be all right and would go as planned.

That night we packed all our things and were up at the crack of dawn. Before six in the morning, we were outside waiting patiently. Six o'clock came and went with no sign of his friend. By seven o'clock, I was very agitated and wearing myself down with nerves. I hate it when people don't keep to their word.

"I don't think he is coming. I have to do something," my husband said, running around, not knowing what to do. Finally, he decided to try to get help from our neighbour, but to no avail. I knew the reason behind our neighbour's refusal to help.

"Karma, what is the use of hanging around your husband," this neighbour once said to me when I was pregnant. "He can't support you and the baby you are carrying. I am rich, I can get a place for you and your unborn child. I will build you a house just by the river." If it was someone else, he was suggesting that to, they might have slapped him hard across the face for saying it, but I am not that someone else.

"Sorry, it is very kind of you, but I love my husband and I want to be with him. Anyway, you are already married. What would you do about your wife and children?" I asked, intending to make him feel guilty.

"Look, I have got my reasons and I don't think you are in a position to ask," he said audaciously.

"What? You are suggesting that I have an affair with you, but you are not ready to discuss your wife. I don't think that would work, please leave me alone," I said with finality.

When thinking about the comfort he could provide for me and my baby I was tempted, but the thought of sharing a bed with him made me feel nauseous.

"It would be lovely to go to bed with someone that has false teeth," said one of my neighbours facetiously, when we were once talking about him.

"Imagine kissing him without his false teeth. It would be like kissing a toothless granddad," another added.

"I knew he was into you. Do you remember how he once offered some nuts only to you, even though you were in a group of people?" asked the neighbour.

"He is not that old," I added irritably. I didn't even know why I was defending him.

"He is too old for you. I think he is as old as your dad." I did agree with her but that did not mean she had to go on and on.

"Poor guy, what is he supposed to do?" said another neighbour.

"What do you mean?" I asked.

"Didn't you know that his wife became pregnant by one of his friends?"

"Really?" I said wide-eyed, surprised by this revelation.

"Apparently, he had a vasectomy against his wife's wishes after their second child. He was never to be a father again, but fate has got something in store for him—his wife's pregnancy."

"That's what you get for going against your wife's wishes," I said, my need to defend him fading into the background.

"You are pregnant, and your husband has a tendency of flirting with other women, he might have thought of you as an easy target and that you would succumb to his blandishments," said my friend, Thuji.

"Really, I don't know what he took me for. I know my husband is not fully committed to me, but I can't give up on my relationship just like that," I responded.

"That is good of you, Karma. I think that guy was surprised when he found his wife was pregnant," Thuji added.

"Isn't it possible that the child is his? I heard that even after a vasectomy some men are capable of making their wives pregnant?" I asked.

"How is that possible?"

"I don't know, maybe it is just hearsay."

"What? When his balls were singed, how is that possible?" another one of our neighbours said with incredulity.

"I don't know, I just heard somewhere," I repeated.

"I think men become impotent after a vasectomy, unable to get an erection. So maybe his wife was not having enough and started to venture outside," added another neighbour, facetiously.

"Really, I think you are talking nonsense," I said, not believing a word. I know I had heard the same thing, but I didn't know how true it was. Apparently, after a vasectomy, a nerve is affected that is directly connected to a man's erection. Over the years, I heard people making fun of their friends whose husbands had had a vasectomy,

"I would rather have millions of children than go through the excruciating pain of having my balls chopped off," added another neighbour seriously.

My husband was not able to arrange another lift to my college and I didn't make it to my exams. My life went downhill from there, and even though my health didn't deteriorate overnight, it did gradually worsen.

At the age of 20, I lost my dream of going to university, studying engineering and medicine. It afflicted me adversely, but I hung on to my motto: *Whatever happens, happens for good.*

Chapter 4

Confinement.

I was too embarrassed to go for prenatal care. I had only visited the hospital twice throughout my pregnancy and that was my prenatal care done. This was not a great idea of mine as I was bedridden for about a year after my son was born.

We didn't realise then that it was due to a lack of prenatal care and not because, as we thought at the time, that I was afflicted by the spirit *Lu* (the god of serpents). My leg and hand movement had started to deteriorate, but instead of going to the hospital, my parents and I ended up offering an oblation to Lu and visiting a *Lama* (monk). It was foolish of us to choose religious ceremonies over medical treatment, but oblations are part of our tradition and custom. I know there is a certain truth to religious ceremonies, it does work for some things, but not for all, and the same applies to medical treatments. Nothing is guaranteed in this world, even scientific research. One day you are told that chocolate is bad for your health, but at other times you're told it is good for your health; so nothing is concrete and every idea has a flaw.

I had to be blessed, and the Lama made me inhale incense smoke and drink holy water, this was so an evil spirit wouldn't be able to invade me. At one point, I breathed in a lungful of smoke emanating from the burning incense which made me cough. I am not saying it was horrible, but I was poorly and even the nicest scent would put me off. I love the smell of incense sticks, but not when I am ill. There is a right time for everything.

"You should avoid eating meat products from now on," the Lama instructed.

"Why?" I enquired.

"Lu does not take kindly towards carnivores," the Lama said. From that day on, I had to live on dairy products and refrain from eating any meat products. I was becoming as emaciated as a skeleton.

My health deteriorated even further and we had no option but to go back to see the Lama. Some more oblations, but no improvement. I started to lose faith in praying. Since my illness I had done nothing but pray, but like my mum said, "God is not at your disposal, you can't summon God and ask for help only when you need it. Pray all the time and he may listen to you one day." I found that absurd when I was younger. Why should I pray when I don't need it? Like most people, I only like to pray when I need help.

During my second visit to the Lama, his verdict had changed.

"You must stop eating all dairy products now, it seems to be interfering with Lu, that is why you are going downhill."

"Surely, we can't do that. The poor child had some dried beef before giving birth and since then has lived on nothing but dairy products. I just think she should get back to a normal diet." My mum tried but protested feebly; she was never the one to assert her feelings. This time she did, even though it was a feeble attempt; nevertheless, it was better than no protest. She too might have had enough by then.

In Bhutan, it is normal for a leg of beef to be cut into strips and dried, that is the only cut we know, not like in the west where a cow can be dissected into different cuts e.g., fillet steak, rump steak, sirloin steak etc.

"It is up to you *Ama* (lady)," the Lama said, not very pleased with my mum's protest. I thought that was a bit harsh, but we were depending on him so much that we had no voice of our own. So, not enough protein or carbohydrates—it was no wonder that I became malnourished.

After six months of this, we decided to go to the hospital; I was diagnosed with a weak heart (a vague diagnosis) although the ECG result was fine. However, I didn't understand why I had to have a nasty injection. I had no idea what that injection was called and didn't bother asking. Just the thought of it made me feel nauseous. When I saw the nurse digging out the biggest needle I had ever seen in my life, I had to look away; it was fit for a horse, and I was no horse. What seemed like minutes later, I turned around and saw her filling the syringe with a white liquid. I looked away and shut my eyes. It was awful waiting there with my bare, skinny bum sticking up in the air, which is where I was to be injected. The worse bit was knowing that it was going to really hurt. I didn't know what the health assistant was playing at, she seemed to be taking much longer than needed; it felt like a lifetime for me, but in reality, was probably less than a minute. My eyes were hurting so much after squeezing them shut as tight as possible, and wishing I could faint or drop dead! The sudden touch of a cold hand brought me back to reality.

"Don't worry, it will not hurt," I heard her say, and within a fraction of a second, I could feel a needle making its way between the interstitial tissue of my cells, inciting sharp pains along its way. Millimetre by millimetre it made its way into my bony behind. I felt the bum-numbing pain after she had emptied the whole contents and I could feel it spreading throughout my body. It was worse than pins and needles. I wanted to cry out loud, but I had my pride, so I bit my lip to stop the cry from escaping. In spite of the bum-numbing injection, my health didn't improve.

Before I fully recovered, we had to move to Thimphu and find a place to live, as my mum and dad, who we were living with at the time, had decided to move down to our village due to financial constraints. We managed to find a single bedroomed flat, with a small kitchen and a communal toilet which stank. We lived there for almost a year as husband and wife. In Bhutan, once you start a family together, you are considered husband and wife, even though you are not legally married.

That year was the worst time of my adult life as I was bedridden. I used to lie by the window looking out, watching the world go by, wondering when I would be able to walk in the fresh air again. My only connection to the outside was the window. It was big enough to poke my head through, but not big enough to escape through in case of fire. Being constrained to bed was not easy, but it could sometimes be fun watching the world go by.

One day I was gazing out, bored to tears lying in bed. I spotted a nervous, edgy woman walking down the street. As soon as I laid my eyes on her I was thinking, *don't trip over!* As soon as this entered my thoughts, she went flying over and fell flat on her face. I didn't know why but I always found people tripping over hilarious. I went into convulsions of laughter. I went on and on laughing uncontrollably, having to hold my stomach as it hurt so much and tears streaming down my face—I couldn't stop.

Laughter is the best medicine I have heard, but I did not fully understand what it meant until then. I could feel the tensions leaving my body. I might have been in that state for a few minutes and it was the most relaxed I had felt for months. I was in momentary elation, which soon lapsed into misery. The cry of my baby brought me back to reality. I crawled back to feed him and all the aches and pains came back with a vengeance.

There were days when I would just sit there crying. It was so depressing, constrained to the bed, wishing this and that, and my little son fast asleep. There is nothing worse than being ill and confined to a claustrophobic room. My husband was always tired after a long day at work. He was having to cook, look after our baby's needs, especially washing nappies; this had to be done at the outside tap with icy cold water. By the time he came to bed, he would be so flat out even a bomb wouldn't have woken him up.

The daytime was the only time my little one would sleep. He used to cry from dusk to dawn and keep me awake the whole night long. I used to gently rock the hammock that we had made; that would sometimes work for a bit, but it wouldn't last long, and before I knew it, the crying and wailing would start again at the top of his voice. Poor baby, by morning his voice would be hoarse. I tried every trick possible: breastfeeding, rocking the hammock, holding him or ignoring him. No matter what, the crying would go on and on until dawn. Dawn was like a reverse alarm clock for him, and he would be fast asleep the whole day, waking up only for feeding. When my boy slept, I tried crying myself to sleep, but it was still hard to come by. I wished I had known the trick of counting sheep. Nowadays, when I am not able to sleep, I count sheep and it works like magic. Being new parents, we did not know how to deal with it, but now when I look back, I should have kept him awake during the daytime; this would make him sleep in the night, but we were not to know.

Sometimes I would try my best to get up and walk around, which took a huge amount of effort. After God knows how many attempts, I could manage to stand up with the aid of my elbows, which were the strongest part of my body. I even managed to take a few steps some days. It was like winning the lottery, my joy knew no bounds. *Failure is the pillar of success; if you fall once, try to get up twice.* That was what I did, I fell a hundred times, and tried to get up two hundred times. After a few months, I could at least get out and sit on the veranda and breathe fresh air rather than being stuck in that stale room. I could take a few steps here and there, but the pins and needles restricted lots of movement and the soreness of my feet did not help either. As soon as dusk settled in, the pins and needles would start with a vengeance, and I would be in agony the whole night long. One night, my husband decided to give me a treatment by sucking my toes through a hot bamboo straw, but even though it never took away the soreness, it was nice to be cosseted, pampered and looked after.

Our one-room flat was a squeeze for the three of us. To make matters worse, my sister-in-law and her husband announced that she wanted to stay with us for the latter end of her pregnancy, just in case she needed medical attention. I was not happy. Most people in Bhutan are family orientated. We tend to do lots of favours for each other, but this was a favour too far. My husband had decided to accommodate them without even discussing it with me. I know he was the breadwinner, but it would have been nice if he had asked for my opinion. After all, it is my home too. No job, no say I suppose. I hated being in that situation, but what could I do?

I distinctly remember one occasion, my husband bought me a pair of walking boots. I liked them so much, I used to virtually live in them. One day, another sister-in-law came to visit us and she immediately took a shine to them and wanted to exchange them for her cowboy boots. They were that beige colour which was not my favourite. As usual, without even asking me, he decided to exchange. I was so angry that I flung the boots into the field behind our house. I screamed at him when he arrived home later that evening.

"Why did you exchange my boots with your sister's cowboy boots? I don't even like them! You knew that!"

"OK, stop shouting. I will buy you another pair," he said indignantly.

"I don't want new ones. I want my old ones!" I shouted sounding petulant, but there is no comfort like your old boots, and for me too, there was nothing more comfortable than *my* old boots. It took me almost a year to break them in. Petulant or not, they were my boots and I think I had the right to act the way I did. Forget about being petulant, I could even murder someone for that!

"You always do things without consulting me," I said to my husband.

"I don't remember any occasion. Name one," he replied.

"Firstly, you decide to make me pregnant. And I lost everything I like, especially my education."

"Oh, shut up, you are not going to let me forget that, are you?" he said.

"Why should I? You maliciously made me pregnant?"

"I didn't rape you. You came to me in your…"

"Secondly, you decided on your own to buy stuff for your family without even letting me know." I had interrupted him before he could finish his last sentence.

"That's my money not yours. I work hard for it," he said proudly.

"Thirdly, you decide to swap my boots for the cowboy boots of your sister. Do you remember what you said when my sister Dorji wanted to borrow them for a day? And now this, you decide to invite your sister to stay with us when we don't even have enough room for…" I was not able to continue as tears started to stream down my face, making it impossible to go on. It was painful to think of what he had said about my sister Dorji.

"She is not staying here," he said, "she is only leaving her stuff. She will deliver her baby at the hospital, not here. Give me a break! Let's not talk about the past!" he said angrily.

"Yeah, I know, let the past be the past. Even dried shit will stink if you try digging it up, as my mum used to say." I regretted saying that as soon as I had said it. I realised that it was me who was digging up the past, not him. Too late to take it back.

A few days later, his sister turned up with all of her luggage. I didn't have time to regroup my thoughts and I couldn't go and say things in front of his sister. Luckily, she stayed only a night before she was whizzed off to the hospital. His sister left behind things like dried beef, a change of clothes and baby stuff at our place. Our room was more like a storage area than a bedroom. All her things were piled up at the foot of our mattress. One bag caught my attention as it was lying casually at the base, tempting me to explore it, but I didn't dare rummage through it while my husband was at home.

The much-awaited opportunity to explore the bag came sooner than I expected. My husband left for work and told me he would be going to the hospital to visit his sister. On this day, nothing interesting was happening outside when I poked my head through the window, so I decided to check the contents of the bag. I made my way to it taking a small step at a time. When I was within its reach, I plonked myself on the floor and dragged the bag between my legs. After a strenuous effort, I managed to untie the knot which held it closed. Inside were strips of dried beef.

I started to salivate as soon as I set my eyes on it. Dried beef, my favourite! Not being able to afford it, I hadn't had it for ages. The last time I had eaten dried beef was a year ago when I was pregnant. I knew it was so wrong to help myself to it, but the more I tried to suppress my temptation, the worse it got. It was just greed for dried beef; the more I tried to keep my eyes off it, the more I was drawn to it. So, I decided to help myself. I just managed to have a bite when my husband burst in with good news—a baby boy was born! As soon as he saw me with the beef, he accused me of stealing. I was so embarrassed; I had no other option but to burst into tears.

"Hey now, I didn't mean to accuse you. Just forget I said that OK? I will never breathe a word about it again. Now calm down and help yourself to some more if you want," said my husband as I cried. I had heard that tears can bring about sympathy from others. However, I wasn't seeking sympathy with my tears, it was purely out of embarrassment. I was truly mortified and tears just came flooding down my cheeks in runnels.

Dried beef is a special diet for a new mother. The new mother savours the dried beef dish even when it is made without chillies. The Bhutanese diet always includes chillies, but during these times the new mother must refrain. All they would be fed is red rice, and a simple dish of dried beef cooked in garlic, red onion, butter, salt, and water. Sometimes it could be chicken, fish, eggs, and cheese, but never pork. Pork is considered unhealthy for a new mother; don't ask me why.

Unfortunately, I never got to enjoy my maternity feast after the Lama (highly learned monk) instructed meat was not suitable for me. It could be because in the past I had more than my fair share, eating the leftover of my mum's five maternity feasts, two of which I could remember distinctly.

My husband got a few strips out of the bag and gave them to me, but I refused to accept. He insisted. I grabbed one and flung it across the room. I was too embarrassed and humiliated to behave in any other way. In the end, he left the beef where it landed. Then he tied the bag and put it back on top of the pile.

I ignored it for a day, but I lost my resolve on the second day. I happily munched on it when my husband was at work. Three days later, his sister was discharged from the hospital and after spending another night with us, she left us with all of her belongings, and the dried beef scenario was not mentioned again.

Chapter 5

Unexpected recovery: summer, 1999.

When life throws up the unexpected, no matter how strong and optimistic you are, it is very difficult to keep up with a Panglossian nature. Dr Pangloss, a character in Voltaire's *Candide* said: "All is for the best, in the best of all possible worlds." My optimism could only stretch to, *whatever happens, happens for good*, but nothing good seemed to be happening and my patience was wearing thin.

My mum never gave up looking for remedies, and she carried on offering solemn oblations. We had a huge stone in our village, near my aunt's house, which was believed to be Lu's (the Serpent god) shelter. Mum cleaned around the shelter, bathed it with milk and lit incense sticks every day for a week. I started to feel better, the pins and needles gradually abated, and I started to take small baby steps on the road to recovery. My shaky legs got steadier, I could manage to sit on the veranda and bask in the warmth of the winter sun. Then lo and behold, a week or so later, I was up and running; maybe not running, but I could walk without any aid. My euphoria knew no bounds and that was one of the happiest days of my life.

"*Kadrinchay*," I said to my mum, for persisting with the oblations.

You don't know how your body parts are interconnected and vital until you have an injury or are deprived of them with illness. Not being able to walk and move around for ages, it was nice to be heading back to normality, but I knew it was not going to be easy, and I had miles to go before I would have full use of my limbs again.

My nit endemic also disappeared quicker than it had started, and I could see the light at the end of the tunnel and envisage a happy future, but the light at the end of the tunnel turned out to be nothing but a chimera; happiness which I hoped for, but was illusory. It was just a dim bulb lighting the tunnel, and before I managed to reach the end, the bulb decided to pop leaving me in semi-darkness, and soon my life headed in the opposite direction of what I had hoped for. One should expect the unexpected. My relationship with my husband started to decline rapidly, and our amorous feelings were melting away like ice under the scorching sun. We were becoming a pugnacious and belligerent couple. Sometimes after a fallout, I would disappear in the middle of the night, carrying my baby with me on my back in a *kabney* (a handwoven long shawl) to my sister's house. With my unstable step, it was like walking on a cobbled path in high heels (I love wearing high heels!) very unsteady, but I managed to walk a kilometre from the top of the town to the bottom where my sister Dorji lived.

I didn't know why my husband never stopped me from walking away in the night, maybe he too had enough. After all, he was only human, not a saint.

My sister, Dorji, was as accommodating as ever. She would take me in no matter what time of day or night it was. I had done it dozens of times, but she never got sick of it, even though I would rush back into my husband's arms when he would come to get me the next day. I think that is unconditional sisterly love, to be there whenever she was wanted. She might have thought that I am silly, but sometimes this is how life goes, *C'est la vie*, things happen, but life goes on. Whenever my husband came to get me, looking apologetic, my anger would melt away and I always forgave him.

I know that Dorji could be blunt most of the time, but she never said anything like *leave him.* I am glad that she didn't, as this kind of thing needed to be sorted out in my own time. If she had encouraged me to leave him, I would have ignored her and that might have ended up building a wall between us.

Dorji was a godsend. She and her then husband used to come to visit me every day with snacks while I was bedridden. One day, she came with potato crackers which were a new product in town, from India. I had never tasted such a tasty cracker before. It was heavenly and ambrosial. I think it was down to the law of relativity, that nothing is good or bad, big or small…until you relate it to something else. I hadn't had a decent meal for a few weeks now, and to eat such a sybaritic snack took me to the higher realms of taste—like a King in this fable:

The king was so used to feeding on sybaritic feasts all the time, and after a while, he was getting fed up with it.

"I want to find someone who can cook a delicious meal, and I will reward him handsomely if I am impressed. If not, he will have to face the consequences," he announced to his crowd one day.

"I will cook for you, but your majesty must follow my rules strictly," a man volunteered in a chirpy voice. He came forward, bowed and fell to his knees in supplication, looking at the King through his lowered eyes.

"Prove it then!" ordered the King.

"Your Highness, starting from now, you are not to eat until I cook for you," the perturbed man said anxiously, but surprisingly, the King gladly accepted his proposal.

The man starved the King for two days, and while he slept the King was whining about his hunger.

"Bring me horses," the King said on the first day. "Get me a cow or an elephant. I want to eat anything," the King demanded on the second day. Then on the third day, the man appeared.

"Time to cook!" he said. He took one big, red potato and threw it onto the open fire. Immediately, all eyes fell upon him with curiosity, wondering what kind of special meal he was going to produce for the mighty King; one made from a potato that had been tossed onto a fire. When it was roasted to perfection, with a crispy skin, the man took it out, placed it onto a warm plate and cut it open, dividing it into four equal pieces. Finally, he added a big knob of butter to the potato. The hot steam from the potato sent melted butter running down its cut valleys.

"Time to serve now!" shouted the man confidently, seasoning it with salt and pepper.

"Looks yummy," the King said, itching to get his hands on it.

"Go slow now your highness. You are not supposed to gormandise. You must savour it, relish the melted butter and the hot potato." The man handed over the plate proudly to the King.

The King was sat there salivating, relishing the luxury of warm food. He took his first mouthful; it was unbelievably delicious!

"Mmmm very nice! I never thought potato could taste so good. Delicious! Thank you, thank you, you can now go and collect your reward."

So, like in the story, it is all relative. For me, even now, I like to buy potato crackers whenever I lay my eyes on them. It is still nice, but not as delicious as it was then. However, it brings back a happier memory of my confinement, and seeing my sister was one of the happiest times during my sickness. I would be like a child waiting for my mother to come back with a bag full of goodies!

Dorji was younger than me, but she was the first of the sisters to earn money and help the family. She gave up her schooling for me. I know education is free in Bhutan, but sometimes educating a child was not just about paying school fees. Things like uniforms, books, meals etc. The expense always adds up.

But whatever happens, happens for good, and there was a lucky happening for Dorji, in fact for all of us. She was taken on by the Bhutan Archery Federation to train and compete in international competitions. With her stipend, she was able to help support the family. By 1998, my parents started to run out of my father's army pension and had to move to the village. My mum inherited one acre of land and thirty terraced paddy fields, but without a house. They had to stay with one of the neighbours until they built their own. With the help of Dorji, they were able to build a tabernacle—a temporary shelter. My parents and four younger sisters lived in it for a few years. She helped my family whenever possible with the little money she was earning, but she didn't have enough to support them all the time or to build a proper house.

Years later, me and my fifth sister, Pinka (this is a pet name for my sister Ugyen Lhamo), were reminiscing and Pinka spoke to me with tears in her eyes.

"You know *Ashim* (elder sister), when I was little, we had just a roof over our head which was paid for by Dorji. We didn't have enough food and used to feed on dried, fried corn and black tea, which was not even made of proper tea leaves, but tea leaves made of dried wildflowers which would stick to our clothing like leeches."

"I know," I replied, also with tears in my eyes, "there was a time when we were starving and barely had one decent meal a day. I was in tears one day, as there was no more rice to cook.

My husband disappeared for a while. When I looked out of the window, there he was coming out of the shop with three packs of Maggi instant noodles. He bought them on credit. How sad is that?"

"When we didn't have enough for everybody, Mum and Dad used to have empty stomachs so they could feed us children. Aren't we lucky to have such parents?"

"*Kadrinchay*, *Apa* and *Aie*," we both said at the same time.

"I know we have the most wonderful parents in the world," I reminisced. "I love them so much. Do you remember our dad used to say never waste rice? One day, when rice abandons you, you will suffer."

"Did you go on buying Maggi on credit?" Pinka asked with inquisitiveness.

"No, the next day, he came home with fifty kilos of rice; then he disappeared and reappeared with five hundred grams of pork which had a thick layer of fat. I cooked that for dinner, and even sixteen years later, the taste of that pork still lingers at the back of my throat! That was one hell of a meal. I can never forget it!" I said salivating.

"That was nice of him," said Pinka.

"I know. There were good and bad times, but there were more bad times than good. Sometimes, we are so engrossed in our misery, that we don't tend to look beyond the end of our nose. I think we just ignored the good and brooded over the bad times."

"I know, it's not good, is it?"

"I think we saw a crack in our relationship and were determined and intent on making it wider," I added, with my eyes welling up again. "Do you remember? Oh, why am I asking you that? You weren't to know, you were so little then."

Our mum used to say: when you struggle, you will struggle even for a *cheltrum* (a *cheltrum* is equivalent to 0.1 British pence). I did wonder why someone would struggle over a *cheltrum*. I told her, I can see them lying around the house and I can pick them up. Now I know what she meant. Aren't we gormless when we are children? Every problem that adults face, we wonder why do they have to put themselves through so much misery; why can't they sort it out? Now as an adult, I wish problems could be as easy to sort out with a child's way of thinking.

"We had to get an advance on his salary to buy rice and pork," I said, "but what would we do next month? That was the big question and that was my situation; how could I help my family?" As I said that, I burst into tears.

"All is not bad, is it, *Ashim*? I could remember how our life changed after you got a job with the airline company in 2001. It was a turning point in our life, with yours and Ashim Dorji's income, we never ran out of rice or milk powder, and we started to have proper tea then. I know we didn't have a luxurious life, but we had all the necessities." Pinka spoke appreciatively, which consoled me.

"I suppose so. I think 2001 was the making of my life." I said drying my eyes.

"What more could you ask for? We don't need luxury. We are in a better position than most people from third world countries. We live in a beautiful and peaceful country. Gross National Happiness is our motto." Pinka said.

Bhutan is a beautiful country, located at the eastern end of the Himalayas. Even though we are sandwiched between two mighty powers, we are not well known to the world. We Bhutanese proudly say *Druk Yul, Land of The Thunder Dragon, Kingdom of Bhutan*. We have very rich vegetation and most of the population depends upon agriculture. Our fourth King came up with a policy called Gross National Happiness rather than the usual Gross National Profit and it consists of four pillars: promotion of sustainable development; preservation and promotion of cultural values; conservation of the natural environment and establishment of good governance. The people are happy. We have never been invaded by another country as we haven't any minerals, gold or things of high value, except when the British tried to take over during their time in India, but they never managed it. So, Bhutan is a most beautiful and peaceful country, with more than a hundred years ruled by a Monarchy. We are extremely lucky to have good and caring kings.

Even with my adult brain, I failed to foresee what was happening to our mum, which was evidently a chronic disease. I remember her suffering from gastritis; she was constantly in and out of the hospital, so I thought she was being looked after properly, but little did I know that her health was deteriorating. One day, I was asked to come down to the village to look after my younger sisters as my mum had to undergo some more treatment.

My parents and my four sisters were still living in our neighbour's house. We didn't have a car then and had to hire a taxi. I was not fully recovered and couldn't face such a long journey. I was feeling apprehensive, but I must go when duty calls.

We set off early one morning, in September. The sky was thick with clouds and ready to burst. It was the monsoon period when it rains cats and dogs. The day was very gloomy. We all set off: me, my baby and my husband, Dorji and her husband. The taxi boot was full of our luggage.

The taxi took us up the winding road towards Dochula (mountain pass) and down more zig-zagging roads towards Wangdiphodrang (another district in Western Bhutan). The road was as slippery as anything, and at one point, the driver misjudged the corner and we nearly went off the cliff. Luckily, he managed to steer back. From Wangdiphodrang the road is a bit wider, but this does not necessarily mean a clear road. To prove this, there were two major roadblocks due to landslides. We ended up waiting two hours for them to be cleared.

It was a very long journey. It took us six hours of driving, and two hours having to stop for the roadblocks. In Bhutan, landslides are very common and we get them mostly during the monsoon. These are major landslides, and every year many people die in them. During one monsoon, a southern Bhutan village was washed away; Bailey bridges and roads collapsed, and many people were caught up in it and died. Lucky for us that during our journey we had no more than roadblocks.

As the road condition worsened, the driver refused to go any further. We were still an hour's drive from the village or three to four hours on foot. Good job we had left very early in the morning and it was only one o'clock in the afternoon when the driver refused to go beyond that point. My husband had to head back in the taxi to Thimphu, as he was working the next day. After a brief valediction, we went our separate ways. Dorji, her husband and I to the village, my husband and the taxi driver back to Thimphu.

Dorji and her husband carried all our luggage, and with my son Yeshi on my back we set off. I think that was my actual journey towards recovery. We went along the crop fields and across the mountainside and then gently dropped down into the valley. Then we went up the mountain on the other side and through the dense forest. The journey was treacherous, and me being so unstable on my feet, I was slowing the journey. I had to let them go ahead of me, so they could reach the village first and send someone back to help me.

I had to crawl on all fours at times as the path was so slippery, and when I did this my baby would whine as it would make him uncomfortable. The path is easy to follow when you go with someone who knows the way, but I had never climbed this path before on my own. I was always with my parents leading the way. I followed footprints, which was a big mistake as I ended up on a wrong path. I seemed to be climbing and climbing with no sign of the straight, flat path that I distinctly remembered from the past. Suddenly, I came to an opening and looked down in dismay when I saw our village down in a distant valley. Then I realised that I had gone the wrong way. I had to drop down and take another difficult path, which eventually led me home.

As Dorji and her husband lost their way too, they were not able to send help for me, but they got there only a few minutes ahead of me. I did well. Actually, not just well but good. Indeed, I would say very good! I know I was tired at the end of the day, but I felt good to be on the road to recovery. Mum, Dad, Dorji and her husband left for Thimphu the very next day and I stayed behind.

For two weeks, I looked after my sisters; I cooked, cleaned, and washed for them. One day, I had a problem with my ears, and thinking my aunty would have a remedy, I went to see her.

"Karma, nice to see you. Are you well?" my aunt Gyemo chirped.

"I am all right, apart from some unease in my right ear, and you?" I asked.

"I am all right. Enough rain and river not running dry." (What she meant was, we're just surviving). Come in and have a cup of tea and I will have your uncle look at your ear. Come Kulu (the pet name for my youngest sister Yeshey Choden), come in." Aum Gyemo picked her up and placed her on the veranda, whilst stroking Yeshi's cheek who was fast asleep on my back. Over a cup of *suja* (butter tea), we chatted.

"I am glad you are looking after your sisters while your mum and dad are away," Aum Gyemo said.

"I haven't got a job or anything now and I don't mind looking after them," I replied. Just at that precise moment, my uncle burst in full of ebullience after cow herding.

"Karma, are you OK?" he asked.

"Yes, no, I mean my ear is hurting a bit. I don't know why," I said touching my ear.

"Have you been in my storeroom?"

"No."

"I have got spirits in my stores and they are very protective of my swords, bows and arrows," my uncle said solemnly.

He had a jovial manner and you never knew whether he was serious or not. My aunty used to moan about his uselessness and being drunk all the time, but when he died, she repented and told me that you should never complain about someone being useless. He might have been useless in making money, but he kept the house and she had freedom to go where she wanted. However, after his death, she was drowned under house chores and lost her freedom. So, as she advised me, *never say someone is useless without knowing their full depth. You don't realise how useful they were until they depart from this world.*

"No, I haven't been anywhere near your stores," I said. "This is my first visit, and look where I am sat, nowhere near your store," I said, gesturing at the area where I was sat.

"Don't listen to your uncle, he will say anything," Aum Gyemo interrupted.

"It is true, Karma, now you know, keep away from my stuff," he said jovially, and my aunt laughed with me. There is a spirit that is called *Nawan*, a deity or spirit that protects weapons. I supposed that was the spirit that my uncle was referring to.

"Let me have a look," he said, holding onto my ear. I angled my ear in such a way so he could peer inside. "Look here. Sometimes to get affected by *Nawan* you don't have to touch anything, just your presence could disturb them. Your ear is red. I must blow on it whilst reciting an incantation. *Om mani pad may si de hung*, he recited, and huffed and puffed down my earhole.

Surprisingly, the pain subsided instantly, it was such a relief. I didn't know what to make of it.

"I heard your other aunty is being awkward, about letting the water run through her paddy field onto yours," Aum Gyemo asked.

"I think so. I didn't have time to have a proper talk with my parents. They left the day after I arrived with Dorji and her husband," I said.

"Why don't you go and talk to her? Be polite and say that you need water for a better harvest from your paddy," Aum Gyemo advised.

"I will," I agreed. "OK, I need to go now. Thanks for the tea and the nice afternoon. See you later Uncle!" I shouted and left with Yeshi and Kulu.

The house where my parents staying was further down the valley. It was paddy time and very difficult to navigate our way around. The field edge is very narrow, and the fields being filled with water was not helping. I was holding Kulu's hand and leading the way, when suddenly she decided to sit down and refused to move.

"Come on Kulu, we haven't got the whole day," I said.

"No!" she started to scream the place down.

I was so annoyed. I slapped her hard and she burst into tears as always. I grabbed her arms and dragged her with me. Screaming, she dug her heels in and refused to budge. I had enough by then, Yeshi on my back was not a lightweight to carry. I spanked her, trying to shut her up, but without success as she wouldn't shut up; she carried on crying and screaming at me. I gave in after a while. There is a limit to how much you can hit a child. I carried her as well as Yeshi. As soon as I picked her up, she gave me a winsome smile and started to chat incessantly, *look at those rice heads, aren't they beautiful with their golden heads bowing? Oh look at those dragonflies, aren't they beautiful?* To see her this happy, my heart went out to her because of my earlier cruelty. But it was hard work for me, and we nearly went headfirst into a paddy field a few times.

"Listen Kulu, you can see I can't carry you both. Did you see what just happened then? We nearly went into the paddy field. You don't want us to get wet, do you?" I asked cajolingly, and she nodded. "Will you walk from here? Hold my hand. Yeshi can't walk and I have to carry him, OK?" she nodded again.

We set off along the muddy banking of the paddy fields. Everywhere was green and lush and Kulu carried on pointing at things.

My village is like any other village in Bhutan, a sylvan area with scattered settlements, surrounded by terraced paddy fields, and a river flowing swiftly down the valley in the distance. A family of hornbills were making a hasty escape, flapping their wide wings from one tree to another, looking for food. Monkeys were up to mischief, either destroying crops of rice or making a vociferous noise. Different types of little birds, happily tweeting away all day. It is a Shangri-La, a heaven on earth.

But I was not able to take in everything as I was brooding over the incident of spanking and slapping Kulu. I could be so vicious sometimes. It was not fair raising my hand to a child, and I regret it to this day. That was not the only occasion when I raised my hand to my younger sisters:

One time, Dorji and I were coming back from school and we ended up having a row over a book. Dorji sat down and refuse to budge.

"Move now, shift!" I shouted

"Go to hell!" Dorji said indignantly.

"Don't you dare speak to me like that!" I said and slapped her hard across her face.

"*Randi, Cheytom* (prostitute)," she screamed and ran ahead of me. She can be so stubborn at times. Although, I can talk as I am like that too—I guess it runs in the family! Authority doesn't work with me. If someone wants me to listen, they must ask me politely. Bullying may work to a certain limit, but not to an extremity.

Another incident. As a child, I was never afraid to be left alone with my younger sisters. I took good care of them, except on one occasion when Nidup, my fourth sister, started to cry and was inconsolable. I tried everything I could think of, feeding her tea, water, fruit, but she kept on wailing and whinging, like all babies do when they were not happy about something.

I pinched her so hard, thinking that it would teach her a lesson to keep quiet, but instead, she wailed louder and screamed the place down. I had to console her by patting her back and speaking gently to her. Nidup was only three then. I don't know what gets into me sometimes. I could be so cruel and aggressive.

When Nidup was seven, she was with me looking after Yeshi and she was not happy about something and was sulking. This girl could sulk for Bhutan, just like me.

"Nidup, please don't block the path for the neighbours to pass," I requested, but she ignored me and carried on sitting there, deaf to my plea. "Are you deaf?" No response and I could feel myself filling with rage and slapped her.

These are four incidents that fill me with compunction, whenever my mind decides to bring them up. They pull at my heartstrings and it hurts. I have heard that if you repent enough, you will be forgiven one day, and hopefully, that will be my case. They may not even remember, but I do, it is not nice, and I hate myself for doing these things. But every coin has two sides; my behaviour was overruled by my caring and sisterly love towards them. Even though they are all adults now, I feel that I am still responsible for them.

Two weeks after being in the village, we were having dinner when we heard a whistle blow. *Pew pew pew* it went. We all went very quiet and listened intently. *Pew pew pew* we heard again. I was nervous to go out as it was starting to get dark. As soon as the sun sets, the landscape just disappears into pitch black. We could hear crickets chirping all night long, a soft breeze making the trees leaves rustle, and in the distance, we could hear an owl hooting. Children don't tend to have such a fear of darkness if they have an adult with them. They all ran out to see who was whistling.

"It is *Acho* (elder brother)," they said excitedly, running back in. It was my husband.

When dusk begins to set, we must make sure all the oil lamps are filled and ready to be lit. It was difficult to navigate around anywhere without light, especially when there is no moonlight filtering through the gaps, and all around the wooden window frames which contributes to lighting the rooms. We had to make sure that we never ran out of wicks in the lamps. You get a long thread or a piece of cloth to make a wick which needed to be threaded through the narrow neck of the lamp. If you hadn't seen someone make a wick and fill lamps before, it would be very difficult to work it out on your own.

"How did you find your way here?" I asked.

"Oh, it was not easy. I met a guy on the main road, and I enquired about your family. He pointed out this house which I could see from where I was standing, and he told me to follow the path. It looked easy and simple to get here when he pointed, but the actual path was not easy to follow. With the help of your dad's directions and the guy on the road, I managed to get so far, but somehow, I got completely lost. Luckily, I met a cousin of yours and he pointed out the way here." My husband spoke looking exhausted.

"I know, it's not easy, but I am glad you made it here before the night settled in properly," I said relieved.

"What was the name of my cousin?" I asked.

"Karma."

"He is my mum's sister's son. So, you met him for the first time. What do you think?"

"I think he is OK. You can't really judge people from a first meeting."

"I suppose so. I don't know much about him, the only time I see him is when I come to the village," I added.

I know that me and my husband didn't get on when we were together, but absence makes the heart grow fonder, and I was happy to see him. And like a besotted teenager, I decided to go back to Thimphu with him, leaving behind my sisters in the village with no one to look after them. Now, I expect my son to behave well and be thoughtful all the time. Sometimes, when my son begrudgingly agrees to help me with cleaning and the dishes, I am filled with indignation and self-righteousness. Writing this book made me see Yeshi's behaviour through different eyes, and put things into a better perspective. I started to understand him better, and know that he doesn't do things to annoy me or without respect. Sometimes, I think I expect too much from him.

When my parents saw me back in Thimphu, my mum was not happy. I don't think that she forgave me for a long time.

"Where are your sisters, Karma?" my mum asked anxiously.

"I left them in the village and asked Aum Gyemo to look after them."

"Why have you come back so early?" she said.

"I need to study," was my lame excuse.

"Whatever for? Can't you do that in the village?"

"Yes, I can, but I prefer to do it in Thimphu where there is electricity," I said, wincing and avoiding looking directly at her. I knew I had been very inconsiderate and thoughtless. I have no other words to describe my action but pure folly.

"I was not expecting this from you, Karma, I thought you are a sensible girl. Now I have to go back to your sisters before finishing my treatment," my mum said, with tears in her eyes. It hit me then what an idiot I was. I was not helping my parents or their needs. I had stupidly followed my husband to Thimphu, leaving my younger siblings to fend for themselves.

I wish I could turn back the clock, bring the wheels of time to a stop. The words of a Johnny Hates Jazz song kept ringing in my ears. When things go wrong, I always think of that song, but I don't think I would have done anything differently, even if I had managed to turn back the clock.

"It was my husband, he said he misses me," I said.

"You watch that man of yours, he will never be a good husband to you," my mum said angrily. It was not a nice thing to say but what did I expect, abandoning my younger sisters in that manner. It was heartless of me: no compassion. This is what it makes you do when you think you are in love, and I must have had stardust in my eyes. Stupid heart!

I thought I had been an angel to my parents, but I wasn't. At that age, I didn't seem to understand the difference between good and bad and I could be selfish.

As my mum used to say: *You have got your share safely tucked up on the shelf. You may repent later, but it may be too late as I might be gone from this world.*

Chapter 6

Whatever happens, happens for good.

Even though I missed the chance to sit my exams, it didn't dissuade me from giving up.

After becoming a mother, the return to education was not easy. I had to approach the Bhutan Board of Examinations and had to go through megillah—a tedious explanation of why I missed my exam; obviously I had to lie, I couldn't give the full facts—before they would permit me to enrol. Oh, how I wished I was in the west, I wouldn't have been kicked out of school in the first place for being pregnant.

I finally managed to enrol myself, but I ended up failing some of the end of year exams. I wondered, *why I had bothered trying?*

How true for me was the saying *be careful what you wish for*. I had to pay a big price for my silly wish.

When I was in primary school, my wish was to study in Thimphu, at the college where our Princes and Princesses were educated. I used to write the name of the school repeatedly in my exercise book and recite incantations: the six Vajara verses of Guru Rinpochey, praying for my wish to come true.

Du sum sangye guru Rinpoche.
Ngodrub kun dak dewa chenpö shyab.
Barche kun sel dudul drakpo tsal
Solwa deb so jingyi lab tu sol

Chi nang sangwe barche shyiwa dang
Sampa lhün gyi drubpar jingyi lob

Translation:
Embodiment of buddhas of past, present and future, Guru Rinpoche;
Master of all siddhis, Guru of Great Bliss;
Dispeller of all obstacles, Wrathful Subjugator of Māras;
To you I pray: inspire me with your blessing,
So that outer, inner and secret obstacles are dispelled,
And all my aspirations are spontaneously fulfilled.

Lo and behold, one year after my son was born, I finally gained entry to the school which was my long-time wish; I could never have imagined it would be in such circumstances.

Once I started the first term at the college, I soon realised my IQ level had diminished. My brain was *full of cow dung*, not able to process what was being taught. I had never felt like such a ninnyhammer, a simpleton in my life before, and then I knew how my best friend Yanki had felt, when she was not able to learn anything, no matter how hard she studied. I failed miserably, passing only three subjects: English, Dzongkha, and Biology, and failing the rest which were Physics, Chemistry, and Maths, all the main subjects in the science stream. What a disaster! So much for wanting to go to that college! I thought it was going to be so different from the others I went to, but it wasn't. The same kind of teachers taught there, and even though I did see royalty, it was only from a distance.

After failing my exams miserably, my career went out of the window, and I reverted to my role as housewife and mother. One day, I was visiting the library to borrow a book and I spotted an advertisement for basic computer training. The training was supposed to commence at the youth centre in Thimphu, free of charge. This is one positive thing about Bhutan, despite being such a small and poor country, the citizens' welfare is good. We get free education and medical care. If needs be, we could be sent to India for major medical operations. Aren't we lucky to have been born Bhutanese? *Kadrinchay La*, to our kings of Bhutan, for caring for people's welfare.

I therefore took up computer training and started looking for jobs. I got a job in a restaurant and then in an airline company. Now I am glad that I had prayed. If it was not for praying, I would not have got pregnant. If I wasn't pregnant, I wouldn't have missed my exam. If I hadn't missed my exam, I wouldn't have had the chance to study in my dream college. If I hadn't studied in my dream collage, I wouldn't have failed miserably. If I hadn't failed miserably, I wouldn't have done my computer training. If I hadn't done my computer training, I wouldn't have got a job in the airline company…

Despite my misfortunes, I wanted to say *Kadrinchay*, thank you for everything. I am glad things happened this way.

Chapter 7

Betrayal 1999–2000.

I used to wonder, was it me or him to blame for the failed relationship? When it came to a disagreement, I could equally be very intransigent, obstinate and obdurate, ready to point a finger.

I was a good mum and wife. I cooked, cleaned, washed, and looked after our son. When my husband came home after work, all he had to do was put his feet up. I did everything for him, but still, it wasn't enough; he had to go and find comfort in the arms of other women.

The year 2000, four years into a serious relationship and with a two-year-old child. I thought I was happy and had everything I wanted in life, being a full-time housewife and looking after our son Yeshi.

I was with Dorji, my mum, my mother-in-law, and his aunt; we were sat around a single rod, electric heater chatting, trying to keep warm on a cold, autumn night. In Bhutan, we don't have central heating, and we were not able to afford a wood-burning stove as wood is very expensive. It's ironic, isn't it? Wood, wood, everywhere, but not a single stick to burn. It was government policy: we are not allowed to cut down trees willy nilly, but must get special permission and it is only allowed in certain areas. So many people use electricity as a source of heating, or use a nice warm blanket wrapped around the body—my favourite way of keeping myself warm. Not surprisingly, my sisters had a special nickname for me, *Jili*, meaning cat, who loves to curl up in the warmth. I am the middle *jili*, my mum was the big *jili*, and my youngest sister Kulu, the little *jili*!

My husband was supposed to be home by ten thirty in the evening, and it was now midnight, but there was no sign of him. I knew then he was up to something. I couldn't help but have a presentiment, sending an uneasy shiver through my body. I hate it when I have this kind of foreboding thought, a feeling that something is about to happen. My intuition was rarely wrong when it came to him. The first place I wanted to look for him was in his office.

"Can you come with me, Dorji?" I asked my sister. She was living with me after her divorce. When the others heard me speak, they looked at me like I had gone mad.

"What on earth are you thinking of?" my mum said, looking at me and then the others.

"I was wondering where my husband is. I know he told me he is with his boss for a dinner party, but I don't believe him."

"He will be home soon. Don't worry," my mother-in-law said reassuringly.

"I think something is wrong. He should be home by now. His boss never stays later than ten. In the past, when he went for a formal dinner, he would be back by half ten at the latest," I said.

I was not worried about him going missing or meeting with an unforeseen accident, but there was a nagging feeling that he was cheating on me. In those days, we didn't have mobile phones, so I couldn't find out where he was. Anyway, it was high time I caught him *in flagrante delicto*, and I wanted to catch him red-handed. Enough was enough.

Keeping that to myself, I asked Dorji, "Do you want to come or not?"

"Give me a sec, I will put on some warm clothes," she said, and hurriedly put on a sweater and a coat.

"Where on earth are you going to look for him?" my mum added, worriedly.

"I don't know, I will check his office first," I replied, with a sense of purpose.

"What if he is not there?" they both said.

"Then we will come home, and wait to see if he has the guts to show up and explain his nocturnal life," I said, filled with righteousness.

"Be careful, it is pitch black outside," my mum said, looking perturbed.

"Don't worry *Aie,* we will be fine." After dispelling my mum's fear, I put on my coat. Minutes later, we were setting off on a mission to hunt for my adulterous husband.

We made our way to his office while the whole world was sleeping, some with good dreams and others with bad. I wished I was the one with the good dreams, but I was nothing but a bag of nerves, filled with apprehension; forget about good dreams, I wouldn't have slept a wink at this rate. It was annoying not knowing what was waiting for me, but the sooner I found out, the better it would be. I knew some things are better left alone, but how long was I to put up with this? I knew that finding things out tonight would turn my world upside down, but I was prepared to do it. Better that than living in ignorance. Ignorance is bliss, people say, but do I want that kind of bliss? I don't think so. With no torch to hand, but with fortitude, we headed towards the distant light emanating from Tashichho Dzong.

A *dzong* is a distinctive type of fortress built around the fifteenth century. It amazes me how such a simple building could last for hundreds of years. The architecture is uniquely Bhutanese, with tall, exterior walls surrounding a complex of courtyards, temples, administrative offices, and the monks' accommodation. It was built with stones, mud, and wood. No sign of concrete, but just the mud holding the stones together, shaping the great walls of Tashichho Dzong. Our monarch's throne is situated there and the day-to-day administration is run from there. Our monastic body uses it as a summer residence and Punakha Dzong (Punakha is another western district) as a winter residence.

The closer you get, the grander it is. Such a majestic sight, the building's silhouette at night-time did not disguise the grandeur of the dzong. It was standing there solemnly, and I couldn't stop admiring it, even now in the middle of the night with my mind in turmoil. I am proud that my dad took an active part in rebuilding this dzong, not as anyone important but as a labourer in 1966. He was only thirteen then. In those days, each household had to make a compulsory labour contribution. My dad was the only child of a single mother. His mother died when he was very young, and his mum's land was inherited by her nearest relative who took the responsibility of looking after my dad. In return, he had to volunteer to contribute labour to earn his keep. Poor Dad, it was not enough that he lost his property, but he had to pay his keep as well. Where is the fairness in that?

I cannot imagine Yeshi volunteering to do this kind of labouring job today. Is it the time that is changing or the people? ***Dhue nam menjur mee nam jurwa enn*** - *time is constant and never changes, but instead, as time progresses, it is the people and the way they live that changes, sometimes for the worst. Time is constant, but people are not,* Bhutanese saying.

Almost four and half decades later, two of his daughters were heading towards the magnificent dzong. We got closer, but we still had to go past the dzong, through a maze of stray dogs to get to my husband's office; we had to pick our route carefully as we may have ended up getting mauled. Getting your heart mauled was one thing, but getting mauled physically would be too much. So, we climbed up onto a terraced paddy field to give the vicious dogs a wide berth. It took us half an hour extra to get to his office, but we were safe from the mongrels. It was not easy to find our way in the dark, but we managed it in the end.

His office was situated behind the dzong, amongst the rest of the offices, chalets in rows with red roofs, whitewashed walls, and wooden windows painted in intricate Bhutanese designs;

flowers, swastikas and, instead of a typical wooden shutter, glass windows were used. A tarmacked road ran around in a circle to give easy access to the offices. Who would have thought that my so-called first love was two-timing me?

When we were close, I could see the light coming from one of the rooms in his office building. I pressed my ear against the window; I could hear people conversing in English—a woman and a man; the man's voice was his. When I heard him conversing in English, it was a blow to my pride. I know it was nothing to vilipend me, as they didn't even know that I was there listening. But my rage knew no bounds, which brought up the mighty strength of an elephant in me.

"Oi come out! I know what you are up to!" I shouted. *BANG, BANG, BANG,* I hammered on the window viciously with my fist. "*Wai chetom and chetola*, (slut and man-slut come out)."

If people judge me by my appearance, they could never imagine that I could use such profanities; but looks can be deceiving. I can be demure, modest, diffident, and as timid as a mouse—when I am calm and nothing is making me unhappy. When I am angry, I transform into a roaring lioness, ready to pounce on whoever dares to cross me!

It went quiet for a few seconds, and then the main door opened. There he was, the two-timer acting all innocent, like butter wouldn't melt in his mouth. He can't fool me. I was far from caring. ENOUGH is ENOUGH! I could tell that he had been up to something, but he thought he could pull the wool over my eyes. He didn't know me well enough then, did he? Me and my sister rushed into the room, but no one was there.

"Where is that *Rundey, chetom (*slut)!" I shouted at him.

"*Chetom*? who's a *chetom*?" he asked, looking amused.

"Where is that bitch? I am asking you again before I destroy everything in your office," I said contentiously, my eyes moving furiously down the corridor. I could see the guilt in his eyes; whoever said that the eyes are windows to your soul, how true is that? He looked so doleful and pitiful and momentarily I was wrong-footed. I wasn't expecting that. For a second, instead of a cheater, I saw my first love standing there, looking handsome. Until, he opened his mouth, trying his best to coax me out of my temper.

"I am alone and watching movies on the computer." He might have been thinking that he could fool me, but I didn't walk five kilometres in the dark, alongside the fields, avoiding vicious dogs to be lied to.

"Look, don't try to fool me. I heard you and a woman talking, I can tell the difference between a Hollywood English accent and a Bhutanese accent. I may be naïve, but I am not gormless. If you can remember, I have got a higher level of education than you. Now tell me where she is!" I said, screaming at his face, but he didn't even flinch—bastard! Then I went into a coughing fit; I might have tickled my vocal cords, shouting that loud.

"No, there is no one here with me. I am alone and I am watching a movie. Look around if you like," he said, unwavering, making him look so unattractive. At that precise moment, I had never hated anyone as I hated him for being so deceitful; he was lying blatantly through his teeth.

"No, what do you mean no? How can you tell such a barefaced lie? I am not going to fall for it," I said, hysterically. "Where is she?" I went directly towards his boss's office, but it was locked, while Dorji checked the rest of the offices. "Where is the key? Give it to me now," I demanded.

"I haven't got the key. The PA might have locked it," he replied.

"No sign of her, Karma," Dorji said, coming back after a few minutes.

"Can you go and get our mums and his aunty?" I said to Dorji, hoping against hope that he would admit his affair, rather than being humiliated in front of his mum. I would rather not have involved them, but he was resolute and stood his ground, insisting he was alone.

"Be careful, Karma!" Dorji said, looking perturbed. Just that word and a concerned look made me cry even more. I knew that no matter what, she would be there for me. I know she couldn't beat the hell out of my husband as a brother would, but at that moment, I have never been more grateful to have a sister like Dorji; *Kadrinchay,* for blessing me with my staunch, stalwart sister. I knew then without a shred of doubt, I would do the same for her. I couldn't speak, so I nodded and carried on crying.

"I won't be long." said Dorji, and saying that she disappeared into the night. She was so brave to go back on her own in the dark.

I plonked myself on the floor and said, "It is your choice, tell me where she is now. If not, I am going to sit here until the office opening time, and I will see how you will face your colleagues." I spoke filled with an iron will.

"There is no one here, I swear I was watching movies on the computer on my own," he said, taking a step closer to me.

"Don't you dare come anywhere near me! Why are you doing this? You have done it before, and I forgave you, but this is going too far. I don't know… I am so fed…" and I was stammering and couldn't go on. I knew if I carried on talking or shouting, my sentences would be full of anacoluthon, breaking between words and not able to form sensible sentences, as it involved too much emotion. So instead, I started crying. I know that I didn't want to give him the satisfaction of seeing me hurt, but it was difficult to hold back the tears.

"Wo wo wo," I wailed in *cri de coeur*, sounding like a wounded animal.

"Please, Karma, don't be sad. I love you," he said, coming closer.

"Yeah, right, you two-faced liar. Last time, when you decided to sleep with a girl under my parents' nose, I let you off because my mum asked me to. But I think you are stretching the limit now. Don't you dare touch me!" and I glared at him. If looks could kill, he would have been dead.

"Let us go home now," he said, daring to get closer to hold me and looking abashed. I did waver a bit, but I hardened my resolve instantly. I was pretty sure it was a woman I heard, not the movies.

"Don't you dare touch me!" I felt like slapping him hard across his face, which was nothing but a Janus-face. "I am not going to fall for any of this nonsense now. I am serious about what I said before. I am not going to move an inch, and it is up to you what kind of consequences you want to face," I said this as I clenched my fists, ready to punch him if he moved any closer.

He looked alarmed and panic-stricken. It could be because I said I was going to be there until the office opening time. Whatever it was, I didn't care. He disappeared for a while. A few minutes later, I heard a key being used. It went CLICK! I lost no time and I got up and rushed to see what he was up to. He was opening his boss's office which was locked before.

I was there by his side at lightning speed before he realised it. I was aware of the situation and managed to squeeze past him into the office. To my dismay, the room was empty. It took me a few seconds to register that there was an adjoining toilet room, with the door closed. I tried to open it, but it was firmly locked from the inside. With two kicks, I managed to break in, (see, I said I have the strength of an elephant). A woman was stood on the toilet bowl looking very apprehensive. I could see the terror in her eyes.

Chapter 8

Provocative

Dra men nyen tshey - *if you have no adversary get married,* Bhutanese saying.

"What the hell Wangmo? What are you doing here?" I could not believe my eyes. "You *chetom*!" I said with pure venom, seething. She was supposed to be a family friend and I thought she would have some respect for me. My mum used to say, *a trusted friend may steal your faith.* There is some truth in it. When you least expect it, people can turn on you. I thought she was nice, coming to see me when I was poorly. Little did I know, that she had eyes for my husband.

"How dare you?" I said, looking up at her. She was still stood on top of the toilet bowl looking down at me; she looked like a rabbit caught in a car's headlights, nervous and frightened. No sign of my husband, as I might have taken him completely by surprise and threw him off his guard. "How long has this affair been going on for?" I shouted, and charged at her. All I wanted to do was rip her into pieces. But before I got hold of her, my husband grabbed me from behind and pinned me down.

"Run out of the door!" he shouted to her in English.

"Let me go you bastard!" I shouted, and tried to wriggle out, but he was too strong for me.

"Keep still and I will let you go."

"How dare you? Get off me now!" I kicked, pushed and wailed at the top of my voice. I nearly managed to rock him off me, when he slapped me hard across my face and tears sprung immediately in my eyes.

The Bhutanese maxim, *Dra men nyen tshey*, rang loudly in my mind. I thought how true it was for some marriages there was no peace. I felt helpless and vulnerable and here I am now being slapped for no fault of mine.

"Shut up you!" he said, ready to slap me again, but at that precise moment, Dorji, our mums and his aunt made a welcoming entry. I have never been so glad to see anyone in my life.

"How dare you slap me. It is not even my fault, I am just the victim here," I started to sob. "Go and find Wangmo, she escaped," I said to Dorji, still sobbing, pointing towards the direction she had ran.

"Where?"

"Through the front door."

"No, the front door was locked. I locked it behind me when I left." Dorji said—clever girl, she thought about everything.

"Check in every possible room," I said.

It was a big office building with more than twenty rooms. Dorji disappeared for a few minutes, and the three of them: my mum, his mum and aunty, were stood there dumbstruck.

"Get off," I said pushing him off; he rolled off me without an effort. It was such a relief to get him off me, as being underneath him made me feel a bit out of breath. "Look what your son is up to," I said, looking at his mum, but I got no response.

Within a few seconds, Dorji joined us, dragging Wangmo by her hair. Dorji, our Bhutanese Olympic archer, had an athletic build. She kept fit and had the strength of a tiger.

"Haven't you got anyone else to sleep with?" Dorji shouted at her

"No," the girl said curtly.

"Take this then," Dorji said, and slapped her hard across the face and started to kick her. Then, my husband jumped in to defend Wangmo, and I followed suit, defending my sister.

"You bastard! Keep off my sister!"

Looking back on it now, the fun bit was we were two against two, with three older women stuck in the middle, not knowing what to do. I did not go there to display my art of pugilism, but a knuckle fight was inevitable; we're nothing like professionals, but it was enough to satisfy my anger. I punched him many times as hard as possible, but he received them all without flinching.

We were all crowded together hitting each other, with three older ladies trying to keep us apart. I grabbed a hand, thinking it was my husband. I bit it as hard as possible, but the yelp came from his mother! My husband punched, intending to hit Dorji, but he misjudged his target and I heard another yelp from my mum! Dorji went to punch Wangmo, she ducked and Dorji's punch went flying into his auntie's chest and knocked the wind out of her! It might have been a very interesting sight to watch!

We had a very chaotic time, as mad as a hatter's party. In the middle of this fight, his aunty managed to call the police.

Chapter 9

Detention Centre

It took me by surprise when the police turned up in the office, and they escorted all of us to the police station. My husband was begging, "Please, please let us not go to the police station. If it was because I hit you, hit me back." He was pulling my arms to hit him.

"Don't touch me. You should have thought about this before you started to have sex with another woman." I gave him a venomous look. If a venomous look could poison, I would have turned him into a green, lifeless monster.

Going to the police was nothing compared to what I was going through. I felt like stabbing everything that crossed my path, especially my husband. It is mad how one is affected by infidelity. Now I know why someone could end up murdering an unfaithful partner. It felt like a red mist had fallen over my eyes, and obscured my vision for my future—if I had any left after this. We entered the gloomy, police station like criminals. It had a damp and chilly smell.

"Follow me," said the policeman, and we hesitatingly followed him down a corridor and then up some stairs, walking cautiously. I felt a foreboding that if I stop, I would be swallowed up. I held Dorji's hand until we got to where he was taking us. Holding her hand gave me a sense of security. There is no one better than your family to fall back on in times of need, and one should never forget that. They will be there no matter what.

"Sit there, all of you," instructed the policeman, pointing towards a row of plastic chairs. All of us sat down as silent as lambs and without moving an inch. We were all nervous, I suppose. I sat next to Dorji, then my mum, followed by his mum, his aunt and then him, but the girl didn't dare sit next to him, and decided to sit with a chair between them, like it would make any difference now.

By then, my husband was ignoring her completely; *serves her right*, I thought with satisfaction. She got her comeuppance for stealing someone else's husband, but didn't my husband deserve the same comeuppance too? It was beyond my comprehension how he could show such an indifference within the space of a few hours. A few hours ago, he was ready to get intimate with her, or he might have done already… God knows! Now he was acting like she didn't exist. A small part of me felt sorry for her, no matter how much she deserved it, I could not wish bad upon her, but I was adamant not to show it. I felt nothing but hatred towards him. *A true Janus-face*, I thought.

"You must all write a statement," the policeman said, handing us a sheet of paper each.

"Thanks," I said. The rest just murmured.

"You are the injured party, so I will let you go home with the other three ladies, but I need to take your sister into custody as she has beaten Wangmo. Wangmo and your husband must stay also, as they are the main culprits." The police officer spoke sternly while facing me, after reading our statements.

"You can't do that. My sister was trying to protect me," I pleaded.

"I know she was, but in the eyes of the law, she has committed a crime by raising her hand against someone else. I am sorry, but she must be held in police custody until we come to some sort of judgement," said the officer.

"In that case, I am not going anywhere. I can't let my sister suffer on my behalf," I said, putting my hands on my sister's shoulder.

"Ok then," the policeman said.

"What am I going to say to my boss?" Dorji said, panicking.

"I don't know. I am sure we will come up with something. I am not happy that you had to get involved in this. I am glad you are here with me though," I said.

"Don't worry Karma, we will be ok, we will look after each other." And she gave me a tentative smile. We spent the next few days in the detention centre.

No matter where I go, I like to settle comfortably. So, I ended up scrubbing the women's toilet bowl from a dirty yellow to a shiny white. I can't stand a dirty bathroom. I felt sick while cleaning it, but I was prepared to do it for the result. With the horrible smell gone, I could relax, and I even managed to have an Asian shower (a jug and bucket of hot water). I was dreading our time in the centre as I didn't know what to expect, but in the end, it didn't turn out to be bad at all. Fortunately, we were alone, there were no other offenders with us. During the lunch breaks, we filled our faces with mum's packed lunch that she brought each day, and in the evening a meal was provided—rice and potato curry. It reminded me so much of my school lunches and dinners.

During this whole time, Wangmo was curled up in the corner, not eating, and I don't even remember any of her family visiting her. My heart went out to her, but I was adamant that I would ignore her. After all, she was the reason why we were all there, and she was about to break up my relationship, or was it already broken? That hardened my resolve. *Serves you right for stealing my man*, I thought satisfyingly, feeling possessive of my husband, and as blind as a bat towards his infidelity.

An unfaithful man, but why do we women have to blame each other? Now when I think back, why didn't I sort it out with my husband rather than blaming the other women? But how was I to know? He made me feel loved and wanted, not knowing that he was doing the same to her, but this kind of thing you learn through experience.

Another incident of a woman turning a blind eye to her husband's follies. My sister Tshering was attending computer classes in the evening. She was not back at the usual time. Dorji and I were worried sick and didn't know what to do.

It was a cloudless winter's night with a chill in the air, twinkling stars above, and a full moon illuminating the peaceful night, but it was far from peaceful for us. We were all gathered around the electric heater trying to keep ourselves warm, creating a haimish room. The environment was homely, cosy and unpretentious, but our minds were in turmoil not knowing what had happened to Tshering. I was visiting Dorji in Thimphu. She lived in a rented house which was built on the side of a mountain, surrounded by apple orchards and terraced rice fields looking down at Tashichho-Dzong.

No matter how cosy it was, we had to leave and we walked down the road to wait for her, hoping and praying she would be all right. I don't know for how long we had waited, when we saw car headlights coming towards us; it was a taxi and it stopped beside us.

"I brought your sister back home safely," said the taxi driver, winding down his window, his breath full of alcohol fumes.

"Thank you so much," we said, and shook the driver's hand in gratitude. I walked around the car to help Tshering out.

"He is lying!" a trembling Tshering said. "He was trying to sweet-talk me and took me to Dechencholing. I thought he was going to rape me!" A tremor went through me. I didn't even have time to react when I heard Dorji screaming at the taxi driver.

"You bastard!" Dorji said, and got hold of his collar; she started to slap him while trying to drag him out.

"Karma, hurry! Help Dorji!" Tshering screamed, as I hurried towards the driver's side.

"We are not going to let you go until you pay for your sin!" Dorji shouted in rage.

I joined in, grabbing the collar of the driver's *gho* (traditional attire for a man). We managed to pull him out of the taxi. He tried to escape, dragging us both with him. Our strength was nothing compared to his, even though he was drunk. All three of us went tumbling down the hill towards the paddy field, which was surrounded by barbed wire. Rolling down the hill was making me dizzy, and I had to let go of his collar, but Dorji had managed to cling on. I was recovering from my dizziness when I saw the driver on the other side of the fence. I don't even know how he managed to get there. He must have squeezed through the wire when Dorji lost her grip on him. But before he managed to escape, Dorji got hold of him again and wouldn't let go. She is one hell of a strong girl! In the process of doing that, the barbed wire cut her arm and it started to bleed instantly. Her arm still bears the scar.

"Stop Dorji! You need to stop, you are bleeding," I pleaded, but she was way past listening.

"He must kill me, or I am going to kill him," Dorji said in a fury.

"Listen to me!" the driver pleaded. "I am sorry if I was a nuisance to your sister. I wasn't going to do anything nasty to her. I know I tried to sweet talk her and tried to take her to see my relatives in Dechencholing, but when she said no, I brought her straight back home."

We calmed down a bit when we heard him pleading, but we didn't want to let him off the hook.

"Prove your innocence in the police station," we said.

We ended up in the police station once more: me and Dorji, filing a complaint this time.

"Please let me go, I meant no harm. I have a job and I need to be in the office first thing in the morning," the driver was pleading.

"You should have thought about this before you contemplated seducing a teenager," Dorji said.

"Who are those witches trying to set up my husband? All they want is money," came the infuriated voice of a woman. Sharp, high pitched and irritating.

"Calm down, madam," the policeman said.

"How dare you call us witches when it was your husband trying to rape my sister." I said, and went charging at her. I was ready to have a catfight, but Dorji and the policeman stopped me.

"Shhhh, Pema, will you shut up. It was my fault," the driver said, shushing his wife.

"If you are going to behave like that, we have no option but to take it to court. I was thinking of withdrawing the complaint since there was no harm done to my sister," I said.

"Please, please, don't do that. I am ready to compensate for my misconduct," the driver pleaded.

"Are you all right? Are you sure they are not ganging up against you, to get money off you?" his wife said.

Has she heard what we said and what her husband was saying? Stupid woman, I thought.

A wife turning a blind eye to her husband's misconduct and infidelity. How pathetic is that? I know, I am one to talk, aren't I?

I always wondered why I blamed Wangmo, my husband's mistress. Now I know why. In the wife's eyes, the husband can do no wrong, it is always other women's fault when the husband starts to have an affair. It should be the husband who is to blame when he can't keep his dick in his trouser. It is easier when you see through experienced eyes, but back then, I was just a clueless twenty-two year old.

During our detention, I saw my husband in the yard with his *gho* down to his ankles, as the police had taken his *kera* (a belt which holds the *gho* up to knee length), and my heart went out to him. The mere sight of him in that state, emptying a chamber pot, had made me sad and pity soon entered my calmed heart. I ended up sharing the packed lunch my mum had brought with him, as if nothing had happened. When I was younger, I used to say that if my partner ever cheated on me, I would put an end to the relationship, but as the maxim goes, *easier said than done.*

Chapter 10

No end to betrayal.

A few days later, we were in court. We were advised to settle the matter with a *Jabmi* (mediator) and guess what? I went back to square one like nothing had happened. What was all that fuss about? Put up or shut up. What a pathetic life, what a megillah!

The problems didn't stop there. By the end of the year 2000, he moved out after a big fall out.

"Karma, your husband is trying to seduce me," Tshering said as she came to me in tears.

"How dare he? Don't worry, I will deal with him," I told Tshering. *Is she encouraging him?* A parapraxis hit me. *How dare I? She is only a child; how can I even think such a thought?* I told myself. It was annoying when these kinds of thoughts surfaced without warning, and I felt like kicking myself.

"What do you think my sister is? Like your mother who can be easily laid," I said, as I confronted him.

"Mind your own business and watch what you say about my mother," he said.

"I am not making anything up. It was you who told me about it." I said resentfully.

"I've had enough living with you. I can't face it anymore," he said, storming out of the house. After this incident, I didn't see him for a few months. I suspected he was having an affair again, but I didn't know with who. It could be the same woman or someone else, it was difficult to know.

He left me and Yeshi to fend for ourselves. I was not working at the time and was depending heavily upon him, but luckily as always, Dorji was there to help with pecuniary assistance. Dorji, my lucky star. She has helped me a lot and I am truly grateful, but I needed to find my own way now. I knew Dorji was prepared to do anything for me, but I couldn't depend on her forever. I would like to be independent and earn my own money. I had to stop being an albatross to my sister, so I decided to look for a job.

Deciding to get a job is one thing, but finding a job was entirely a different matter. It was a time when unemployment was gradually rising. But I was lucky enough to get a job working as a receptionist in a hotel. I know the salary was peanuts, but I could buy some freedom. Like I said earlier, I didn't want to be a millstone around Dorji's neck. She had her own mess to sort out.

"I have fallen out of love with you and I don't want to be with you anymore," said her husband to her one day. And so they got divorced, but later, we found out he was having an affair.

It is very common in Bhutan, almost like it's going out of fashion, the husband with someone's wife and wife with someone's husband. The husband wants to seduce his sister-in-law and vice versa.

Being a receptionist was not an ideal job, but I was happy as it paid enough keep for me and my son. I might have been working there for a few months when I got a visit from my mother-in-law.

"Karchung has bought himself a motor scooter," my mother-in-law said. She meant my husband.

"Where did he get the money from?" I asked ponderingly.

"He said something about getting a loan."

"Loan, what loan?" I said, stupefied. "How selfish of him, the bastard!" I said this quietly as I didn't want to say it out loud. No mother wants to hear anything bad against her son.

The love of a mother is blind I was once told. She knew her son was a womaniser, but at the end of the day, she would take her son's side. And when this relationship terminates, I would be nothing, just another acquaintance in her life.

Lo and behold, a week after my conversation with my mother-in-law, I was on the way to work when I saw him ferrying a woman on his scooter, all lovey-dovey. Suspecting was one thing, but witnessing is quite another. When I saw them, my heart took a massive leap and it wouldn't settle. All I wanted to do was wail, but in the middle of crowded pedestrians it was difficult, and I had to control my tears. As soon as I got to work, I started to cry. Incomprehensible, how could he have an affair with a different woman in the space of a few months? Who did he think he was, Casanova?

"What's up Karma?" I heard my colleague say with a reassuring tone, gently placing a hand on my shoulder. I burst into hysterical sobs.

"It is my husb…and, I know he walk….ed out on me, but I had a sm…all hope he wo…uld come back to me and my so…n." I stuttered. I was in agony and it felt like my heart was going to burst open at any time. My colleague looked at me sympathetically and full of pity, but he said nothing and let me cry.

"I was not expecting him to move on so quickly. We are not even divorced yet," I said, calming down a bit and trying hard not to cry, but it was impossible.

"I think you need to get to the bottom of your problem. Either get divorced or sort yourself out. You can't leave your relationship hanging like this," my colleague said.

"I know, I know, I must get in touch with him and sort it out," I added.

"Don't worry if things do not work out between you two. It is not the end of the world, one goes, a thousand come," added my colleague, reassuringly. "There is nothing to worry about. Go and freshen up, and I will take over the reception until you come back."

"Thank you," I mumbled

Is it worth trying to salvage our relationship, hoping that he will change one day? I had to question myself.

I can't go on like this forever. I think it is high time that I put an end to this pickle of a situation, my conscience says when I was angry with him, but whenever he came begging, I would go back to him as nothing had happened.

My mum would say. "Stop behaving like a faithful dog. When the owner shows a bone to you, you happily follow; when he kicks you, you leave with your tail tucked between your legs. I think dogs are treated better than you. You need to grow up Karma, stop being so naïve." My mum didn't say this without a reason.

My defence to my mum's criticism was when your heart is involved, you can't think straight. While in a relationship, you think you could give it up, but when it comes to ending, your heart cries out for him. It is never a straightforward business. I didn't want to accept that our relationship had come to a junction where we needed to go our separate ways.

"Husbands are like firewood. When you have burnt one, you will find another to replenish. You are still young. I am sure you will find plenty of fishes to fry," my mum said philosophically, every time she saw my heart broken.

In 2000, I decided to file for divorce or dissolve our partnership. I still didn't know how to define my relationship with him: husband, boyfriend, partner… it was a big question.

In Bhutan, when a boy and girl start dating seriously, move in together, and have a child, they are considered as husband and wife. We don't have to get any form of proof to state that we are married. *Once you start to live together and have a child, then you are married*, was a Bhutanese notion.

Now the complicated bit. First, we had to form a civil partnership to get a marriage certificate, and based on this marriage certificate we had to file for divorce. I know it was a very strange way of doing it, but then it made sense. Being a woman, you have no legal right to claim your child as yours without the father's consent. Therefore, I didn't have the right to claim my child without dissolving the civil partnership first. You can't even register a child if you don't know who the father is. And that was the first time I hated being a woman.

My dad used to say, *men are ten generations ahead of women*. I did believe him when I was young, but now I know it was nothing but patriarchal talk. I don't blame him for coming out with such nonsense. He was from that era where men bring home the bacon and women kept the fire burning. And he did a good job of bringing up us six daughters; he gave us the love we wanted, fed and clothed us, and kept us away from any danger. I have nothing but gratitude towards him.

After few trips to the court, I got what I wanted: custody of my son and free from my husband's infidelities.

Freedom, here I come!

Part II

Family and Prelapsarian.

"In a prelapsarian world, the necessity of language is unnecessary and only exists in a postlapsarian world, when questions of emotion, nature, and creation come into existence. What's there is to be so envious of postlapsarian life. I wish I could go back to be a child."

John Milton (Paradise Lost).

Chapter 1

My parents.

There are some selfish parents out there in this world, but I was fortunate to have two wonderful parents. They were self-sacrificing and unselfish.

When it was time for them to come home after a day's work in the fields, we girls would be eagerly waiting for them. Like faithful dogs waiting for their owner to turn up with doggy bags. As soon as they walked in, we would get hold of the doggy bag and dig straight into it, but not before sharing. We were never selfish, we shared everything. *Sharing is caring*, as my mum always used to say. We watched each other's back and took care of each other. We were best friends and we still are.

One day, one of my sisters was spanked for being selfish. As a child, you unwittingly can be both, selfish at one time and unselfish at another, but being born to altruistic parents makes you realise that being selfish is not the way of life. The spanking did the trick, as we learned to share and care; love became part of our life. They showed us what compassion is: help people in need, be gentle to people, and never be harsh to one another. I like to think both my parents are philosophical, as I do remember Dad being ethical; although not as much as Mum. My mum liked to rain pithy maxims and aphorisms on us. She was a sententious woman. Dad brought home the bacon and didn't have much to do with educating us; he would rather discipline us than educate us—this is why I felt closer to my mum when I was a child. But now, as an adult with a child who you need to discipline sometimes, I understand that Dad loved us as much as Mum did.

As most partners do, now and then my parents did have disagreements. As a Bhutanese saying goes - ***Day ni mang na za ru da zencha ya thru -*** *even ladles and spoons clash when handled too many times.* There are always going to be disagreements between couples.

My dad needed to work hard when he was angry. One time, he was not very happy with Mum for some reason. It was paddy harvesting time and he stormed out with a sickle.

"Where are you going, Dad?" I asked.

"To harvest our paddy," he said, "what do you think I am going to do with a sickle, kill myself?" he brandished his sickle like he was going to war. Indeed he was, but with paddy fields, not with people.

"You don't seem very happy. I am asking to make sure you are OK."

"Don't worry, I am fine. I just need to harvest. It may rain while the harvest is left on the ground to dry, and I can't risk losing the crops." My dad gave his explanation and left. That's the downside of agriculture: you tend and care for your crops and sweat over them, and sometimes, nature will strike, flushing all your hard work down the drain.

"Can I come?" I asked, ever ready to assist, even though I could be more of a hindrance than a help!

"No, stay here with your sisters, I won't be long," he said, and jumped over the fence and disappeared along the road towards the fields.

At dawn, he was stacking the sheaves into piles, which had to be left throughout the winter. Completing the job of three people in less than twenty-four hours. I still can't comprehend how he managed to do that; he must have worked so hard and nonstop.

Autumn is beautiful, full of brown colours and fresh, crisp, salubrious air. The day started with a white sheet of frost, spread across the village and surrounding fields. I can still remember walking, on that frosty morning, to check on my dad before setting off to school. As soon as I stepped out of the warmth of our house, I could feel the cold hands of air stroking my face, soon chilling me to the core. I could feel my nose run. Rubbing my hands together, I started to run and soon warmed up. How does rubbing hands together warm you up? I used to wonder, not realising that rubbing hands causes friction which generates heat, and the heat travels to all the parts of your body, warming you up through and through. So, I think it comes naturally to people to rub their hands when they are cold. Very instinctive, innate behaviour of human beings towards a particular cause.

I could see my dad in the distance after climbing a few terraces of rice fields. I kept running carefully, not to drop the flask which contained Dad's hot *suja*, butter tea that Mum had prepared; even though she was not happy with him, she got up early to make suja for him. I suppose that's what couples do: fall out then mend fences. I finally got to Dad and could tell by the redness in his eyes that he hadn't had a wink of sleep. He looked exhausted, but that was my dad— strange and funny. Who else would be wanting to work the whole night long when one was angry? Not me. When I am not happy, I tend to sulk, go into hiding or lie down, and go to sleep without having anything to eat or drink. People are like snowflakes. I don't mean as in the snowflake generation; I mean where two people are not the same in thinking and behaviour.

Another funny side of my dad was when he was drunk; he could eat a whole pot of rice, enough to feed the whole family, all by himself.

"Have you got a hole in your back?" we would say as we teased him, feeling his back to see whether there was a hole there or not. It is incomprehensible how one man could eat enough for five when drunk!

"I like to eat when I am drunk. It is a mystery and I haven't got a clue why," he said, jovially winking at us. Funny how alcohol made him so jovial and affable. But no matter how drunk he was, he would always find his way home—except for one night.

He once said to us as he was reminiscing. "No matter how hard I tried, I was not able to get up what I thought was a hill towards home. An inch was the furthest I got. The harder I tried, the harder it became. Finally, after three attempts, I managed to get to the top, only to roll back down again. I knew it would be useless to try again, but I didn't give up. I tried again and again. I must have fallen asleep exhausted. I didn't wake up until the rain was beating down on me. I opened my eyes and it was morning, and I was in an apple orchard near our house, lying next to a fence. I could have just walked alongside the fence which leads straight to our house, but I was not to know as I was drunk."

All he was trying to do was climb the fence, and for some reason he thought it was a hill. Alcohol, what is in it that makes you lose your sense? After this incident, people made fun of him, saying he intended to roll down the hill to end up on the doorstep of a woman who he fancied. I didn't understand that joke, and I always wondered how my dad could roll down onto the doorstep of a woman. From my understanding, if he had rolled down to the bottom, he would have ended up in a stream instead!

My dad had an interesting life. His dad had abandoned his family when he was little. When his mum died, his uncle took away his property. Instead of showering him with avuncular affection, my dad was nominated him for labour contribution, so when he was thirteen, he had to contribute labour in building the *Dzong* in Thimphu with one of his relatives who had looked after him. In gratitude, he accepted to help his relatives.

They made the journey, full of acclivities and declivities, to the Dzong with some other villagers. They had to walk steep hills and along narrow trails which were known as monkey's paths; they were called this as they were very narrow and headed down into the valley, through tropical forest and up towards the highest point between the destination and the village. The hike was at times treacherous, and when they could take no more, they stopped for the night in Dagala.

After Dagala, the hike got easier at first, downhill all the way. The more you descend, the harder it gets on your knees, but my dad was a young boy full of enthusiasm and he didn't feel it all; but he is facing the consequences now, sore knees and hobbling whenever he goes downhill. But in those days, he could run down until he got to the Phuntsholing – Thimphu highway, which was still under construction.

He had never seen a vehicle before in his life and it amazed him. Black and yellow colours, with an open back and a shelter in the front. It intrigued him; he was not able to take his eyes off it. He turned to his other uncle, who was the brother of the uncle that had inherited his property.

"What is that?" he asked.

"What that?" his uncle said, pointing towards the moving vehicle.

"Yes, that."

"That is a truck and it transports materials for the construction site."

"Oh OK," said my dad, wondering how something like that can move of its own accord. It was obvious he hadn't noticed someone manning the steering wheel.

Up the mountain, then down the valley and across the river they went. The forest eventually turning from tropical to conifer and then to deciduous as they gained height in the mountains.

Once they got to Dompa, the forest was thinning and the temperature had dropped by a few degrees. It was never easy on this kind of journey, especially on foot. Summertime was too hot and wet, and winter was too cold and sometimes it snowed, making it harder to cross the passes. One time you would be looking down at the torrid *Wangchu* (Wang River) from above, and other times you would be down in the valley, close to the gushing water, looking up at the mountains.

From our village of Durjeygang to Dagala, it takes two days on foot. And an overnight stop at Gangtakha, Dompa, Gekeha, and Babesa, which brought them to the last stretch of the journey. They ended up taking shortcuts some of the time, so they could complete it in six nights rather than ten. I can't imagine how tired they would have been, but that was life then.

My dad, at the age of thirteen, travelled six days on foot to contribute four months of labour. Imagine children doing that kind of thing these days? Forget about this day and age, I don't think I would have done it during my time.

Then he spent a further four months labouring on the modern replacement of *Lungthenzampa* (Bridge of Destiny). Only because a great Drukpa Kayug lama, Phajo Drugom Zhigpo from Tibet, came to Bhutan in 1224. He meditated in Paro Taktsang (Tiger's Nest) where he had a vision instructing him to meditate at twelve places: *Dzongs Zhi* (four fortresses), *Drak Zhi* (four rocks) and *Phug Zhi* (four caves). Then he met Acho and married her, but he was restless because he was destined to marry another girl who was a Dakini. At last, he found her in Wang Simo, but unfortunately, she was on the other side of the Wangchu River. He wooed her by singing, and she followed him along the other side of the river, and they eventually met at a bridge ten kilometres upstream from Wang Simo. Here they met and got married, hence the name *Lhungthenzampa* came into existence.

Then my dad followed his eldest-half-brother to Wangdiphodrang (the Western part of Bhutan), and lived there for a few years working as a farmhand.

In 1969, he was back in his village, Thangna, Durjeygang. He felt like a foreigner in his hometown. He could still speak his mother tongue, but he was sounding foreign to everyone. Five years was a very long time to be away from home.

He left as a young, curious, shy boy, and came back as a fine, young and handsome man. He was happy to be back home, and soon felt like he had never been away.

By then, two of his half-brothers were married. He wanted to settle down and have a family of his own, but he was selected to join the army two years later; again he found himself hiking to Dagana. He passed the entry test, and was sent off to an army training camp in Balung, Wangdi. In those days, without any road connections, it took him a week to hike to his destination.

His younger half-brother's sister-in-law, a shy eighteen-year-old girl, captured his attention, and soon they were married. It was very common in Bhutan in those days, with in-laws marrying in-laws, but it is less common now.

My mum and dad led an uncomplicated life, no stress and simple living and a journey to bring up six, beautiful daughters. It would have been eight if it was not for mum losing two during pregnancy.

I am the eldest and I am the only one without a nickname. They called me *jili* (cat) sometimes, but it never became my pet name. The second sister Dorji Dolma (Aum Hitler, because she is the big boss of the family), then Tshering Dema (Aum Burkey, because when she was little, she used to have a snotty nose). Nidup Dema (Tata, because of her big head), Ugyen Lhamo (Pinka, I am not sure why) and Yeshey Choden (Kulu, as when she was little, she was like a little puppy).

"What's wrong, Kulu?" I asked, when I saw my youngest sister's grim, sad and tear-stained face. She can be a character of emotion. If she was not happy, she could easily burst into tears or sulk.

"*Ashim* Dorji said I was a mistake, and it is because of me that our mother died," she sobbed.

"Now, now, look at me. I know it was horrible of Dorji to say that to you, but we know she didn't mean it. She says things without thinking and there is no malice in her action. She is short-tempered, have you forgotten that is why we call her Hitler?" I said as I consoled her.

"I know," she said, with a smile on her face.

"That's better. You were never a mistake, and never will be. I know we may not always be lovey-dovey and affectionate, but deep down we all love you the same and never think you are a burden," I said, embracing her.

My parents had given us the life we deserved. We were never rich, but very happy and we had a comfortable, loving home and food in our belly. What more do you need? Money cannot buy happiness. There are some families, very rich and who could afford anything they wanted, but happiness is not always a part of them. It takes labour to build the house, but it is the beautiful hearts of the people living there that makes it a home.

Three of us, Dorji, Tshering and I were born in Thimphu. When I was nine, my dad was transferred as a palace guard to a village called Namseling, where the palace was situated. Mum and dad left Dorji and me with my maternal uncle to complete our year in school. We hated being with our uncle and aunty as they never treated us well. Poor Dorji was only six then, and she couldn't eat chilli, but she didn't dare pick it off the plate. I would surreptitiously pick it off her plate when my aunty was not looking and eat it. One night, she soiled our bedding. To avoid her being told off, I rolled the mattress over to one side, and laid a *kira* (women's national dress) on the bed instead, and the very next day after school, I washed the bedding and her soiled clothing. Dorji failed miserably in her mid-term exam, and Mum and Dad decided to take her out of school for half a year. After spending the summer holiday with my parents, I returned to Thimphu to complete my education. I didn't mind it that much as I was treated better than Dorji, me being my uncle's favourite. A year later, I was moved to a school closer to my parents.

    The best part of my childhood was spent in Namseling, frolicking and skylarking. Like John Milton said: "In a prelapsarian world, the necessity of language is unnecessary." We were ok if our belly was full, and we had parents to look after us.

Chapter 2

Childhood home.

The palace my dad was guarding belonged to our Queen Mother, now our present King's grandmother. It was a beautiful building: four stories high, traditionally built out of clay, stone, and wood, with the unique Bhutanese art décor; the walls all whitewashed and then painted with *yuerung* (swastika) as part of its beautiful patterns. It is surrounded by a courtyard of big slabs of stone, which themselves are surrounded by a high, stone wall, making it impenetrable for intruders.

The swastika is very common in Bhutan. It takes western visitors by surprise when they see it for the first time, but it is included in almost all the houses and monasteries. It is also seen in paintings. For the Bhutanese, it is a sacred sign.

The Palace grounds, where we were housed, had such an intriguing nature. The whole time we were there, the Queen Mother didn't even visit once. When I was ten, the Palace enchanted me, and was beckoning me to explore her. I was stood at the bottom of the mighty walls, contemplating my moves. No matter from whichever angle I explored, I couldn't see a single way of getting my footing right. I couldn't try it from the front, which was possibly an easier route, as my parents may see me and I would be in trouble.

I tried to shimmy up the wall, and only managed to get an inch off the floor. I climbed a peach tree, to try to get on the surrounding wall, in the hope of reaching as close as possible to the lower veranda, which was two arms' length away. I tried to swing, but the branch was not flexible enough. I wished I was a monkey, so I would have easily made it with my long limbs.

My mission was unsuccessful. There was no way I could have climbed that building, and I had to declare it "Mission Impossible". I was trying to overcome my disappointment, but then the day came for the annual cleaning. I had to beg my dad to take me with him to see inside.

"All right then, but you will have to behave," my dad warned. "Don't get in anybody's way."

"I won't, Dad," I said gratefully. "Come on everybody! Dad is letting us see the palace!" I shouted at the top of my voice with gaiety, trying to get my sisters' and friends' attention, but they barely acknowledged my call.

"Come on, Karma."

"Coming, Dad." I followed with a spring in my step. I couldn't stem my excitement, all I wanted to do was go exploring.

What a difference, so much easier walking in through the front door; rather than trying to sneak in like a thief.

"You can go and explore on your own, but don't be a nuisance. I will come and find you when we are done."

"OK Dad," I said, skipping ahead of him.

The ground floor was used as storage for rice grain, but originally it was a dungeon. It was believed prisoners were left to rot there. It did not surprise me at all. The place was awful, cold, and dark. The floor was made of stone, and it had very close, confined spaces without windows. I started to hyperventilate, and my breath was coming out in gasps. *What an awful way to treat another human being*, I thought, feeling sorry for those people who had been locked in there. It had an eerie feel to it, and I could feel a chill run down my spine. If I let my imagination run wild, I would be able to see ghostly apparitions floating around, infesting the room. I had to get out before I scared myself to death, or exhaust myself trying to keep up with exhalation and inhalation.

The eerie feeling soon disappeared when I started to climb up the large, wooden ladder, taking me to the first floor which was warm and airy; the sun rays were filtering through the cracks in the wooden shutters, making it much more pleasant than the ground floor. I don't know what it was used for originally, but now it was used for storing more rice grain.

Another wooden ladder, but shorter than the one before, took me to the second floor, and again another contrast. The walls were beautifully decorated with the intricate design of eight auspicious signs: The Treasure Vase, The Endless Knot, The Victorious Banner, The Wheel of Law, The Golden Parasol, The Golden Fish, The White Conch, and The Lotus. It was a very lively room. It may have been used as a parlour because it was filled with divans, with intricate, woven silk draped over them, and a beautifully carved and painted *Chok-drom* (low wooden table) in the centre of the room.

The excitement did not end there. The ladder which took me to the top floor had a very interesting handrail; carved into it were a pair of dragons, painted in green, red and gold, looking upwards as if to defend the top floor. All the bedrooms were as exquisite as each other. King-sized beds were covered in handwoven silk throws. Tiger skins were also thrown, ostentatiously, over the bed atop the throw. The beds stood on four legs which were carved into the lion's claws, big and mighty. The room smelled of opulence and sybaritic luxury. No wonder the dragons were looking so protective up from the stairs.

It would be very nice to sleep in those, what a luxury to have, I thought. In our house we didn't use beds, instead we slept on a thin mattress on the floor. I know a bed is luxurious to have, but sleeping on the floor has its beauty.

The toilet captured my imagination, it was the cleanest I had ever seen in my life. It had a toilet bowl rather than a toilet hole, and it sparkled like white gold. I went in and sat on it, wondering how someone could have a poop sitting there. I didn't think I would be able to! Firstly, it looked too clean to use, and secondly, sitting on the bowl was not the best position. It is too relaxing and comfortable, and having a poop whilst sitting there was next to impossible. I was so used to doing it out in the open air, or with a squatting toilet. I was glad we didn't have such a complicated toilet.

There are vast differences between our toilet and the palace toilet; our toilet drops straight into the running water below, but the Palace toilet was more like a stool made of white ceramic. Ours was meant for squatting, but the other was meant for sitting. We used old notebooks, magazines, newspapers, and leaves to wipe our bums with, but this one had paper as soft as silk. What a sybaritic toilet, but I preferred ours—it is more adventurous and exciting by far!

Next to the bedrooms was a sitting room or morning room. The walls were whitewashed, and one wall was filled with the paintings of *Tak* (Tiger), *Seng* (Snow leopard), *Chung* (Garuda), and *Druk* (Dragon); the four, animals considered to be highly symbolic and powerful.

Another room was filled with the paintings of four harmonious friends: elephant, monkey, rabbit, and bird, stood on top of each other next to a prolific tree. The story goes, the bird finds a seed and plants it. Then, rabbit waters it and the monkey fertilises it. Once the tree is grown, the elephant protects it.

The other walls were filled with painted flowers. Our home did not have such a luxury like beautiful walls and amazing paintings, instead, they were covered in old newspapers. Every year we redo our walls. We would get as much newspaper as we could, paste it in rice starch mixed with flour, which acts as glue, and then plaster it all over the walls and ceilings. I know it hadn't an expensive look like the palace, but it was alluring. We could read whilst we were lying on our mattresses, and most of the night we would play a game of finding a word. One would shout out a word, and others had to find it. Whoever finds the least words loses. The papered walls kept the wind and dust out, making the house nice and cosy.

I wandered back to the main bedroom of the palace, and I could see the sun rays were impatiently breaking through every gap of the wooden, window shutters. It was bewitching, cosy and beckoning me to crawl into the big, luxurious bed, or lie on the sofa, pull a silk throw over me, and go to sleep. It was very enticing, but I had to stay away from this temptation. Firstly, if caught I would get into trouble, and secondly, I wouldn't know how to handle such a luxury.

We lived in a two-roomed house, six of us, including Mum and Dad, sharing the bedroom. Since I was the eldest, I was given a choice of which side to sleep. I always ended up choosing the righthand side of the room. Old habits die hard, and I still like to sleep on the right-hand side.

My parents would share a mattress with the youngest sister, the remaining sisters shared a mattress, and I would sleep on my own. If I had to share a bed, I wouldn't have minded. It was always nice to sleep next to a warm body.

There was a time, I would lie awake at night wondering what my parents were up to. I sometimes overheard adults discussing the night rituals that a husband and wife would have. I didn't know how they did it. It was very difficult to catch them, and I never caught them once. They might have been very quiet. Maybe that is why the Bhutanese use the euphemism 'Blanket Moving' for having sex.

I don't know what I would have done if I had caught them, and I am glad I didn't catch them blanket moving or anything. It makes me cringe whenever I think about it, but as a child, you tend to be inquisitive, and inhibition is never a part of you.

The Palace top floor windows give a 360-degree view of the village. Apple orchards surround the palace bound by fencing. Gala apples dominate the orchards, followed by golden and cooking apples.

Groups of houses were scattered around Namseling, the village. All the buildings are made of clay, stones, and wood. In the middle of it lies the temple, painted in horizontal, white and red stripes beneath the roof, a white circle painted on the red stripes. Next to it, lies a big Cypress tree surrounded by prayer flags being blown in the gentle wind.

Deep down in the valley flows the majestic Wangchu, and a hill on the right adjoining the mountains would look forlorn if it was not for the small temple on the top. Instead, the temple takes the forlornness and makes it look deeply pious, filling the surrounding area with an aura of calm and peacefulness.

Every year, for a big religious ceremony held in Namseling temple, the ritual books were borrowed from another temple and transported on people's backs in a procession. It is such an interesting ritual to see, where all the able-bodied villagers from all walks of life amalgamate in transporting the books. The procession always starts early in the morning. A group of monks playing *jali* (religious flutes), leading the way and burning cypress branches with full of veneration, could be seen far and wide along the path. The religious ceremony lasts for twenty-one to twenty-three days.

It took me by surprise how different the four floors were. It was like they were competing against each other in design. The higher you climb, the more magnificent and marvellous they got. The juxtaposition of these floors was amazing. A cold, eerie ground floor, an airy first floor, an ornate second floor, and swanky bedrooms on the third floor were starkly juxtaposed. I would like to own this kind of house, but how is the big question? On second thoughts, I didn't think I would like such a big house.

For me, there was no better place to grow up than my childhood home. It was beautiful, and had everything a child would want. Unfortunately, when I went to re-visit in 2010, the guard wouldn't let me anywhere near the building.

"I tried to visit Namseling Palace yesterday, but they didn't let me anywhere near the place," I said, when I met my childhood friend Thuji in the town.

"They are not particularly friendly like your dad and the other guard were. They try to be imperious over the villagers, and I don't think I have been up there since your dad left," she said, sighing, "people don't get along with them."

"It is sad, isn't it? We always got along very well with the villagers, I miss my time there," I said recollecting. When my father was a guard, everybody was welcomed except for the problem creators. I even remember having a school picnic on the grounds.

Our quarters were built adjoining the surrounding wall of the palace. We had a clay, wood-burning oven in the kitchen where we cooked our meals. Next to it, there was a large, metal, wood oven, used only by the royal cooks during a royal visit.

We lived there for a few years, and the fourth King with his family visited only once. I was excited about the prospect at first, but my excitement didn't last long. We were not allowed to go outside our homes and we had to lock ourselves in. Being an outdoor child, I was feeling claustrophobic. We were so used to running wild, and being cooped up in a room was not very pleasant.

"If you dare to come out in the open, I am going to feed you all to a demon," said a young, evil, male voice.

There were no boys amongst us, and we didn't know where it was coming from.

"Open the window!" he demanded, and then we realised that the annoyed voice was from outside.

It was one of the princes shouting at us for no reason. How did he know we were there? It is still a mystery. We didn't dare look. It was bad enough being cooped up in a room, and getting threatened was the last thing we wanted.

"Open the window!" he demanded again

We said nothing and huddled close to each other in fright. We had no clue where our mother was, and my dad was guarding the Palace. Having no comfort at getting any sort of protection from our parents, we nestled even closer.

"BANG BANG!" he hammered as he shouted "open the window!"

We had no option but to comply with his order. The responsibility fell on my shoulders, and with shaking hands, I opened the window.

"You, did you hear what I said?" he said, pointing at me

"Yes, *Da...sho..,*" I said, it all came out squeaky and shaky. I decided to nod instead of speaking. He continued speaking on and on, and I nodded for all of his inquisition. And it was over before I knew it.

"Good, now behave," he said, and marched off.

"What have we done?" Dorji said, quivering.

"I don't know. I wish Mum and Dad were here with us now. If they were, we would not have to go through all this," I said, and I missed my parents terribly. My dad was attending to the King's needs the whole day, and mum told us later that evening that she was out in the fields, working with the other women.

Luckily, they stayed only a night. When they left, the first thing we did was escape out into the wild. We spent the whole day playing in the woods, climbing trees, and sledging on pine needles that covered the ground.

"Keep off my wood you brats! Sledging destroys pine needles, and it is no good for my cattle." We scarpered as soon as we heard the farmer, but sneaked back in as soon as he left.

"We are doing nothing wrong here. We are only using a small part of his woods. I think he is just being awkward," said one of our friends, and we readily agreed with her and carried on sledging.

Every winter, farmers collect the pine leaves for bedding for their cattle, which will turn into manure to spread in the fields.

We used to give a helping hand to a farmer, shifting manure in the field. We would get up early, washed and off we go to contribute labour. We were fed three meals a day, but we needed to carry our plates and mugs. So, with our little luggage bags on our backs, we skipped down the path around paddy fields, and hopped as fast as possible over the fields until we got to our destination.

The breakfast started with red rice, sun-dried chilli powder paste, dried beef and *suja* (brewed in our unique tea leaves, and churned with butter and salt).

Lunch was red rice with a Bhutanese curry, made with any vegetables or dried beef, chilli, and cheese. Or sometimes *emadatshi*, a curry made of chilli, cheese, red onion, and seasoned with salt; this is a delicacy of the

Bhutanese, and it is my favourite. I prefer this to the meat dishes.

Then, afternoon tea with *suja* and *zaw* (toasted rice), mixed with butter and sugar. It is so yummy, we would end up licking our fingers to our hearts' content.

Dinner would be the same as the lunch, but with a different vegetable curry, also cooked with chilli and cheese. I couldn't believe it when I heard that Bhutan was the only country in the world that uses chilli as a vegetable. The earliest harvest for chilli will be in early spring in Eastern Bhutan. It is expensive, but people don't mind paying, and it sells like hotcakes.

When Mum used to get these chillies from the Sunday market, we were not able to wait to get our hands on them. Even as children, we used to make a feast out of it, and we were not scared of the chilli heat. My favourite was to slit one side of a big, green chilli, and add a knob of butter, salt, and then roast it in a fire, and then munch it or have it with rice. But we had to be careful not to eat too much, as it tends to give horrible tummy aches. The craziest thing we used to do with chilli was to fill a dried red chilli with hot water and salt, and rub it until it became soft, then we drank the juice; it was flavoured with chilli heat and salt. It would be mouth-wateringly hot. Another one of my favourites was the café bought chilli chop; chilli dipped in batter and deep-fried.

We would spend the whole day carrying manure on our back in hand-woven, bamboo baskets. Chatting away happily about this and that, and the day would go in the blink of an eye. And at bedtime, as soon as our heads touched the pillow, we would fall into a blissful slumber.

We got along well with the villagers in all aspects of life. My mum likes planting paddy, and she played a vital part in contributing labour to the villagers, for which she was paid in goods. She would come home with red rice, butter, and cheese.

Just below the palace, there were acres of paddy fields that belonged to the current king's grandmother. She held the tenancy of the paddy fields, and most of the villagers put their life and soul into working in the fields. Terraced paddy fields on a mountainside make a beautiful scene. In springtime, the greens started to shoot everywhere, and in summer the green deepens, becoming all lush with tall, rice stalks dominating the fields. In autumn, all rice heads turn into golden-brown, swaying in the breeze.

Before being piled into a rice dome, the rice needed to be laid on the ground to lose all moisture. After a few days, farmers tied the rice into sheaves, and stacked them on top of each other to make a dome. When winter comes, the rice domes were dismantled, and the sheaves of rice were beaten on a piece of large stone to free the grains. Whatever was left over, after paying the tenancy charges, was stored away for winter consumption. I feel sorry for all the farmers who work so hard, and at the end of the day, they only get to keep one-quarter of the harvest. They didn't seem to mind, but instead thank their lucky stars for such a bountiful harvest. When all traces of domes were removed, the farmer then ploughed the field in preparation for next year's plantation. And that was where we children came in, transporting manures onto the fields, which was laid in heaps of giant molehills, and then later, the farmer spread the manure evenly on his fields. Thus, the cycle of a farmer carries on. We got equally involved with the villagers in farming. We went wood collecting, shifting manure to the fields, and helped to plant paddy. We didn't hesitate in getting our hands dirty. We worked hard and our hard work was rewarded in goods or cash. We preferred cash as we could have it as spending money, but we would happily accept goods if it was necessary.

Your childhood home doesn't have to be surrounded by luxuries. The necessities of life are all you require.

Chapter 3

Sunday vegetable market (*Sabji Bazaar*).

On Sundays, my mum would go vegetable shopping, I had the responsibility to look after my sister Nidup, who was only three and the youngest then. With Nidup on my back followed by Dorji and one of our friends, we went to meet our mum. Instead of taking the normal route, we decided to take a shortcut along the stream. The stream made her journey from the mountain, running smoothly down the valley. The further she travelled, the older she got. She had turned into a beautiful woman with flowing curves, moving gently through the valley, making everything she touched lush and green. She looked very clean and fresh, and we were not able to resist sticking our feet into the water. The soft touch of her travelled through my body, cooling me down to the core, and making it more bearable to walk under the scorching sun.

With Nidup firmly latched onto my back, we ambled alongside the stream to our destination. I was not looking where I was going and I misjudged my step. It was so sudden, and I didn't have the time to react as I went tumbling down headfirst—Nidup still attached to my back like a baby monkey. Luckily, we rolled brushing past a thorny bush. The fall knocked my senses sideways, and it took me a while to gather my thoughts. Dorji saw it all, and was jumping up and down, wailing and crying at the top of her voice.

We were lucky to land on soft grasses. Dorji and our friend came running down. My first thought was to check Nidup for cuts and bruises. There were no bruises, but a small cut on her forehead.

"Are you all right, *chechey* (baby)?" I asked with concern. She didn't say anything but nodded. That meant she was ok.

"Don't tell *Aie* (mother) that we fell, all right? I will give you some sweets when we get home." I knew I would be in serious trouble if Mum found out about the fall. I was fine, not a single scratch, but Dorji was shaking like a leaf and couldn't stop crying. "OK?" I asked, and she nodded again. "Good girl," I said, "come on now, hop on my back, I promise I will be careful this time." And with Nidup on my back again, we made our way to meet Mum.

I was dreading that my mum may notice the cut soon, or worried that Nidup would blurt out what happened one day. You know what children are like. If you tell them to be quiet, they get very loud, and tend to do exactly the opposite of what you ask of them. Despite that, I must admit they are cute. I am sure she may have said it one day, but by then water was under the bridge and I was not in danger. I could not believe my luck that the cut went unnoticed, but it worried me for awhile, and I was on edge every time I saw Mum feeding Nidup. For a couple of days, every time I came home from school, I was worried that Mum might be ready to shout and pounce on me—it was nerve-wracking. Fortunately, that incident went by without my parents noticing.

I always enjoyed our trip down to the main road to meet our mum. While waiting we would frolic about, and as soon as we saw a taxi approaching, we stood still and waited. We knew that one of them was bound to have our mum in it. When that moment came, we ran down to meet her. I took a shopping satchel from Mum, but not before she distributed goodies of toasted rice balls equally amongst the children, and then we all trooped back home. That night, we would always have a dinner of beef—short ribs cooked with potatoes and dried chillies. A Sunday treat!

I don't know whether Dorji and Nidup would remember. Reminiscing about my childhood brings happy memories. I can still feel the warm, gentle breeze stroking my face as we were heading to meet Mum. That tumble had shaken me, but I pulled myself together. I know I was a child myself then, but I knew my responsibilities. I was always told, with great power comes great responsibility. I had great power to treat Nidup how I wanted, but I had an immense responsibility to look after her too.

Recalling my childhood memories are always special and wonderful. I love every bit of it, and I can recall another incident with Dorji and Nidup.

One Sunday, when Mum was preparing to go Sunday shopping, I was pestering her to take me with her.

"Can I go shopping with you, *Aie* (mother)?" I asked.

"No, why?" was her firm response.

"I want to go with you and see what the vegetable market looks like." What I wanted, was for Mum to buy me some new shoes. "I promise I will carry your bag."

"Who will look after Nidup?"

"Dorji will, won't you Dorji," I said pleading. "Say yes, say yes," I sotto voce.

"I will, *Aie*," Dorji said, fortunately.

"Are you sure? Will you take good care of Nidup?" Mum asked apprehensively.

"Don't worry, *Aie*. I promise," Dorji said, pinching her throat between forefinger and thumb, "don't worry, I will be fine with Nidup. You take Karma and go." Dorji spoke sounding all grown up.

"Don't worry *Aie*, Nidup will be fine and *Apa* (father) is around as well. If anything goes wrong, *Apa* will be there to help," I added, looking at her with puppy dog eyes. "*Aie*, it makes me wonder why you are apprehensive about leaving Nidup with Dorji?"

"You will understand one day when you become a parent," Mum said, before adding, "Are you sure? I hope you won't get into any trouble Dorji Dolma," she said sternly, first looking at Dorji and then at me.

"I won't, I promise *Aie*," Dorji said again, pinching her throat between her forefinger and thumb again. That was her favourite gesture when she promised something. So, trusting Nidup in the good hands of Dorji, we left, walked to the road and caught a taxi. Half an hour later, we reached our destination.

The vegetable market was quite big, open stalls all spread out. Vegetables were freshly laid out in lots, and the vendors stood next to them selling. The other end of the market was filled with local produce: rice, wheat, *zaw* (toasted rice), wheat flour, rice balls covered in brown sugar… and in one corner, it was full of dairy produce: fresh cheese, butter, dried cheese, and tea leaves for *suja* (butter tea). Everyone is busy in their world, selling and buying. The hustle and bustle of the market enthralled me.

A boy of my age was helping his mum weighing things. He was using traditional scales and we still use them today. The way he was holding the scales looked precarious, and I could see a contretemps was about to happen at this scene. He tried to balance it, but the weight of the rice was too heavy for him, and he let it fall out of control. It landed with a thud, sending rice flying all over the place. *Oops, his mother is going to go mad*, I thought. Sure enough, the woman started to shout at him.

"You little brat. Can't you even hold that damn thing?" She rushed towards the boy and rapped on his head as hard as she could. *Tok*! Indeed, Tok is the perfect onomatopoeic word for the sound made as she rapped the boy's head! The boy stood there as if frozen to the ground, and I could see his eyes filling up with tears. *Tok!* The rapping went again, and the boy wailed at the top of his voice then ran away as fast he could. I didn't know where he was going, probably to someone who would console him. I could feel his pain. It is not pleasant being rapped. Rapping seems to be a Bhutanese mother thing. I got rapped plenty of times by my Mum, but from Dad, I would get kicked and slapped for being naughty. But I didn't think it was fair on that boy to be punished. It was not his fault for not being able to keep up his heavy load.

I was so engrossed in this drama, that when I turned around my mum was nowhere to be seen.

Where is Mum? How will I get home if I never see her again? I thought, as I started to panic, and all kinds of thoughts were running through my head, but I didn't give in. Before too long, I spotted my mum near a vegetable stand going through some vegetables. I ran as fast as my little legs could carry me.

"*Aie!*" I shouted.

"What?" my mum said, not even looking up, so engrossed she was in selecting the vegetables, I don't think she noticed that I was not with her. *How can she be so careless not even noticing my absence*? I thought angrily.

"I thought I lost you," I said aloud, tears blinding my vision.

"It is all right, Karma, I am not going to leave you and disappear. I was keeping an eye on you, and was aware of where you were," she said comfortingly. Immediately, my opinion changed: she had such a caring nature, and I feel safe when she is around.

"How long was I stood there?" I asked wondering. It seemed like a few minutes.

"Not for long. I called you but you were so engrossed in that mum and son drama, you didn't hear me. So, I thought I will look at these," my mum said, pointing at vegetables.

Mum and I hopped from one vegetable stand to another, looking for fresh potatoes. Mum was very fussy, wanting them nice and fresh without any marks on them. Even if there was slight damage, she wouldn't buy it. After a while, it was wearing me out, and I was bored stiff; I wished Mum had never agreed to bring me with her. After an hour, we managed to get all our shopping done, but by then I was yawning my head off. I tend to do that when I am bored. So, with me carrying the bag, we left and started looking for my shoes.

"Look, *Aie*, aren't those shoes nice?" I pointed to a pair of plastic shoes with a slightly raised heel.

"They are nice," was her reply.

"Can we buy them?" I asked, apprehensively

"No," was the reply.

"Why?" I asked, my eyes threatening to fill with tears again. I could cry at the drop of a hat. It was like a permanent well was fixed in my eyes, ready to burst open as soon as some tension builds up.

"Because you don't need them."

"I would like them, and I can wear them when I go to school on Saturday."

"Why Saturday?"

"Because we can be dressed casually. You should see some of the girls, dressed up to the nines. I am sure they like to preen in front of the mirror for hours on end. I am telling you *Aie*, they dress very smart. Look at me, forget about dressing up to the nines, I don't even have a decent pair of casual shoes."

"What is wrong with your school shoes?"

"School shoes are awful. They are not even smart and they are made of rubber. By the end of the day they make my feet stink," I said this with emotion, tears welling up in my eyes again. I meant what I said about those shoes, they were horrible, ugly and smelly, and they made my feet itch like mad when it was too hot or wet. I had to wash my feet and socks every day to try to keep them smelling clean. I didn't know why it was and I was sick of it; they smelled like a sewage tank.

"We haven't got enough money now. I will buy some next time," Mum said, cajolingly.

"Please, *Aie*," I said, looking longingly at the beautiful shoes. It was love at first sight, but I never got a chance to own them. If I see this kind of shoe now, I will buy it and see how it feels. It may be nice or it may be not.

The taxi ride home was tiring, and the humming noise of the engine lulled me to sleep. It was tiring to walk about looking for perfect vegetables. I didn't understand why slightly damaged vegetables can't be cooked. My mum, nit-picking over vegetables, might have been too much for my child's brain to cope with. As an adult, whenever I went vegetable shopping, I used to throw everything in a bag without even checking. I realised now why my mum was so selective when choosing vegetables. If you don't, the vegetables tend to go off quickly. It is all because one rotten one spoils the lot. The phrase *one rotten apple spoils the whole barrel*, might have originated in this manner. I am still not as fastidious as my mum, but now I pick and choose carefully. The overall experience was not as exciting as I thought it was going to be, but when I reminisce now, it was fun, and I am glad I insisted on accompanying my mum, even though I did it only once.

We got out of the taxi, and we were climbing up the hill towards home when we spotted a figure rushing down towards us with a child on her hip.

"Ta da!" Dorji said, proudly.

"What?" Mum and I said in unison, as we didn't know what she meant.

"Ta da…" Dorji said pointing at Nidup's head. Until that time, we had completely forgotten about the baby.

"I am a professional hairdresser now," Dorji beamed.

Mum and I focused our gaze on Nidup. "Is that Nidup?" I asked bewildered.

The baby looked nothing like Nidup, with the roundest and funniest haircut I have ever seen in my life! A straight, dark brown mop sat on her little head, with the sides shaved to almost nothing.

"I gave Nidup a Japanese haircut," Dorji said proudly.

"What do you think, *Aie*, Karma?" She said, looking at Mum and then at me anxiously.

"Ha ha," I laughed out loud looking at Mum, who was wearing a shocked expression.

"What are you laughing at?" Dorji asked pointedly.

"Look at her! She looks like *Sangay Shamu* (a Matsutake mushroom), ha ha ha!" I pointed at Nidup and went into fits of convulsion. I had to hold onto my sides to stop stitches from bursting any further!

"Umm...you may be right," Dorji said, glancing at Nidup.

All this time, while I was laughing hysterically, Dorji was showing off her latest achievement. After Dorji had finished with her presentation, and I had recovered from my fits of laughter, I saw that Mum was stood there dumbstruck. Not able to get any reaction from my mum, Dorji didn't dare move an inch, with Nidup still latched firmly on her hip. At the start, Dorji looked like a young, excited entrepreneur presenting her new project, but now I could tell by her face, that she was seriously worried.

Suddenly, Nidup said, "Aie," breaking the awkwardness between mum and daughters, and reaching across towards Mum. Her hair flowing freely down to her ears...but no further.

"That is the most hideous haircut I have ever seen in my life," my mum said, trying hard not to smile.

"Phew... you are not angry then? I got worried for a second," Dorji said, letting out a big sigh of relief.

I don't know what it is with children and scissors. My second youngest sister Ugyen, once cut her fringe into a V-shape. She didn't go, "Ta da!" as Dorji did, instead she was hiding behind

Mum when we came back from a pilgrimage. I was so tired after our long walk to the monastery on top of the mountain and back. But that didn't stop me from laughing hysterically when I saw it!

"What's there is to be so envious of postlapsarian life. I wish I could go back to be a child."
John Milton (Paradise Lost). Sometimes I wish it too.

Chapter 4

Hitch-hiking to school.

"Enjoy your childhood while it lasts, it is a once in a lifetime experience, so embrace it with open arms," I heard someone say. I did wonder what they were talking about, but now I know.

I had a very happy childhood, nothing to worry about, loving parents and spending joyful times with my sisters and friends. We used to walk to school and back every day, ten kilometres in total. These days, children moan about walking even a kilometre. I happily did it then, I got enjoyment from it. I am glad my parents never had a car as we would have missed all the fun, hitchhiking, walking, playing hide and seek, picking berries, climbing cliffs by the roadside to munch on clay. Delicious!

I know it is ironic to say that I am glad that my parents never owned a car, but we always tried to hitchhike to school. In my defence, it was more fun hitchhiking. Sometimes we were lucky, and sometimes not. Despite being the eldest, I always shied away from being on the frontline. However, the younger ones in the group would line up by the side of the road, confidently sticking out their arms and asking for a lift. Meanwhile I, and some other older girls, would hide behind the bushes, or walk in front nonchalantly.

With luck, they would be able to stop a truck, and we would all scramble up into the cab. I had the responsibility to help the younger ones to climb into the giant vehicle. I would push them up, until they could get a handhold to hurl themselves into the back of the truck. Once they were up, they were nimble on their feet, and would climb easily over any obstacles. Once they were safely on board, I would climb after them, finding a foothold on the big tyre, then find a place to grip, and gently swing in—and off we would head towards school. We were a good team, and took our responsibilities in our stride. This was the fun of hitchhiking, an entirely different experience from getting a lift with your parents. It was always a treat when we got a lift to school to save us walking the five kilometres. But if we were not able to hitchhike, we walked to school without complaint. During severe weather, depending upon how wet we got, we would be given the day off, or had to stand close to the fire in the school kitchen to dry our uniforms. It never entered our heads to cheat by getting wet on purpose. We tried to stay as dry as possible on the way to school, but sometimes, despite getting under a big bush or a tree, we would still get soaked, especially during the monsoon, when heaven decided to pour buckets of rain over our heads.

We were always on time, never late for school. We would always try to be early so we could play marbles, ring goal, skipping, rubber band, hide and seek, or chase each other, depending on the season.

In springtime, we would play the game 'rubber band'. It was made of lots of rubber bands knotted together to make one, big, circular band. There would be two teams. Two people from one team would stand in the loop, legs apart facing each other, stretching the band into two parallel lines. Firstly, the other team had to jump over the first band, and then over the second band. If they succeeded, they had to jump and land on the bands one at a time. If the first team fails, then the team swaps positions and the other team would have a go. The game would begin with the band at ankle height, and gradually the height of the band would increase. Whichever team was the first to jump the band at head height were the winners.

In the summertime, we played marbles. Boys play '*peel*', where a small hole was dug in the ground for the marbles to go, and girls played '*ring goal*,' where instead a circle was drawn to roll the marbles into.

In autumn, we play '*ring goal*', and despite the same name, this is a different game to the one mentioned above. A big grid was marked onto the ground, with three columns and three to five rows, depending on the number of players. One group had to occupy all the rows with one person on each row, and the other group had to run past them without being tagged. The winners were the group that managed to run back again without being tagged. This game was a good way to keep warm as it involved a lot of running about, and girls and boys would play this game together.

In winter, we did skipping and knitting. These were more of girls' pastimes than boys'. Some boys joined in, but most wouldn't. I don't remember what those boys got up to. Mischief I suppose. In all the games, I did well and taught my sisters well. They carried on with the legacy when I left primary school.

These days, you hardly see children playing those games. They are more technical and IT orientated. All they do is sit in front of a computer or TV, getting square eyes or exercising their thumbs. It is a shame they don't get all the excitement we had, but nothing stays the same forever and changes are inevitable.

My primary school life was full of fun. I distinctively remember one of my classmates, he was a funny boy. When I said boys get up to mischief, he was one of the most mischievous and impish ones. We had a beehive in our classroom that was situated in between the ceiling and the roof; this is not unusual in a Bhutanese building. This boy was not tall enough to reach the beehive, so he climbed onto a chair.

"Tandin, Tandin, Tandin," the rest of the students cheered, encouragingly.

"All right, all right. I am doing it. Leave me alone," he shouted back, like a pro.

As soon as he dug his fingers into the beehive, we could hear bees buzzing around. We all ducked, hiding, and covering our heads.

When we heard slurping sounds, we all looked up and there he was licking his fingers, and smacking his lips. When he saw us watching him, he put his right forefinger on his cheek, making a delicious poppysmic noise. The bees were getting madder every minute, but he was beyond stopping. He stuck his hand in the hive again and licked the honey, but this time no poppysmic sounds; instead we heard him yelp, "*Atsha!* (ouch)."

We all ran outside to avoid being stung, panicking, but they took no notice of us. They were attacking the main culprit from left, right and centre: on his nose, his eyes, arms, legs, every exposed bit of skin. He would have been stung to death if it was not for one of our teachers. He spotted the chaos, and came back with a smoking branch which drove the bees back to their hive.

When Tandin finally emerged from the smoke, we could barely recognise him. His face was swollen, making his eyes mere slits, a nose as big and red as a clown's, lips so thick, he looked like 'the elephant man.'

"You look like a Hanuman (Hindu Monkey God), ha-ha-ha," laughed one of the classmates. While they laughed, clapped, whistled, and cheered, some others with tear-stained faces struggled to smile; those were the faces of those who thought Tandin was being murdered by hordes of bees. From that day on, we nicknamed him Hanuman. We used his nickname all through primary school. He might still be using his nickname to this day. I haven't seen him since I left school, and that was more than twenty-five years ago.

I had a huge responsibility for being the eldest. My school day started at six in the morning. There would be a shout from my mum, "get up Karma!"

"*Ya, ya, Aie!*" I would shout back, then I would get up and get on with my morning chores which included making breakfast; this consisted of rice and milk tea with sugar. The ingredients all came with my dad's army ration: rice, milk, tea leaves and sugar. It was not the best of quality, but it served its purpose for a growing family. There was only three of us in the school then: me, Dorji and Tshering.

"*Ya ya, oie oie*, get up, get up, breakfast is ready!" I would shout, but it was not easy to get them up. At the first call they would barely stir. On the second squawk, they would lift their heads off the pillow and back down again, but when I shouted a third time, they would be wide awake, and still refuse to get up! By that time, my parents would join in to rouse them, and they would rise begrudgingly.

"Why do we have to wake up so early?" they would complain.

"Because we need to get to school. Now get up or I am going to leave without you," I would say, thinking that threatening them would make a difference, but instead of hurrying, they would drag their feet.

Finally, when everybody was up, we would all troop outside to the tap to wash our faces and clean our teeth, brushing furiously.

I had to dress first, which was OK as I knew my style, but dressing Tshering wasn't easy. Dorji was no problem as she could get herself dressed.

"Come here Tshering, we need to get moving." I would pull her to me. She would be stood there lost in her thoughts with her *kira* (dress for Bhutanese women) draped around her shoulders, dazed and yawning time and time again.

Pinning the *kira* on her shoulders was the easiest bit, but the hard bits were adjusting the length.

"It is too short," Tshering moaned if I raised her *kira* up to her ankle.

"All right, all right. Tell me how long you want it."

"Down to my heel," and she would start stamping her feet.

"Like this?" bringing the length down to her heel.

"No, a bit higher. I may trip if it is that low," she would say, pulling it higher. "Like this, not like that." She would put it to the length she wanted.

"All right. I wish you could dress yourself," I said, losing my patience.

"Me too!" came the petulant reply. She could be a right little madam sometimes.

It was hard work to look after my younger sisters, but I got joy and satisfaction out of it. I loved every bit of it. I know I didn't spend a long time with them in school, but the short time I did was wonderful. I liked being the big sister.

"All right, it is done now," I said satisfied. Getting the length right was always a problem for some reason, it was a daily ritual. But after a while, Tshering would start again, killing my feeling of satisfaction.

"Too short! I want it a bit longer," Tshering would moan. "I think it is the *kera* (belt) pulling up the *kira* when you are tying it around."

"All right, all right, come here and I will sort it out again." So, back to where I started, pinning the *kira* at the top of her shoulder. I put my hand through the inner layers of the *kira* to get the inner layers closer, then I pinched the outer edge together, which makes it easier to adjust the length.

"Is this the right length?" I pointed with my free hand. After her firm approval, I secured the *kera* around her waist. "Is this comfortable enough? Shall I secure it now?" She nodded again, and this time with a big grin.

Later, over breakfast, I spoke to Dorji feeling indignant. "I wish she could dress herself. It is frustrating when I can't get things right. Why can't you dress her?'

"She is too fussy," Dorji replied simply with a shrug, and carried on eating.

Eating breakfast was the easier task of the day. We all knew what we were doing. Each one of us would fill a big, white, army mug (we called it an 'army mug', as in those days my dad would get free utensils: a big, white mug; a white plate, and a white Tiffin-box) with rice and milk tea until it was nearly overflowing, and we'd gormandise with chilli paste. What a breakfast—rice and chilli!

The Bhutanese love chillies. We grow our own chillies, and during winter, after harvest time, the roofs of houses will be covered with red chillies to be dried. In Bhutan, we tend to use corrugated iron for a roof, which makes it easier to dry chillies. The chillies would be spread out in a single layer, completely covering the roof. When the sun shines, the iron roof absorbs so much heat making it good for drying the chillies. Within a few days, fresh, red chillies would turn into a dried, dark red. They would shrink to half their size, exposing the iron roof beneath them. Some houses still have the traditional wooden roof, and this works almost as well.

Green chillies are dried too, but first they needed to be blanched, and then dried in the same manner as red chillies; when blanched green chillies are dried, they turn a light brown colour. The Bhutanese winter being predictable, dry and cold, is good conditions for chillies to be dried quickly. It is such a beautiful sight to see—patches of red and brown chillies covering the rooftops.

In the summertime, my dad went fishing and would come home with the day's catch, most of which he would dry above a pinewood fire. With the remainder, he would cook a simple trout curry with chilli, red onion, ginger, and of course rice; that made summer meals always delicious. My dad didn't cook often, but when he did it was ambrosial, a meal fit for a god. It always makes my mouth water when I think back.

Our summer breakfasts would include dried fish. We would grab a piece each to munch on the way to school. This eudemonic pleasure would make our day.

The memory of good food and beautiful moments of childhood are the foundation of genuine happiness, I think.

Chapter 5

The guardian angel.

Being the eldest sibling is a blessing and a curse in equal measure.

As a big sister, I was bound to be solicitous to my siblings.

"Pem's brother Nima beat me, Karma," cried a wailing Dorji, as she came to me one day, tears streaming down her cheeks.

"Stop crying and tell me all about it," I said, with concern.

"I fell out with Pem, and she told her brother Nima, and he is threatening to beat me," Dorji said in distress. I could feel my anger surge and my blood beginning to boil.

"So, he didn't beat you then?"

"No, but he said he is going to put me straight later. I am so scared. Do something Karma," Dorji pleaded.

"All right, all right, calm down now. Tell Pem that I am challenging her brother to a duel. You can do that, can't you?" I said, emphatically.

"I will do that. I can't wait to tell her, and to make her feel what I felt," Dorji said, with the biggest grin I had ever seen in my life. I didn't know how she managed to change her appearance, from a sobbing mess to a heap of happiness.

I made the challenge out of sheer protectiveness, but the big question was, would I be up to it? I was sick with apprehension. It was easier said than done, but I had no choice other than to face the music. Was it pride? I didn't know. I was just a child who wanted to be strong for my sisters and to protect them. As the challenge got nearer, apprehension was replaced by a boost of confidence. We hadn't decided on a place, but we just knew we were bound to cross paths, as we lived in the same village.

The last bell at school rang, and a trail of students came streaming outside eagerly wanting to get home. The path leading up to the main road was jam-packed with school children, ages ranging from ten to sixteen years old. Some in big groups, and some in small groups, and some loners trying to fit in with the rest. It looked like an army of black ants on a mission.

On the main road, students flocked in all different directions: east, west, north, south. I was in the group heading north. My rival was nowhere in sight, but I knew that he wouldn't be far. We normally hang out together, and my eyes were automatically searching for Pem and her brother Nima.

"Where are Pem and her gang?" I asked Dorji.

"Oh, they left earlier," Dorji replied, shrugging her shoulders. "Pem told me that they will be waiting for us somewhere. I don't know where though."

"Oh, are they now? I think they have chickened out," I said, confidently.

We walked through a village market, Khasadrapchu, and were not able to pass it without spending our pocket money. We were all stood there admiring the latest trend in sandals, especially the pair I had seen when I went vegetable shopping with my mother. I know they were nothing fancy or high end like Jimmy Choo or Ralph Lauren, but it was something that gripped my attention. They were just cheap, plastic sandals, with rubber straps around the ankle, and a slightly raised heel. I love high heels. I was drooling over them wishing I could buy them. I would have spent the whole evening gaping at them, but as Robert Frost said: *The woods are lovely, dark and deep but I have promises to keep and miles to go before I sleep.* I composed a poem for my beautiful sandals. It went like this:

Red Sandal, you fill me with joy.
You look lovely and beautiful.
Giving me a tempting wink,
But if only I had few ngultrums to spare,
Or if I had the eternity of doing nothing.
I would stand there gawking, gawping and goggling at you,
But I have got kilometres to walk to get home.

"Karma. Come on! We must go. Stop drooling over those sandals. COME ON!" my little group cried.

"COMING!" I shouted back, and I had to drag myself away from my temptation.

I was in heaven, so caught up with my dreams of owning those beautiful sandals, and for a short while, I had forgotten all about my dual.

Half a kilometre away from the town, I saw a group of boys and girls by the side of the road. All of them were doing different activities: playing marbles, singing, and running around. My inclination told me that our rivals were waiting for us.

Then I saw Nima was walking towards me, rolling up his sleeves, trying to show his biceps, which were probably no bigger than his testicles! He was followed by his sister and friends.

"Ooh…scary," I remarked, sarcastically.

I needed to do something. Forget about a proper bicep, I didn't even have egg sized biceps! But I had to do something to show my feistiness. So, I tucked my hair behind my ears with such force, I nearly pulled my ears off.

"Ooh…I am scared now. Karma is going to beat me," said Nima, roaring with laughter.

"Whatever. Come on then, let's fight," I said, gesturing with my forefinger at him to come closer.

Someone had already drawn a white line between us. We tacitly understood that we were not allowed to cross the line before the fight starts. We looked like boxers, both of us jumping up and shielding noses with our fists.

A white line, I don't know how that came into existence. It was very common amongst children, especially when they were fighting. The fighters would stand on either side facing each other, surrounded by spectators, daring each other to cross the line.

"I dare you to put your foot on the line," Nima challenged.

No sooner had he said that, I stuck my foot out and was preparing to stamp the line. I can be fearless if someone dares me, and I can take up any challenge, but he was quicker than me, and had his foot there before me. I stamped on his foot hard, his face started writhing in pain, but then he barged into me with such force, and I lost my balance and went flying backwards. Luckily, my sisters supported me from falling. Nima took advantage of my lost balance, and didn't lose any time in kicking me. He kicked me so hard on my shin; the pain was excruciating. I nearly burst into tears, but that was not the done thing in front of my younger sisters—portraying weakness. I had to blink hard to keep my tears at bay.

"I am not soft. I am strong and feisty. I can fight and beat him to a pulp." I lectured myself.

"You are going to die at my hands!" I screamed, and ran like an alley cat towards him.

"Karma! Karma! Karma!" My supporters were applauding and cheering. That gave me the strength of a tigress, and I jumped and pounced on him, pulling his hair and scratching his face.

"Karma! Karma! Karma!" shouted my supporters.

"Nima! Nima! Nima!" shouted Nima's supporters.

We were onto each other. He was kicking at me like a wild horse, and his short hair was impossible to keep a hold of. I was like a wild cat trying to scratch him. We were equally matched in different ways: me scratching and him kicking.

"Stop fighting now!" A disembodied voice spoke, but we took no notice of the voice and carried on. Suddenly, our school captain appeared between us shouting "stop!" We were beyond caring, school captain or not. We managed to get around him and carried on fighting.

"Right, that is enough! If you lot are not going to give me a hand in separating these two, you will all be in trouble as well." The school captain looked furiously at our spectators.

Instantly, we were torn apart by the group. I was wrestling, wriggling, and writhing to wrench free, but one against five was impossible.

"Nima, never threaten my sister again. If you ever do that, I am going to kick your balls," I screamed contemptuously.

"Mind your language, Karma. Calm yourself down," the captain said sternly.

"Tell him, not me. He was the one who threatened to beat my sister," I accused.

"See what she has done to me? I am bleeding all over the place!" Nima was wincing.

"Right you two. I am putting you in detention, starting tomorrow."

"Whatever," I said enraged.

"Why me?" Nima moaned

"You are as bad as each other. See me tomorrow after the morning assembly. And now off you go. Karma you go first, and I am going to see to Nima's wounds," said the captain, in such an emphatic tone, we all cowered away from him.

The next day, I was not looking forward to school. I knew I had to face detention. I wouldn't have minded if our detention was sitting in a corner not doing anything, but our detention was cruel. We were made to kneel on pebbles for a whole period—an hour. It was very painful, but that taught us a lesson for life.

"I am never going to fight again," I swore to myself.

My guardian angel episode does not end there. Pem's elder brother was not there when we fought. Nima and Pem must have told him, as since the fight I had the feeling that he had it in for me. A perfect day came to get his own back, when I was walking back home with some of my friends and sisters. On the way, he joined our group and started teasing one of my friends that he fancied.

"Put me down," I heard my friend Thuji say.

"Set yourself free if you can," Pem's brother said.

"I am telling you to put me down!" she screamed.

"You have to free yourself," he said again.

I felt sorry for my friend and so I went to help her. I got behind him and started to pinch and kick him.

"You little mouse, keep off me!" he said, picking me up and dropping me heavily on the ground. "Sit there, if not I will slap you!" he said, pointedly.

"Why should I?" I said, getting up.

"Because I said so. I have already had enough of you. You brat!"

"What are you going to do? Hit me?" I said, and charged at him like a raging bull. I don't know what I was thinking. He was as big and strong as Tom the cat, but I was not as fast and witty as Jerry the mouse, and I wouldn't stand a chance against him.

"Have this," he said, and slapped me right across my face, "I have wanted to do this for a long time now for when you tried to beat my brother and sister," he said, with satisfaction.

"*Tshay mata mae* (don't mess with me)," I said in fury, and went at him like an alley cat to scratch him, but to no avail. He picked me up, held my hands behind me, and no matter how hard I tried to free myself, I couldn't.

"Leave her alone. She was trying to help me," my friend said.

He got distracted by my friend's shout, and I took full advantage. I managed to wiggle myself free, and kicked him on his shin as hard as possible. I then ran as though my tail was on fire towards home, but not before shouting, "I am going to tell my dad."

"*Apa*, Pem's brother slapped me," I told my dad.

"He is nearly an adult. How can he treat a little girl like this? I will go and talk to him tomorrow. Now go and wash your face. You look a right state," Dad said, without even asking why he hit me. I didn't even bother to explain, as I couldn't wait to see my dad knock his lights out. At that moment, I couldn't be any prouder of my dad's protectiveness, and I felt blessed to be his daughter. Our guardian angel.

"Why did you hit my girl?" my dad asked, as he confronted Pem's brother the next day.

"Because she is a brat," he replied, with malice.

"Whether she is a brat or not, it is none of your business. If she was misbehaving, you should tell me rather than hitting her like that," my dad said.

"Shut up, old man!"

"Say that again," my dad said, and shoved him against the wall, ready to punch him. Then my excitement of getting revenge was replaced by fear.

"Dad, stop it!" I said.

"I need to teach this boy a lesson. From now on, if I even hear you have pointed a finger at my daughter, I am going to knock the living daylights out of you, do you hear me?" my dad said.

"Yes, *leybay (sir) Thinley*," Pem's brother replied, a bit shaken. I was not surprised, my dad sounded like a giant with his sonorous voice.

"And don't you dare call me an old man. Do you understand?" my dad said, jabbing his finger on his nose.

"Sorry, I won't do it again," he said.

From that day onwards, Pem's brother ignored me completely and vice versa. His sister and my sister Dorji, having forgotten this episode, soon became friends again.

This is what you do as a child. Have a big row one time, and become firm friends the next. I don't think it was a good idea for an adult to get involved. There is always a chance an adult would end up making a lifelong enemy.

My mum, and the wife of my dad's colleague, didn't talk for a few months because of us children. Me and my three siblings, and their two children, had a quarrel one day over who was going to pick the pears from the trees. We didn't manage to agree. Dorji, being light-footed, managed to climb ahead and picked the pears. The second eldest daughter of my dad's colleague, threw a tantrum and hit me with a stick, and we ended up fighting. Their mother came out from nowhere and started throwing abuse at us. My mother must have had heard it, as a few minutes later, she appeared and joined the shouting match.

It felt good to have someone behind us, watching our backs. Our guardian angels! *Kadrinchay la.*

Chapter 6

Misbehaving.

Summertime is the season for *Sisi shamu*, wild yellow mushrooms (Girolle). I don't know how or why it got its name *Sisi shamu: sisi* means oak and *shamu* means mushroom. They are not grown on or under oak trees, but tend to flourish well under holly and pine trees.

One morning, on the way to school, maybe a kilometre away from home, we decided to change our course of action, and go mushroom hunting for the day instead. We were heading home after a fruitful day, in a euphoric state, thinking that it was well-timed with the normal school home time, until we were confronted by our dad as we were about to cross a wooden bridge over a stream. Dad had appeared so quickly that it made both of us jump over the stream in surprise.

"Why are you two home early today?" Dad shouted at us.

"It is not early. We spent the whole day mushroom picking, oops, I meant the whole day at school," Dorji nervously mumbled. I had to shush her before she got us into more trouble. My heart was in my mouth, and I hoped against hope that dad hadn't heard her. But no such luck.

"Come here you two. You think I was born yesterday, don't you?" I could feel the heat of dad's anger travelling along the stream in waves toward us. We were stood there like two scared kittens.

"Tell me now why you didn't go to school."

"We just felt like going mushroom picking," I said honestly.

"Haven't you heard that every year people get mauled by bears in the forest? I don't know what you two are playing at!" Dad shouted at us even louder now.

"We are not far from the road. It is not the place bears will come hunting." As soon as I said that, I wished I had kept my mouth shut. I could see my reply was infuriating him. Smart answers bring nothing but trouble in this kind of situation.

"Did you want to be mauled and disfigured like the guy who lives in Ramthogtok?" he yelled; I could see the vein on his neck getting bigger and bigger.

I remember seeing that guy. He was out picking mushrooms in the wild when he was attacked by a bear and mauled, he lost an eye and his nose. They tried their best to repair his nose to its former glory, but instead, it was made to look like a balloon. Whenever he breathed in, his tiny balloon nose would shrink, and on breathing out it would expand. Lucky that he survived, as not many people do. But as a child, that kind of thing did not bother me. When we saw him for the first time, with his balloon nose inflating and deflating, we thought it was funny, and we had to stifle our giggles in front of him, out of sheer politeness. We burst out laughing as soon as he left. My alertness was so engrossed picturing the man in my mind, I didn't notice Dad leaping towards us. Dorji yelled and escaped, but I was too slow to gather my wits. Unlucky as always, I got my share of a whipping, and Dorji's share too.

"This is for missing school." A flexible, willow branch went THWACK! on my bum.

"This is for not being a responsible, elder sister." And he thwacked me again on the same spot. I had to bite my tongue not to cry out loud.

"This is for misleading your younger sister." THWACK went the whipping again, harder than last time. The pain went rippling through my body, and it was so painful I had to roll on the ground to try to ease the pain.

Lucky Dorji, not getting caught, I thought in tears, trying to brush away my pain. Dorji may be able to get away once but not twice. She had a lucky escape that day, but months later she was disagreeing with Tshering. She made Tshering wail at the top of her voice.

"Dorji, what have you done to your sister?" I heard Dad shout.

"Dorji smacked me. Wo, wo, wo," Tshering wailed.

"Seriously, do you want a smack Dorji?" I heard Dad's shout getting louder.

"*Jaydha* (swear word), I haven't done anything. She stole my marbles," Dorji argued.

"What did you say?" And Dad was charging towards Dorji.

"*Jada* (swear word) I haven't done anything. She is being so…." she didn't quite finish her sentence, as she saw Dad approaching fast to spank her, and she raced off like a frightened fawn.

Dad chased her around the Palace and into the apple orchard. She told me later, that no matter how fast she ran, Dad seemed to be only a pace behind. She was aged ten then, I don't know how she thought her short legs could make her run faster than Dad, silly girl! She gave it her best shot though. Dad caught her when she was struggling to open the gate. We were following them, not knowing what to expect.

"Are you going to use that kind of language with me again?" we heard Dad shout at Dorji.

"I won't Dad, please, please, forgive me," we heard Dorji wail.

"Are you going to behave from now onwards?" Dad said, looking angrily at Dorji.

"*Kuchay*, *Kuchay Apa* (forgive me Dad), don't hit me anymore. I will never repeat those words," Dorji pleaded, looking up at Dad with one blackened eyed, her hands cupped with palms touching, and thumbs tucked inside as she pointed towards dad.

"*Kuchay*, *Apa*," she supplicated. We were very quiet, and stood there not even daring to breathe.

"Enough, stop!" my mum interjected. But Dad was beyond listening, he looked like a raging bull.

"You, go inside, and the rest of you," he said, pointing angrily at Mum and looking menacingly at us. We didn't need telling twice, and we scarpered, dragging Dorji with us at lightning speed.

"Why is Dad so mad?" we asked Mum; we were not able to comprehend why saying *Jaydha* or *Jada* was such a big deal.

"Because you can't talk to your dad like that. He is your father, and out of respect, you should never use those words. Do you hear me?" Mum warned.

Being a child, you tend to misbehave not because you want to annoy your parents but out of innocence. Innocence is bliss, but not when you get punished like that.

We were playing 'Bearing': a go-cart made of a wooden plank, attached to three car wheel's bearings to roll on: one in the front, which pivoted to steer us so we could negotiate curves and bends, plus two at the back.

We would roll downhill at the speed of light, and with each fall rip our clothes and scrape our skin, but that never bothered us. We would lie on the road, wincing in pain, until the pain subsided and off we go again, down the hill on the plank, then back up the hill carrying it on our back. It never seemed to tire us and it was part of our delectations.

I forget how many pairs of Dad's army camouflage trousers I ripped playing Bearing. Trousers were not girls' quotidian wear. Forget about wearing trousers, underwear was an unknown piece of clothing for girls. A *kira* didn't provide much protection against a fall. As soon as you fly downhill, your *kira* would billow up around your legs, and when you fell, scrapes and cuts were inevitable. Borrowing Dad's trousers were the only solution I could think of to avoid the injuries. I knew borrowing without permission was stealing, but that didn't stop me. I felt like a professional racing driver in my dad's camouflaged trousers, but I was no Mario Andretti. The ripped trousers I would hide at home, and then I would go back to wearing *kira.*

"Has anyone seen my camouflage trousers? I had four pairs but can't find two of them, where are they?" Dad would ask Mum but looked at us knowingly. He might have had some inkling about us being the culprits, but I am glad I had never been caught in them.

"Don't know." We shrugged in unison.

As an adult, when I was looking after three children, mugs used to disappear at an alarming rate.

"Do you know where all the mugs are children?" When asked, they would either give me a blank look or would say in unison, "No idea." And shrug my inquiry away.

When I think of it, if one of them had broken a mug, then in fear of getting spanked they would have hidden it, after all, if you can't see it, then you can't prove it. I had to buy a replacement every time a cup disappeared mysteriously. Children are children no matter where you go.

One day, we were booming downhill on our bearing, Dorji holding on tight behind me, when suddenly Dad appeared out of nowhere.

"Stop you brats," Dad said, sticking his foot out to stop us.

We had to put our feet down to stop running straight into him, and instantly, a foul smell emanated off the burnt rubber of our shoes.

You idiot! we would have shouted if it was someone else, but being Dad we dare not. Before Dad could grab us, we jumped off and ran as fast as our legs could carry us, along the road, and then into the woods between pine and oak trees. By the time we got to the top of a steep ascent, we were out of breath and panting heavily. When we looked behind us, Dad was nowhere to be seen.

"Phew, that was lucky," Dorji said, panting.

"The danger is not over yet, the bigger the gap, the better the escape, run, run," I said, dragging Dorji uphill again, and then scrambling on all fours: through the woods; through apple orchards; down to a vegetable garden, and into our hiding place—an outdoor toilet.

"Ssshh…" I signalled to Dorji, pressing my forefinger to my lips as her panting was getting louder; we couldn't afford to be seen and get whipped again. Dorji was trying her best to control her breathing but was failing. Her cute little head was dripping in sweat and soaking wet, but in contrast, mine was bone dry.

I don't know how long we had been hiding in the toilet, but it seemed to be for ages, when through a crack in the door, we saw Dad walking down the path towards the village.

"Phew… that was a long wait," I said.

"I don't know how we managed to escape," Dorji said, with a shiver. I am not surprised Dorji was shaking after her last race with Dad.

"Do you think he let us off because we didn't swear at him? If he wanted, he would easily have caught us."

"I don't know," Dorji said, scratching her head.

"OK, let's go home. I don't think Dad will be home soon. We will go home, eat our dinner, and be in bed before he comes back."

"What if dinner isn't ready?"

"If that is the case, we must go to bed without food," I said smartly.

"I don't think I will be able to. My stomach growls like mad when it is empty," Dorji said, with a sorrowful look.

"Do whatever you like. If dinner is not ready, I am going to sleep. When he sees us in bed, he won't have the heart to punish us, and hopefully it would just be a distant memory by tomorrow," I added.

So, hand in hand we headed home. That was a lucky escape, as Dad seemed to have forgotten all about it in the morning.

Adults see mischief as misbehaving, but for children, there is no such thing as mischief—they are just having the time of their life!

Chapter 7

Adventure.

I always enjoyed our walks home from school through terraced rice fields, and in all seasons, whether the fields were lush and green or frosty and white.

In spring, rice plants would be thick and green and ready for transplanting. Once planted, they would grow into ripened, brown paddy which needs a constant water supply through summer.

Croaking frogs could be heard everywhere in early summer; a sign of them courting and mating. Sometimes, they jump onto the path like Siamese twins joined in the middle, scaring the life out of us. Fortunately, we didn't suffer from ranidaphobia. Dorji always used to pick them up by their hind legs and toss them back into the water, but I didn't dare touch them, as I hated their slimy body.

Within a few weeks, we could see glossy, slippery, black dots of frogs' spawn, covering most of the water in the fields. Whenever we tried to pick up a single spawn, the whole lot came out together like a wet, black, dotted cotton net. It was impossible to get a single egg out of it.

We used to capture tadpoles in jars and clear plastic bags. I guess jars and plastic bags are the closest we could get to an aquarium. We would let them go after a few days, some would live and some wouldn't, but we meant them no harm, we did it out of curiosity. We were filled with remorse when we saw the dead ones, and we always sought solace in offering prayers.

"***Om Mani pemay hung, mashay ma thong tho lu zha*** (forgive the innocence)," we would recite, and put them back in the water—both the dead and alive ones.

Then comes the little, black creature swimming furiously, with its large head and tail wagging as fast as possible. The bigger the tadpoles got, the less cute they looked, and then they would develop into small frogs with distinctive arms, legs and head, but with the tail still intact.

Finally, when the tail disappears, a tiny frog emerges, hopping all over the place like excited children skipping along. The cycle goes on and on.

But our excitement did not stop there. Dragonflies swamped the place when the paddy is ready for pollination, and we watched them fascinated. They would hover like a helicopter for a few seconds, make a quick landing, and then take off just as quickly. It made me wonder how they could pollinate the rice if they were there for a fraction of a second. They are fascinating to watch, and with their two pairs of translucent wings, they can easily fly from one rice stalk to another in no time. It was a joy being able to watch dragonflies buzzing around rice fields.

It would take us an hour to get home, a journey which would normally take fifteen minutes.

Sometimes, we got so engrossed in picking wild strawberries. Sweet, juicy, and succulent when taken in the right amount. But we didn't know our limits. We would fill a plastic bag to the brim, sprinkle lots of sugar on them, and then gormandise like hungry wolves. Within minutes, the pain would hit you in the stomach with a vengeance, making you restless and in agony, but we never learned our lesson and kept repeating our feasts.

"Knowing the limit is the sign of wisdom," Mum told us, but it did not make any sense to us, and besides, it was nothing but a platitude.

The source of water which generates the lives around the paddy fields was not enough to irrigate all the fields at once, and farmers had to take turns to irrigate.

As night fell in the village, farmers would stay up guarding the water source the whole night, as they did not trust each other. Some are so vigilant and others very sneaky. Some cunning farmers could easily winkle the water source, and redirect it to their fields. I would say it was stealing, but farmers have no compunction. They would go to any lengths to supply enough water for their rice field. As soon as another farmer finds out, he would come marching to take it back, but the other wouldn't give up without a fight. It would be like mad monkeys in the zoo trying to outwit each other. The whole night, they would go back and forth guarding the water source. It was a pain in the neck when nuisance farmers got involved in stealing water. No peace on these tranquil nights. Even the beautiful Milky Way was not able to ensorcell them. The stars above them ran in a line, lighting the empyreal sky; the Plough on one side, and Seven Sisters on the other. Even those stars shining bright did nothing for belligerent farmers, and it was wasted on them. Every summer, this nightlife came alive without fail.

At other times, it would be courting time. Normally, it would be hard work for parents to ask the younger ones to guard the source. But at the time of courting, they don't need any motivation. They would volunteer, no persuasion needed. For girls, romance under the starry nights is everything. Boys would have different intentions, and would take full advantage.

In a small village, it may be difficult to comprehend, but life did coexist between nocturnal and diurnal in the summer.

We would be sneaking out in the middle of the night to witness all the goings on. Sometimes, we played tricks on those who were guarding / courting by throwing stones and making strange noises; we would have fun scaring them. However, we too were in danger of being frightened to death. We had to be on high alert, ready to run off at the slightest crunching noise or unfamiliar noise in the distance. Even the distant shadows would make us jump. **Drobe hangka dray** - *if you are chicken-hearted, anything can scare you*, Bhutanese saying. It was easy for us and them to be scared, as we believe in ghosts and spirits. In our village, if you walk outside in the dead of the night, spirits are known to frighten you by throwing pebbles and soil at you. Crazy I know, but if you believe in this kind of thing, it is difficult to be insouciant.

Sometimes, right after school, we would head straight for sledging before going home. Once, I ripped my school uniform sledging. I knew I would in trouble if Mum found out, and I had to wear it upside down so the torn bit was well hidden inside. Trying to outwit Mum, I ended up wearing the ripped *Kira* for a year. By then, I had enough and I was ready to confess.

"*Aie* my *kira* is torn," I said.

"How did you managed to do that?" Mum inquired.

"I have worn this for a year now. Maybe life is running out for this *kira*," I said, guiltily.

"Show it to me."

"Oh…ok…" I said, and thought that I'd have no choice but to face the consequences.

"That damage is not because of its age. Stop lying!" said Mum. I knew then that I was cornered and had to come clean.

"I went sledging a year ago and ripped it then," I admitted.

"In future, if something like that happens, mention it to me earlier *marey* (ok). If you don't tell me, I won't know, will I? And don't go sledging," she said, waving her forefinger at me.

"Sorry, I will remember this in future," I added, thankfully.

"Promise me you won't go sledging."

"Promise," I said, with fingers crossed behind my back, as I had no intention of keeping my promise.

The very next day, I got a new uniform and I went sledging. Not because I wanted to wind up my mum. It was all because sledging would entice you into flying downhill as fast as you dared.

While we were sledging, we decided to climb a fallen tree. I got up first and waited patiently, giving instructions to the others climbing after me.

"Be careful not to step here, hold there, and hold on tight," I said, sounding very assured and professional.

"All right, all right," they shouted together.

"No need to show off. Do you think you are superior to us because you got there before us?" As soon as my friend Dawa said this, she mis-stepped and slipped; her *kira* got hooked on a branch, and within the blink of an eye, she was hanging upside down, flashing her nakedness all over the place.

"Ha, Ha, Ha!" I laughed, without any inhibitions.

"Look, look, Dawa is upside down. Ha-ha-ha!" I pointed at Dawa and went into helpless convulsions, and the others joined in, laughing their heads off, while poor Dawa was dangling helplessly upside down in tears.

"If all of you have had enough fun for the day, I would like to be helped down," Dawa said, trying to control her sobs. She sounded so small and frightened, and my heart went out to her.

Eventually, we managed to get her down on the ground. She was shaking from head to toe.

"You poor thing. You will be OK now. We are sorry for laughing at you," I said, pulling her to me and hugging her.

"Glad you all found it hilarious," Dawa said, indignantly, her tears threatening to burst again anytime soon.

It was always the same group: me, my sister Dorji, and our friends Dawa, Pasa and Pem that got up to all sorts.

One day, we decided to go picking plums after school, from a farm which was on top of a hill.

"Shall we go plum picking?" Pasa suggested.

"Where?" I looked at him questioningly.

"Up there near the temple." He pointed and my gaze followed. On top of a hill stood the solitary temple.

"Up there?" I pointed, "It will be one hell of a hike. I am not sure."

"Are you sure it is all right to pick them? Won't the caretaker say something?" Pem asked, looking doubtful.

"Of course, it will be all right. We won't be picking many, just a few won't do any harm," said Pasa and Dawa.

Pasa and Dawa could talk us into anything; they were always the main culprits of the group. We went up the hill under the scorching sun, winding our way around prolific thorn bushes, heavy with edible, bright, orange and purple berries that were ready to be picked. It took us an hour to get to the top. On the way up, we would disappear amongst the bushes picking berries, stuffing ourselves, colouring our teeth and tongue blue, and making us look like zombies as we threw rosehip berries at each other.

When we got to the temple, I was surprised that it was surrounded by fruit orchards, consisting of apple, pear, plum, and peaches. We tried to get through the front entrance, which led to a big courtyard of large slabs of stone that were laid out evenly; a typical 16th Century courtyard. In the middle of this stood an enormous prayer flag, flapping its multi colours in the breeze.

Before we managed to get in, I heard a loud whistle from my right. I looked over my shoulder, and saw Pasa and Dawa waving frantically.

"Over here," they signalled in whispered tones.

"Why?" I signalled back. They were beckoning us towards them, frantically.

"What is the matter now?" I said, not very happy.

"You are not going to get any apples standing there like a pilgrim, with your mouth wide open staring at the prayer flag. Come on now, get through the fence."

"I am not doing that. That is stealing. I came here thinking the caretaker would be generous enough to give some to us," I said, refusing to go through the fence.

"Suit yourself. Go and stand there. You will be lucky to get one apple, forget about a bag full," they said, indignantly.

I had a foreboding that something was going to go wrong. Despite that, I acquiesced and followed them.

I filled my school bag with apples and plums. Dorji filled her plastic carrier bag with pears and peaches. Pasa filled his school bag and Dawa her *hemchu* (*kira's* pocket). We were all climbing down when we heard a shout.

"You hooligans, scoundrels, get off those trees this instant!" It was the caretaker, dressed in red *gho* and he was running towards us.

We made a quick exit and ran as fast as possible, fruit spilling out of our bags. Within a minute, we managed to create a big gap although we could still hear him shouting at the top of his voice.

"I think it is safe now," I said, looking back.

"We don't stop until we get to the road," said Pasa, running ahead of us, and we followed suit and didn't stop until we got to the main road which would take us straight home.

You should have seen the state of us: hair all over the place, red faces covered in sweat, shivering, and some of us crying our eyes out. Dawa, with her *kira's hemchu* (dress pocket) down to her knees full of fruit, looked like a pregnant woman. She was a funny sight, and despite being out of breath, I couldn't stop laughing at her, and they all joined in for few seconds, but I carried on laughing as I just couldn't stop.

That was one unsuccessful day. I had lost most of my fruit while we were running; it had gone through a hole in my bag which I didn't notice until then. It was a green bag with a shoulder strap that could be made into a backpack. I loved that bag. It was one of my favourites, and now I can't even remember where it went. Very likely it was passed down to my younger siblings.

"The plastic bag was getting too heavy and uncomfortable. I thought I better save myself than saving the fruits, and I threw it all amongst the thorn bushes. I wished I had never agreed to go with you all," Dorji said, red-faced and panting. "We have to be careful what we do Karma. I don't want to be in trouble again," she added, pointedly.

"I know you managed to get away last time. I got whipped more than my fair share on your behalf, thanks to you," I said.

"If you don't tell, no one will know. Keep this amongst ourselves and our parents will never find out," chirped Pasa. And we all looked warily at him.

Despite all the mischief that we got up to, we always had a nice time: adventurous and audacious. One of my favourite days at school were Saturdays, not because we went stealing apples, but because it was just half a day, and we would finish after a delicious lunch of fried bulgur and deep-fried, dried fish. The food was donated by the WFP (World Food Programme).

When stocks arrived from the WFP, we had the responsibility of transporting them from the road to our school stores, and there would always be some naughty boys who would break into it to steal dried fish, soya milk powder or rice. It arrived in huge quantities and pilfering would go unnoticed. I would have liked to steal some and take them home, but I never had the guts, and I was always worried about any comeuppance.

After filling our faces, we would gambol, frolic, and skylark all the way home. I never remember walking back home in rain, as it seemed to be sunny all the time. Sometimes, we would go swimming in the river. I learned how to swim with the help of a jerry can. I used to hold on to it as tightly as possible, and kick furiously until I started to move forwards.

After a frustrating first stage of learning to swim, we would all lay on a flat rock drying ourselves. Lying facing the sky, we could see eagles now and then whirling above us, picking their target. I wondered how they were able to see from such a distance, when suddenly my thought was interrupted by the whooshing, swooshing sound of an eagle, sweeping down into the river, and flying off with a trout that was dangling helplessly by its head, clutched tightly by the eagle's talons. *Poor fish*, I thought.

In Buddhism, fish in general are supposed to be one of the most unfortunate living creatures on the earth. No one feels sorry for eating fish. Once, a Lama was preaching to a group, consisting of one each of all the living creatures. Everybody was listening intently, except for the fish, who being ignorant and blasé about the preaching and started to swim off. The Lama felt insulted and put a curse on the fish for being an apostate. To add insult to injury, he blew his nose on the fish and sent it on its way. That's why it was believed that no one feels sorry for eating fish, and also why they have slippery bodies.

We would go back into the river, and after managing to keep afloat, we moved on to the second stage of learning to swim, where we learned how to use our arms and legs. We called it *doggy style,* as we pulled at the water with scoops, and kicked with our legs; our heads stuck out of the water all the time. Sticking your head out of the water like a dog was not the most comfortable position in the world, but for some reason, all of us didn't fancy ducking our head under, except when we were trying to dive. This was the furthest we got with our swimming. I was the best! I felt like a professional, and I taught a few fellow pupils over the years.

Chapter 8

Adventure continues.

In the winter there would be less greenery, but that did not bother us if we had a place to run wild. We did not think about beautiful, scenic places if we were playing. Trees would be as lifeless as a scarecrow, with their leaves lying on the ground. The wind would be the only one who could bring the leaves to life: tossing, turning, and rustling them, until they would give in and shift their position, making a perfect playground for us.

My favourite pastime in winter was wood picking, as there would be plenty of dried branches to pick. At least we had the sense to prioritise work. We would collect wood and fasten it into a bundle, so it would be easier to carry back home, but me being punctilious, I would try to stack the wood in such a way that it would sit properly on my back. But it was hard work to get it the way I wanted. I had to try a few times before I got it right.

Satisfied with my bundle, we would spend the rest of the day chasing each other, playing hide and seek, rolling downhill like excited dogs with itchy backs, and covering ourselves in a fine dust of dried leaves. *Kira* was not the best costume for this kind of frolicking. Since it was made of a single piece of material, it did not give much protection; either it would split at the back, or roll up to your waist, and our body would be covered in the dust. It would itch like mad, but we would be too busy to scratch. Eventually, the itchiness would lose its patience and disappear.

But time did not let us have our way. Before we knew it, the bright, golden sun would be at the horizon, preparing to take daylight away from us and retire for the night. Being high up in the Himalayas, we are not fortunate enough to see clouds turn into a golden hue. The first time I saw a golden sun, surrounded by aureate clouds, was when I travelled south with my parents, via the border town of Phuntsholing, on the way to our village for winter vacation. I was mesmerised by the resplendent sky on the horizon. It was so beautiful; I couldn't keep my eyes off it until it disappeared below the horizon. No such luck in our part of the world. We knew then it was time to head home, but we'd tell each other we would be ok to play for a bit longer.

The light seems to dim with each passing minute. Was it our mind playing tricks on us? Or are we losing track of time? It is mysterious: if you are bored, time is a nuisance, bothersome and painful, but if you are busy, time is a pleasure, a delight, and pain free. The final alarm would ring sooner than we had anticipated. The air temperature would start to drop, and the daylight turned into dusk.

"Time to go home!" the sensible one of us would shout.

Reluctantly, we would set off carrying firewood on our backs, wishing that the sun could stay out longer, or that we had the power to hold the sun in one place with a long chain, until we are ready to go home. It is a good job that we don't have this power. If it had been up to us, we would have never gone home, but time and tide wait for no man and we had to hurry.

Now the time was racing against us. It would be a matter of an hour, when the sky changes from a bright, blue sky to a dark, starry sky.

The dusk was approaching with a vengeance when we were making our way home through the trees, with a stream noisily flowing down the valley, and the night birds started to sing everywhere. The atmosphere was very still but filled with woodnotes: birds tweeting and crickets chirping. Now and then, we could hear crows making a vociferous noise, suddenly setting a chaotic atmosphere as the darkness descended. All woodnotes during the day are pleasant to hear, but in the evening, they have an eldritch and spooky feeling to them.

We were getting paranoid, fearful that a vampire bat might come and attack us. There was always someone in the group trying to scare someone else.

"Look, what is that?" Dawa pointed at the far end of the path, where a gigantic being was inspecting us ferociously.

"We can't see anything!" Dorji shouted, trying to sound brave but failing.

"An apparition, standing very close to that tree," Dawa said, pointing towards the tree.

"Oh shut up, Dawa. Don't listen to her and have us start praying," I said, plucking up courage. Although inside, I was turning into jelly with fear. I hate apparitions.

"*Om maney Padmey Hung*," I said.

"*Om maney Padmey Hung*," the others recited after me.

"**Lama la chab syn chio, Sangye la chab syn chio, cho la chab syn chio, gendyn la chab syn chio. Chab ney dampa kencho sum la chasum chio,**" I recited as the others listened intently.

Translation: "*We take refuge in the lama, we take refuge in Buddha, we take refuge in teaching, we take refuge in Sangha. I am under the guidance of the Buddha, teaching and Sangha.*"

I was so proud to know the prayer by heart. In school, we had to recite it twice a day. Once in the morning, as we prayed to *Jamphelyang* (Manjushri) to bestow knowledge upon us, and once in the evening, praying for forgiveness for our sins and to protect us from apparitions in the night.

The above prayer—praying for three deities—was to be recited if we ever encountered spirits and demons. It was supposed to be so powerful, and in the eyes of the demons, we would be nothing but a piece of prayer page floating away.

"Everybody repeat after me," I said, trying to put brave face on. Inside, I was as scared as a kitten. Being the eldest, the responsibility fell on my shoulder instinctively.

"Lamala Chab syn choi…"

"Lamala Chab syn choi…" they recited after me, and we recited on and on until our throats were dry. I could hear plantigrade wild animals crunching on dried leaves. I was not worried about the wild animals who walked noisily, they are normally harmless, like deer and antelope. I was hoping against hope there were no digitigrade wild animals like a tiger around. They can be very quiet and normally come in for the kill.

CRUNCH! I heard a loud crushing of leaves nearby making me jump.

Let me be the only one who heard this noise, I prayed, not knowing whether the others had heard it, or was it my imagination running wild? I think I did a good job as none of them panicked and followed my lead praying.

If it had been daytime, I would have been tempted to lie on the fallen leaves, listen to all the wonderful sounds, and watch animals gambolling in the woods. But with pitch blackness not far behind, every sound was eerie and scary. I felt like a protagonist in a horror movie: creeping around and trying to find the way back, surrounded by hundreds of sounds and noises.

"*Lamala chab syn choi…*" we kept reciting, and I was congratulating myself for keeping calm—*well done.* When Dawa, pain in the backside as always, decided to run, and the rest followed suit like scared sheep, screaming and shouting with wood bundles on our backs. We could run no further than half a kilometre, when Dorji and I decided to leave our wood behind to make it easier to exit from this scary wood, and the rest did the same except for Denka—she insisted on carrying her wood. She had the daftest basket made of bamboo which was very difficult to walk with, forget about running. I wished that she could stop being so stupid, as it was slowing us all down. We were racing ahead of her, and she couldn't keep up and started to wail.

"*Jaydha*, leave the wood behind!" we shouted.

"I don't want to. I need wood for the fire tonight. If I go without wood, my mother will go mad at me." And then she let out a howl of anguish.

We had no choice but to slow down for her. It was getting darker every minute, but this stupid girl wouldn't leave her wood behind and was holding us up.

"Dawa, you have to stop scaring us. I am warning you!" I said angrily, but she just shrugged. "I mean it!" I said.

"I swear I won't do it again, *Kencho Sum* (three deities)," she said, holding her throat between her forefinger and thumb as I looked menacingly at her.

We all calmed down and were halfway home when Dad met us. I could tell Dad was not happy.

"What have you all been doing?" Dad asked sternly.

"We were playing and lost track of time." I said.

"Where is your wood Karma and Dorji?" Dad asked, looking at us and ignoring the rest.

"It was getting heavy when we started to run, so we left it behind," Dorji and I responded

"How far is the place you left the wood?" Both of us shrugged, as we didn't have any clue where we left our wood. "Right! We are going back to get your wood," Dad insisted.

"What? Can't we get it tomorrow?" I said.

"NO! Tomorrow you have to go to school."

Reluctantly, we led him back and found the wood. By the time we headed for home, it was pitch black. In the dark, Dad managed to stay upright even though he was carrying wood, but in contrast, me and my sister were falling all over the place. Dad was getting impatient and started to shout.

"Stop rolling over like an egg. These two children, why can't you walk straight?" I could hear my dad's exasperation.

I couldn't understand how Dad, with his back bent under the weight of our wood, was able to see. He might have had the eyesight of a cat. Dorji and I couldn't see a thing, and had to go on all on all fours to stop tripping over. We had already annoyed Dad enough. We didn't want to agitate him more. I felt like a character in *The Secret Mountain* by Enid Blyton, where they had to scramble on all fours.

"Get behind me you two. You are getting on my nerves," said Dad.

I let Dorji take the middle position. I knew Dorji was paranoid after our run. Dad was leading the way and we felt as calm as anything.

We did not hear a single thing. That was the comfort of being with the grown-up.

I continued reciting on and on in my head:

Lama la chab syn chio, Sangye la chab syn chio…

Dad got us home safely and Mum had a meal ready for us.

"I was so worried. Are you all OK?" Mum said, looking a bit edgy.

"Yes Mum," we said.

"Dinner is getting cold. Let me heat it and we will eat. You two, go and wash your hands," Mum ordered.

Normally, we would have protested, wanting to eat with spoons and not our hands, but being the guilty party, we complied without any protest.

Until that time, I did not recognise the important role grownups play in our life. Again, I sent gratitude towards my parents, *Kadrinchay La Apa dang Aie* (Thank you Mum and Dad).

Life is made of good friends and great adventures. For me, without my naughty friends, I wouldn't have had such great adventures.

Childhood memories are the best part of my life in Bhutan. I had such a wonderful, carefree, enchanting life. I got punished for being naughty, but I was never abused and had such magnificent parents; it makes such a difference. One of the luckiest things that can happen to you in life, is to have a happy childhood and a loving home.

In your prelapsarian life, you wanted to be a grown-up so you could make your own decisions, but in your postlapsarian life, you wanted to go back to the time when you are carefree about making any decision. Children see freedom in an adult's life, and an adult sees innocence in a child's life – my belief.

Chapter 9

Five years later: visiting the woods with my boyfriend.

We could see all sorts of birds in the wild, but there was no one to teach us how to identify them. A few of the Bhutanese names I knew, but I didn't know the names in English. Ten years later, I was wandering in the same forest with my boyfriend, and saw this strange bird sat on a tree with big, round eyes. It was covered in brown, white, black, and grey feathers, but grey was the dominant colour.

We were stood there very still, not moving an inch and not wanting to disturb this remarkable grey bird. As if on cue, both of us placed our palms together and started to recite Guru's supplication, my favourite prayer.

Du sum sangye guru Rinpoche...

We recited this three times. I don't know why we did that; it might be because the bird looked so mystical, sitting on a naked branch of a pine tree, and blending in with the surroundings. Now and then, a soft breeze blew, ruffling its black and white feathers. It was just sat there, under the bright sunlight, very still and unfazed by the breeze. It occasionally swivelled its head, looking at us with its big round eyes as if directing us to do something. We complied and recited all over again:

"I wish to be rich, and happily married in a western style to my boyfriend," I prayed earnestly. I don't know what he prayed for. When I asked he said, "A wish is not supposed to be spoken aloud or shared. A shared wish doesn't come true."

That evening back at my parents' home, we were sat crossed-legged on the floor around the cooking pots. Mum was dishing out our meal of rice and beef ribs, cooked with potatoes and red, sun-dried chilli; Dad was making sure we all got our share.

"We saw a strange bird today," I said, with my mouth full.

"What did it look like?" Dad asked. He frequented that forest many times and sounded intrigued.

"It had two, large, round eyes. Its feathers were brown, black, and grey, but mostly grey," I said, being very precise with my description.

"That could be an owl. They are normally not seen during the daytime, and tend to come out at night for hunting. If you see an owl during the daytime, it is supposed to be a bad omen," Dad added, ominously.

"Oh," I said, thinking back to my prayer.

"Look, there is nothing to worry about. Don't take any note of my ecclesiastical beliefs. ***Na ta mi na nay pa mi*** - *if you don't take things literally, it won't affect you.* Come on, cheer up Karma," he said soothingly, easing my uneasiness; but my mind kept wandering back to the wishes I had made:

To find **THE LOVE OF MY LIFE**.
To be **DELIRIOUSLY HAPPY.**
To be **RICH**.
A **WHITE WEDDING**.

My mum once said that you should *be careful what you wish for*. But I had done it now and there was no going back. Rewards or comeuppance, I had to wait and see. From that day onwards, my wishes were never far from my mind. And then I read something about *The Law of Attraction*. If you wish for something often, it may come true.

I became a firm believer in *The Law of Attraction*. Over the years, when I wanted something, I used to wish repeatedly, and a white wedding was one of them. I used to watch lots and lots of rom-com films, which heightened my desire for a white wedding. I used to go to bed thinking of a white wedding, and end up dreaming of a white wedding with my imaginary man, a *Chilip*, who can love me from the bottom of his heart. Not for a tall, dark, handsome stranger—a cliché description of a male protagonist in a Mills and Boon book. Figuratively, a tall, dark and handsome stranger takes your breath away, but in a literal sense, aesthetics is a physical appearance of beauty. He might be easy on the eye, but he might not satisfy your emotions. A warm-hearted and caring man is all I needed.

Let us see how my law of attraction works –
WHITE WEDDING!

Part III

Postlapsarian Part II.

Chapter 1

My first job.

Everything must start somewhere and everything has a first time, my quote of the day.

By 2001, my life was running downhill and I was losing control. No career ladder to climb, which I had made sure of by getting pregnant in 1997. I often wonder how I managed to get myself in this situation. Therefore, getting a job as a receptionist in a hotel was a godsend.

One day, in my job as a receptionist, I received a telephone call to make a booking.

"Hello, is this Jigdrel Resort?" a friendly voice said at the other end of the line.

"Yes, it is. How can I help you?" I said.

"I'm calling from the airline company, and want to book a dinner for twelve people please."

"Sure, what day and time?"

"7 pm next Saturday?"

"All right, we have a set menu. Shall I read it out to you?"

"No need. I am happy with whatever you pick, we are not fussy."

"OK, we'll see you at seven on Saturday then. Bye," I said, hanging up the phone.

The rest of the week just rolled by, and before I knew it, Saturday was knocking on the door. That day went very quickly too: setting up the tables and preparing for the dinner that night.

At around eight, our guests started to arrive an hour late. Bhutanese like to follow BST— Bhutan Stretchable Time.

They all settled down for dinner, and left around midnight after thoroughly enjoying themselves. Some of them got too drunk and had to bury their head in a toilet bowl before they set off. As they departed, I was handed a couple of business cards.

"There are plenty of jobs in the company. If you need any help with finding a job, give us a call," I was told, as guests handed me the cards.

I will never forget that day when a slightly ajar door beckoned me to explore, which might have cursed me with a Pandora's box, or blessed me with a golden fleece, but then I had nothing to lose.

A few months later, I was reading the Kuensel (Bhutanese newspaper) skimming through the job vacancies, and there was a vacancy for a traffic assistant in the airline company. The receptionist job was paying me enough to keep me going, but I couldn't see myself climbing the career ladder anytime soon. I was ready for a change. On my day off, I made my way to Dorji's office to use the phone, and called the airline company about the job vacancy.

"Hello, how may I help you?" came a woman's voice on the phone.

"Hi, I saw a job vacancy in your office. How can I apply for it?" I enquired, my heart thudding.

"OK, you have to call in and fill in the application form. If you are shortlisted, we will call you for an interview." The word 'shortlisted' was music to my ears.

"Thank you very much."

I went to the office in Paro, picked up the application form, filled it in, and returned it later that day. I didn't want to pin all my hopes on getting the job; I still had the cards the guests had given me, but I was apprehensive to approach them. You know what people are like, they can say anything on the spur of the moment and I had to tell myself, *if you don't ask, you don't get*. I picked one card and called the number on the front.

"Hello," said a voice on the line.

"Hi, my name is Karma from the Jigdrel Hotel, can I speak to Cheten please?" I asked.

"Oh, hi Karma, I remember you, I am Cheten, how can I help?" he said.

"I applied for a job as a traffic assistant where you work. I was wondering whether you could help me."

"I don't know," said Cheten. That was not the response I was hoping to hear.

"Oh ok, thank you very much," I said, wondering why people bother dishing out their business cards, and asking you to call them if you need any help.

There is truth in the Bhutanese proverb: ***Jin gay say wa ga min go. Chay gay say wa dro min go***. - *Don't be happy when someone offers to help and don't be afraid if someone challenges you.*

While my conscience was busy, I heard him say, "I will try, but I can't promise anything."

"Thanks," I said, and was about to hang up.

"Wait, I am just saying that I will see, tell me again what the job is?"

"Traffic assistant."

"I think I could help you prepare for the interview, as I myself have conducted some in the past."

For the next few weeks, I was back and forth with the job application, meeting Cheten, seeking advice on the job interview.

A few days later, my sister Dorji came home very excited.

"You have been asked to attend an interview at the airline company," Dorji said, approaching me with a big smile.

"I never thought I would get it," I said, "I wonder what took them so long to call me for an interview?"

"No idea."

"Good! Anyway, I am so happy, I can't wait!" I said.

"I am happy for you too. I hope you will get it Karma."

"I know. I can't wait. It will be nice to be independent," I said.

Interview. I hated that word: it was scary and nerve-racking. The day came sometime in February, cold but sunny. All the candidates were gathered near a line of *Chortens* (stupas). They sat gossiping, crossed-legged on the grass with their backs to the sun. Some thought they knew what they were talking about. It was nothing but clishmaclaver—all gossip and idle, foolish talk.

"Can you see that girl, standing on her own near the corner?" I heard a voice amongst the group say.

"Which one? The one with red *tego*?" said another voice.

"Yes, that one. I heard that she is related to one of the managers," said the first voice, pointing at the girl that was standing away from the hoi polloi of the candidates.

"Really?"

"I heard the company is full of nepotism."

"We won't stand a chance. What a waste of time!"

We will see won't we, talking nonsense like that, I thought, and turned a deaf ear to them as they were distracting me and spoiling my confidence.

"Karma," called a lady dressed in a beautiful *kira* with matching *tego* and *wonju*; she looked pretty and the red colour suited her. I stood up, nodded and approached her.

"Follow me," she said, and I obediently followed her inside the building.

I wish I was in her place. Apart from looking nice, she looked confident and so sure of herself. I would give anything to be in her place. Stop wishing and concentrate. I had to scold myself.

"Come in and take a seat." I sat down in front of three pairs of eyes, gazing at me like they were going to devour me.

Do they have to look so stern, I thought, and I could feel my blood pressure and stress levels going up a notch.

"Tell me something about yourself, Karma," said a man in a dark *gho,* glaring at me.

"Umm…my name is Karma Chhoden, I am from Dagana," I said nervously, expecting my words to be all shaky and unclear, but they came out nice and steady which boosted my confidence.

"What are your hobbies, Karma?" said the interviewer; this speaker sat at the far end, a nice looking one with a kind face.

"I like reading books."

"What sort of books?"

"Romantic," I blurted out, before I could stop myself.

"Ha-ha!" they all laughed at once.

What's so funny about that? I wondered nervously, and gave them a weak smile. They carried on laughing and whispering to each other, which made me want to run like my tail was on fire and never come back. But I needed the job, so I stood my ground and put on a brave face. I was so relieved when someone spoke, I thought they were going to carry on laughing for an eternity

"I think that is all. You have done the written test, haven't you?" said the interviewer who was sat in the middle, sandwiched between the stern-looking guy in the black *gho* and the happy, nice man.

"Yes," was all I managed.

"OK, you can go now. We will get in touch in a few weeks' time."

"Thanks," I said, as I stood and left, not daring to look back.

"All the best," I heard everybody say, before the door was shut behind me. I did not acknowledge them and got out of there as fast as I could. I saw the other candidates hurtling into the room.

"How was it?" everyone enquired.

"Scary, and I am still shaking. You will see for yourself," I said, extending my hands to show how unsteady they were. I could feel my hands shaking without control.

"Do you think you will get it?"

"I don't know. They said they will be in touch," I said, and left the building. By this time, everyone inside was impatient to get it over with. I am glad I was one of the first few to be interviewed.

Outside, the wind was blowing but the sun was still out. The sun warming my back, I walked to the taxi stand and headed back home to Thimphu, which took an hour.

"How was it?" Dorji asked, excitedly.

"Horrible," I said, disappointed.

"I was really hoping to get this job and gain some independence," I said, with tears in my eyes.

"It is not the end of the world if you didn't get it. I will look after you," she said, as she consoled me. I couldn't thank her enough.

For a few weeks, I drove myself insane waiting to hear about the job. One morning, a few days after I had given up on hearing anything, I was walking back home after seeing off my dad at the bus station; I was pondering whether to give up my job and look for another, as I was not getting paid on time. I hadn't been paid for two months now.

"Hi, you are Karma, right? What are you doing here, wandering like a lost soul? I thought you might have started the job by now," said a boy with a puzzled look.

"Yes, I am Karma. We have been to the same interview, haven't we?"

"Yes, that is correct. I am Dophu, and I saw your name on the notice board against the personal assistant position."

"Really? I did not hear anything from them, and it was very difficult to get hold of them. There wasn't a single day where I didn't try."

"You should go there in person and find out. I don't think they will hold on to your position for long."

"Thank you very much for letting me know. I need to rush; I want to get there before the office closes," I shouted to him over my shoulder as I ran to Dorji's office; I needed to get some money before going to the taxi stand and then on to Paro. It was lucky it was my day off.

After the taxi ride, I arrived at the building of the airline company.

"Hi. I have seen my name is on the board, the successful candidate for PA," I said, approaching the receptionist.

"Your name?" asked the receptionist.

"Karma Chhoden."

"We have been trying to get hold of you for a few days now. You were very difficult to get hold of." I just shrugged as I didn't know what to say, and I didn't want to go into the long story of explaining my ordeal of the last few weeks. It was exhausting.

"Do you know why I was given a PA job instead of a traffic assistant?" I asked, as that was all I wanted to know.

"Oh, that was because one of our PAs wanted to change her job. Since you came second, they decided to offer you the PA job."

"Thanks."

"You need to report to your office tomorrow."

"Oh, I don't think I can tomorrow. What about the day after?"

"Should be fine. Go and see the admin manager through there," she said, and pointed towards an office just opposite her desk.

"Excuse me, sir?" I said, knocking gently on the half-closed door.

"Come in," said a stern voice. As soon I heard him, I knew who he was; it was the guy with the black *gho* and stern face. For some reason, he seemed to have an angry look all the time. "How can I help you?" The room was full of cigarette smoke.

"I was supposed to report to work today. I didn't know I was selected until today, and I haven't brought anything with me to start straight away," I said nervously, not knowing what to expect, and trying my hardest not to inhale the smoke.

"Not a problem. I will give you your appointment letter today, and you can start on Friday, which will give you a day to sort it out. Give me a minute while I draft your appointment letter. Take a seat," he said, pointing at a chair opposite to him, and he started to type furiously. "Here, take this with you when you go to the office. All the best with your new job. I will let them know about your appointment."

"Thank you, sir," I said. As soon as I was outside, I had to take a deep breath to compensate for holding my breath back there. It was awful to get a lungful of the smoke, but I still thought smoking was a sophisticated thing to do.

I was heading back towards the taxi stand when suddenly it dawned on me, I didn't know where the office of my new workplace was situated. I went back to find out. For a second, I thought I would be told off, but he was surprisingly polite and helpful. After the interview, I thought I wouldn't like to cross his path How wrong was I? He turned out to be very helpful. You can never judge a book by its cover.

"Lhamo," he called, and led me to the receptionist. "Lhamo, can you let Karma know where the hangar is please? Thanks," he said to the lady who was on the phone, and disappeared into his office which was filled with cigarette smoke. No wonder it smelt like a chimney; he had smoked three cigarettes while I was there in a span of just a few minutes.

I stood there, waiting for her to finish on the phone. "Sorry to bother you like this..." but before I finished speaking, she held up her hand, signalling me to wait. It was a few more minutes before she was free.

"How can I help you?" she asked, I don't think she had heard what the manager had said.

"Do you know… can you tell me where the engineering department is?" I said, changing my question into a request.

"It is at the airport. Take a taxi, it will be a lot easier," she advised kindly. "It is too far to walk, and you must know the way around to get there by foot. Good Luck," she said, and the phone started to ring.

"Hello," she answered.

"Thank you," I said, and left very excited; I felt like skipping.

That evening, I went to hand in my resignation at the hotel.

"Sir, this is my resignation letter," I said, handing the letter over to my boss.

"What? Why do you want to leave?" he said, looking up from his desk.

"I have a new job now, at the airline company," I added proudly.

"Good for you. Make sure you chase the last bills for dinner. I still haven't received them."

"I will," I said affably, with no intention of doing so.

"Can you pay me my salary, please?" I asked.

"No."

"Why?"

"Because you are not giving me enough notice," he said sternly.

I did not know what to say so I left. On the way home, I walked along the road, looking down at the river flowing swiftly; the vegetable market was bustling with life, and the early spring sun was beating down on my back warming me. I reflected on what my boss, or I should say ex-boss would say now.

It is fair enough if I don't get paid for a month, but surely he can't hold up my previous two months' salary, I thought, but I didn't have the time to go back and argue. I needed to be in Paro by tomorrow.

A colleague of my ex—by this time, we were in and out of our relationship so many times, I didn't know what he was to me, so to keep it simple, I called him my ex—had a wife and children in Paro. They kindly offered to put me up until I found my own accommodation.

Paro, here I come!

Chapter 2

Independence and joy at having your own money.

Two weeks passed by in the blink of an eye. My job was not bad, but starting afresh is not always easy. Whenever I made a mistake, I always told myself to keep calm and I will get there one day.

Staying with the family was nice, but I didn't want to overload an already crowded house, and I wanted to have a place of my own. I couldn't wait to settle down, but finding a place to stay was not easy. To begin with, I didn't know how and where to start.

"I need to find a place. I think I am outstaying my welcome," I said to my colleague, Deki.

"Where are you staying?" she asked.

"Now I am staying with a friend in Paro town," I said, not wanting to go into details about my life; however, despite my reservations, I told her I am a single mother.

"OK. I may be able to help. You know Tenzin has one of the company's houses in Khangkhu, near the place that I live. Now, Tshewang is renting it from him, but I think he will be moving out soon." I nodded, listening intently. "He is off to Bangalore, training for a few years. I know Jamyang wants to move in, but you see they are well off, and I don't think they need a company house."

"If they had agreed to let Jamyang have the house, then I don't want to intrude. I should find somewhere else in Paro," I said.

"Don't you worry. I will talk with Tenzin and Tshewang and let you know," she added.

"I am still not sure," I said nervously.

"Don't worry, everything will be fine. Just relax and I will have some news for you tomorrow, definitely good," she said with confidence.

A few days later, Deki handed me a key.

"Here is the key for the house," she said.

"Thanks, are you sure I will be all right to move in?"

"Positive. Tenzin and Tshewang both agreed to let you have the house, but only on one condition. If Tenzin ever wanted to move back, then you must move out."

"That is not a problem. Thank you very much. I will never forget your kindness," I said, elatedly

Getting myself to Paro was easy, but taking my belongings was not. I needed money to hire a taxi and I hadn't any. My salary wouldn't be paid until the end of the month, and it was still a week to go. I didn't know what to do.

That weekend, I went to Thimphu to see my sister Dorji.

"I found a house in Paro," I said, when I saw my sister.

"That is good then, isn't it?"

"It is, but I don't have enough money to hire a taxi to take my belongings," I said.

"I won't be able to help you, I won't be paid until the end of this month," she added, sympathetically.

"I don't know what to do," I added miserably.

"Can't you wait till the end of this month?"

"No, I can't. My colleague, Aue Deki, said I need to move this weekend, as someone was planning to move in before me. She told me to hurry up. I don't want to miss this chance."

"What about the salary your old boss owes you?"

"That's an idea, I never thought about that. However, it is not going to be easy to get what's owed to me."

"I know, you told me all about it. Now go and approach him and be strong, you can do it," she said encouragingly. It was easier said than done; I didn't have the courage of a mouse, let alone being strong.

I mustered as much courage as I could before Saturday came to an end. I marched up the hill towards the hotel. It was a beautiful, spring day, and the sun was high in the sky warming everything below it. Greenery was everywhere, and lofty mountains started to look like green giants. My marching didn't last long, as I was out of breath after climbing a few hundred meters, and I had to stop to take a rest.

I was apprehensive at the start of the climb, but the closer I got to the hotel, more confident I grew. I was proud of myself, and I thought, *in desperate need, I can look after myself.* I prepared mentally for what I had to say to my ex-boss.

"Hi, is the big boss in?" I asked the new receptionist.

"Yes, what do you want?" she said brusquely. *How can she work in customer services with that kind of attitude? Or was it my simple look that prompted her to speak to me in this way?* I thought.

"My name is Karma. I worked here before you, and I have come to collect my salary."

"Sorry, I didn't recognise you. You look very different from the picture I have seen. Take a seat. I will go and get my boss," she said. Now, looking in as an outsider, she seemed to possess an air of authority. I was thinking, *had I also possessed that kind of authority?*

I was sat there for a few minutes, contemplating how to approach my ex-boss, and running things over and over in my head. I knew he would be trying to find a way not to pay me. *He can try. No one can blame him for trying, but I won't give up without a fight this time*, I thought.

"I thought I made it clear that you are not entitled to any salary," my old boss said, as he approached me.

"I worked hard for two full months without salary. It is not fair. I need this money so I can transport my belongings to Paro," I said adamantly. He did not say a word and stood there looking at me.

"I am not going anywhere without my money, if needs be I will spend the night here," I said indignantly, and I plonked myself down on the stairs. I never thought I could be this bold, but the desperate situation needed desperate measures.

"Ask our accountant to give her three thousand ngultrums, not more than that," he told the receptionist girl after contemplating for a few minutes.

"I don't want to see your face again," he said, looking at me furiously. He was not happy. He owed me more than that, but I was extremely happy that I got somewhere with it. I didn't bother arguing, after all, the world is round and he would get his comeuppance.

"Thank you," I said politely. *I don't want to see your face again either*, I thought, and left with a big grin on my face, and a big weight lifted off my shoulders. All the way to Dorji's place I couldn't stop smiling.

With three thousand ngultrums in my purse, I hired a taxi and headed towards Paro with the few things I owned, and everything that Dorji had given me: a rice cooker; curry cooker; water boiler; gas stove and cylinder; quilt and all the bedding. I was so engrossed in my thoughts about the recent events, that I didn't even chat to the taxi driver.

"*Kadrinchay*," I said, handing him the fare after he dropped me off near the house. I carried all I could up to the front door, but to my dismay, the house was locked with another padlock. I fetched the rest of my belongings and piled them on the steps. I was still a bit confused when I remembered, *Jamyang wants the house too. So that could be his padlock.* I unlocked mine and tried to wrench the other lock free but without success.

I was sat there wondering what to do. Then I saw Deki approaching me and I relaxed a bit.

"Are you OK there?" Deki said, walking towards me.

"Somebody has locked the door," I said.

"That could be Jamyang."

"I thought so.''

"He was not happy when Tenzin and Tshewang agreed to give you the house. Come to my house, have a cup of tea and I will call him," Deki offered, making me wonder why she was going to such an effort. Was it my suspicious mind, or was I being ungrateful?

As I drank my tea, I heard Deki talking on the phone. "Hello, Jamyang, it is Deki here. You know our new PA? She is here in front of Tshewang's house with all her stuff. I am calling to see if you were the one who locked the door." Deki paused while listening to what Jamyang had to say. "You can't do that you know. You haven't got an official agreement saying the house is yours." Deki then paused again as Jamyang spoke. "All that matters now is, you have to give up the key," Deki said indignantly. I don't know what Jamyang said, but I could tell by Deki's look that she was not happy. During the telephone call, she was rolling her eyes and shaking her head. "Hang on, talk to Karma," Deki said, handing the phone to me.

"Thank you, *Aue*," I said. (Aue means elder sister/brother in Western Bhutan. Honorific for someone elder to you).

"He is annoying," Deki mouthed, and I nodded in agreement.

"Hello, *Ata.*" (Ata means elder brother in Eastern Bhutan). "It's Karma here. Please can you give me the key?" I said desperately.

"Why should I give you the key?" he said grudgingly.

Because it is my house! was what I felt like saying, but instead I said, "Please Ata, I have nowhere to go. I will move out as soon I find another place."

"You should have never taken any notice of what Deki said. She is nothing but a meddler. I don't know what she has against me," he said furiously.

"I know, *goma thray show* (sorry) Ata. Can you give me the key?" I said, with a small voice, knowing that I couldn't afford to be argumentative.

"I will give you the key, but only if you agree to move out when you find your place," he said finally; maybe he was feeling sorry for me, but I was glad he was not obdurate and had some remorse.

"*Kadrinchay, Ata*" I said.

I moved in and lived there for a few months, before I could hand the house over to Jamyang, Tenzin wanted his house back. By that time, I had gained confidence and knew what I was doing; finding another place and moving was no more a big deal. Tenzin moved back and Jamyang stayed where he was.

For a long time, Jamyang was not able to forgive me. *"Forgiveness is a virtue of the brave,"* Indra Gandhi once said, but for some people it means nothing. I had compunction, contrition, and remorse; I still felt guilty, but you need to fight to survive in this world.

Settled in Paro and with a steady income, I was happy. Wasn't it nice to have your own money to spend? With my first salary I treated my mum, Dorji, my ex-mother-in-law and her sister to a good hearty meal.

The job was my lifesaver. I had my freedom where I didn't have to depend upon my whimsical ex-husband to bring the money home.

At last, at the age of twenty-three, I had my independence and some authority to run my life the way that I wanted to.

Chapter 3

At a glance.

When Jon first saw the aircraft in the hangar in Woodford, England, with the yellow and orange flag, with its white dragon in the middle, painted on its tail, he thought the aircraft came from a country in South America. He was working in the UK, inspecting one of two of the aircraft that belonged to the airline company that Karma worked for.

Then, BAe had to send some inspection engineers to X-ray the other aircraft in Bhutan. When he found out that he was being sent to Bhutan for the job, he did some research on the internet and was surprised to read that on Wikipedia:

Bhutan, officially the Kingdom of Bhutan, is a landlocked country in South Asia at the eastern end of the Himalayas. It borders China to the north and India to the south, east and west. To the west, it is separated from Nepal by India... this excited him, as the Himalayas had always captivated him.

Looking at the flag on the aircraft, he noticed the upper half to be yellow and the lower half orange with a white dragon running diagonally through centre of the flag. When he got he searched on the internet and the Wikipedia says:

The upper half of it, which is yellow and signifies the King who wears a yellow kabney (scarf); the lower half is orange and signifies Je Khenpo (spiritual leader) who wears an orange kabney. The line runs diagonally on the flag from left to right, signifying equal power between the spiritual leader and the monarch. In the centre, a white dragon spreads its majestic body, which signifies the purity of inner thoughts and deeds that unite all the ethnically and linguistically diverse people of Bhutan. The jewels held in the dragon's claws represent Bhutan's wealth, the security, and the protection of its people, while the dragon's snarling mouth symbolises Bhutanese deities' commitment to the defence of Bhutan.

Sometime in August 2001, Jon boarded the plane that he had worked on and flew with its crew to Bhutan. It was like chartering a plane, and the good thing about him being a *Chilip* (westerner in Bhutanese language), was that he was well looked after on the flight by Tandin, the Bhutanese representative in the UK, who gave him the royal treatment. He formed a friendship with Tandin while he was in Bhutan. They got along well, like wood and fire.

They flew via Corfu, a beautiful Greek island for refuelling, and then on to Dubai, where they had dinner at a yacht club and spent a night in a hotel. From Dubai it was on to New Delhi. After refuelling at New Delhi, they set off for Paro—their destination.

The plane zoomed between the mountains which were covered in pine trees, the ground was beautifully decorated with sunset brown, pinnate leaves, and made its way above the Snaky *Pa Chu* (Paro River). Jon was invited to sit in the cockpit for the final descent. He was enjoying the approach. It was hair-raising to be very close to the mountains, but thrilling at the same time. However, if he had thought being close to the mountains was hair-raising, it was nothing comparing to what he was looking at now. The aircraft was approaching fast, the runway looking nowhere as long as it should be. It looked like they were going to overshoot straight into the river.

Rather than staring intently at the runway, he distracted himself by looking out on his right side; there were houses that were scattered in groups, some in the middle of terraced paddy fields, some on the mountainsides, and some on top of the mountains. On the other side were the terminal and the hangar. He was so engrossed feasting his eyes, he didn't even notice the landing gear hitting the runway with a thud. That landing could be exhilarating for some, and daunting for others.

According to Wikipedia: *Paro airport is one of the most dangerous airports in the world. The airport is 1.5 miles above sea level and only eight pilots are qualified to land there.* Not anymore though, as they have a surplus number of pilots now. Bhutanese would say, *Chu kay ru kay ma tsha*, meaning even the deluge won't be able to drown them.

Once the aircraft was towed onto the ramp, tranquillity and serenity settled in. As Jon took the steps down from the aircraft, he took a big gulp of clean, fresh mountain air deep into his lungs. and breathed out a stream of carbon dioxide. Again and again he took big gulps of fresh air.

Umm… I call this Shangri-La, Bhutan, heaven on earth, Jon thought, taking in the views.

The airport terminal building stood in front of him, beautifully decorated with colourful paints of red, blue, black, and green, with intricate fine art on whitewashed walls, and finally finished with a green, corrugated iron roof.

Behind him on the hillside stood *Ta Dzong*, originally a watchtower and now a museum. It is a beautiful antediluvian structure, protectively looking down at *Paro Ringpung Dzong* and *Pa chu*. He had never known such serenity. It was his dream, wanting to be in the Himalayas, and here he was now breathing the very air generated by the great mountains.

First visit

"Karma, can you come to my office?" her boss said, over the phone.

She wasted no time and ran to his office. Her office was situated at the airport in the hangar. As soon as she walked in her boss said, "We have guests from England working on the aircraft. Will you look after them? Make cups of tea or coffee, whenever they want.

"Ok, Sir," she said, and went back to her office. She was sharing an office with Deki, the administration girl.

Then it hit her, the guy who was looking at her earlier might be the one from England. She was not able to say exactly what he looked like, as all she had seen was his head poking over the aircraft wing.

"Aue Deki, our boss said to look after *Chilips*. He said to look after them and make cups of tea."

"Ok, make them then," she said.

"I don't know where to start. Can you help me?" said Karma.

"First go and find them and ask if they want anything to drink. Then phone our catering and ask them to send things up."

"OK." She went out and approached the man working on the aircraft wing, hesitantly.

"Excuse me, sir, do you want anything to drink?" she asked him shyly.

"Oh, a cup a of tea would be nice. Thank you."

"Sugar? Milk?"

"Just milk, please."

After that, she was a tea girl for him. She was glad he was the only one to look after, and she didn't see much of the other guest engineer.

The next day, when Karma was heading across the hangar floor, Jon was crawling on the aircraft wing. He spotted her and climbed down.

"Kuzuzangpola, choe gaday bay yeo," Jon said, looking sheepish.

Karma didn't catch what he was saying. It did not sit well in her ears. He sounded like her son learning to speak for the first time.

"Pardon, Sir," Karma said quizzically.

Jon tried to repeat the sentence but couldn't, no matter how hard he tried. All his hard work the previous evening, learning the greeting, went down the drain. *What was the use of learning last night, trying to perfect it, and she didn't understand a word I said?* he thought.

"Hi, how are you?" he said, enunciating every single word loudly.

Then Karma understood what he was trying to say. *Kuzuzangpola* (hi) *choe gaday bay yeo* (how are you?).

"I am fine thank you, and how are you?" she said.

"I am fine too, lovely weather," he said, pointing outside the hangar.

"Very nice, Sir," she said. And saying goodbye she went back to her office.

Jon liked the way the Bhutanese addressed him. It was either "Sir" or "Mr Jon." He found it very distinctive, amusing, and endearing. He watched her until she disappeared. She walked briskly along the corridor, past three doors, and entered her office at the fourth door where she let out a sigh of relief. In the safe confines of her office, she could relax. She didn't know why she didn't have the confidence to make small talk. She found it awkward; she could be taciturn when she had to talk to someone she doesn't know.

During Jon's first visit, he found Bhutan a eudemonic country even though he spent most of the time working. He did not have much time to explore. The only exploring he did was with the wife of Karma's boss and her friend. They went by car up to Chele-La.

Chele-La pass is situated between Paro and Haa at a height of more than 3900 meters above sea level. They parked in a layby near the top, and then set off to walk up the final 200 meters.

Before he knew it, it was time to head home. He was disappointed the visit was over so quickly.

Second visit

In September 2001, Karma was asked to go and receive some company guests from the airport. Karma and Deki were stood there in the crowd holding their guests' names up, written on a sheet of paper. Karma didn't know what to expect, as it was her first experience receiving guests. She followed Deki's lead, who was much more experienced at this.

Two guys approached them. "I am Jon, we have met before haven't we," said Jon, looking at Karma.

"Hi, yes we have, Sir, I am Karma Chhoden," Karma said, and shook his hand.

"Sorry, I didn't catch your name. Say it again," Jon said. It was difficult to hear her soft tone amongst the hustle and bustle of the airport.

"Kar…Ma," she said, enunciating every syllable, and trying her best not to sound nervous.

"Karma, nice to meet you." He shook her hand again. To Karma's ears, the way he pronounced her name, without the emphasis on the R, sounded like *Cama*.

These Chilips don't know how to pronounce, she thought

"Hi, I am Jon," he said, introducing himself to Deki, then facing both of the girls he said, "This is Matthew," pointing to his colleague, and Matthew shook hands with them.

Karma noticed Matthew was slightly overweight and taller. Jon is shorter but the good-looking one.

"Hi, I am Deki Wangmo, I am the administrator, and Karma is a PA. Is it ok if we take you straight to your hotel?" Deki spoke confidently, and Karma wished that she could do the same.

Karma was feeling a bit uncomfortable in the proximity of the *Chilips.* The only association she had had with *Chilips* before was with her Canadian boss. Suddenly, she became self-conscious, and hoped she looked presentable with her grey kira, grey wonju and black tego.

She got little information from her second boss when she was summoned to his office; he didn't elaborate much. All she gathered was the *Chilips* were here to X-ray their aircraft, and she was supposed to look after them during their time in Bhutan.

She had seen *Chilips* before as tourists. They have such fair skin, fawn hair, and different shades of eye colour, and she couldn't help but think that they were superhuman. She thought they were to be treated like Kings. She had heard that their tummies could easily get upset. She made a mental note to prioritise hygiene when she was around them. She wouldn't normally, as

Bhutanese tummies are made of iron and do not get easily upset.

One of Karma's friends had parents who had rented a house to some *Chilips*. The way they dressed, talked, behaved, and ate intrigued her friend's imagination as a child. One day, she decided to peek in their septic tank, expecting to see well-scented poo. But lo and behold, all she saw was chocolate logs floating around, exactly like their own septic tank.

"It was very difficult to comprehend," Karma's friend said, reflecting on her little adventurous episode.

"Wasn't it obvious that whatever you eat needs to be digested and becomes poo," Karma said, recollecting what her mum once said. *Food can look delicious and smell divine, but on consumption, it will digest into a thing called poo, which neither looks delicious nor does it possess its original, aromatic smell.*

"I did wonder for a long time, how was that possible? They don't eat rice like us, two plates full at a time. So, I thought that as they ate different things from us, they may have a different poo," the friend said naively.

"Really?" Karma said grinning.

"Yes!"

"Don't tell me you still believe their poo is different from ours," Karma added incredulously, rolling her eyes.

"A small part of me still thinks they could have better poo than us," said the friend, and started to giggle. She set Karma off, and she went into fits of laughter too.

Karma did speak English, but not to the extent where she could converse easily. She had spoken a few English words with her boss for five months now. She was still nowhere as good as she would like to be. She had to try harder, and learn new tricks to fit in this world.

"How was your flight? I hope it was not too long," Deki was saying in her perfect English. Karma felt so inadequate compared to her. Deki was very good at speaking English, operating computers, on the phone, in fact in everything. She hated being second to her, but she didn't have a choice, and everything must start somewhere. They were approaching the staff bus now. Jon and his colleague took the front seat, Karma and Deki sat at the back. Jon offered the front seat, but they wouldn't take it.

"It was long but not too bad, I am glad to be back though, it is beautiful," said Jon, admiring and relishing the peace and calm of the Bhutanese environment.

They were conversing freely as Karma sat there like a spare part, but she was content listening to them, nodding and smiling when Jon cast a glance at her. After meeting his eyes briefly, which made her nervous, she turned away, not able to hold his gaze for long. Instead, she looked out of the bus window watching willow trees flying past, and a murder of crows in the distance.

"So, Karma, how long have you worked here?" she heard him say.

"Umm...five," counting on her fingers to make sure she was correct, before saying, "no, six months. I started in March."

Small talk was not easy. She was thankful Deki was there with her. She wouldn't know where to start after the initial introduction. Even though she was nervous, she was glad he was involving her in their conversation. There is no worse feeling than being ignored completely.

"Is this your first job?"

"Yes."

"Have you got family here with you?"

"Yes, my son, my niece and my mother."

"Ah...ok."

"Deki has all her family here," Karma said.

"Have you?"

"Yes, I am from Paro, all my aunties, uncles..." and Deki carried on chatting happily again with Jon.

Karma was happy to gaze out of the window again and her mind wandered off. She didn't know for how long she was sat listening to them talking, and she would hear the rumble of the bus engine in the background, and feel the fresh breeze blowing through her hair. When the talking stopped she glanced at Deki; she was busy digging into her betel nut bag choosing a nut to chew. Matthew had dozed off, and Jon was intently absorbing his surroundings.

They were driving at forty kilometres an hour on the airport road, which was straight as an arrow. They soon came to a junction, then turned right into a village of about thirty houses built of beaten clay, wood, and stones; some were two storeys high, some only one. They all had to be built in the traditional style.

Karma was glad their government insisted on traditional buildings to create uniformity, even the modern buildings must look traditional from the outside. The architecture is uniquely Bhutanese. Walls are all whitewashed, the ground floor has a few wooden windows, and was used as storage or a shed for cattle. The first floor consists of living quarters, a living room/bedroom, a kitchen, and an altar. The window frames are of carved wood, all handcrafted. There is an open attic, and a slightly raised middle roof gives enough fresh air to dry beef. Roofs are either corrugated iron roofs, or a traditional wooden roof which is tied down with strong bamboo strings; this is weighted down with stones from the river.

Willow trees were planted in rows by the roadside, and were shedding their greenish, flavescent leaves on that autumn day. Chirping crickets were making a vociferous noise whilst clinging onto the trees' hard, brown bark. A slight breeze would send fragile but beautiful leaves tumbling through the air onto the road, and some onto our bus, a sign of impending autumn. Paddies were fully grown now, ready for harvest, and they could see the golden heads of paddies with bountiful grains; now and then, a fresh breeze would sway their heads left and right. The stalks looked very thin, but they have got enough strength to hold the rich heads in place. Most Bhutanese villages are surrounded by paddy fields, willow trees, fruit orchards, and mountains. Building styles change slightly throughout Bhutan, just like in any other country.

They drove up a winding road into the pine forest, and then towards the hotel where Jon and his colleague were staying.

"Thank you very much for seeing us to our hotel," they said gratefully.

"You are welcome," Deki answered.

It was the airline's policy to look after their guests, make them comfortable, and make sure their every need was met, but within reason.

Some visitors are grateful, some are not, and some try to take advantage, but Bhutanese are who they are: pleasant, amicable and gracious!

Chapter 4

Hike to Taktsang: a full day together. Did it signify something?

The second time Jon and his colleague came to Bhutan, they caught a commercial flight via Bangkok. However, as they sat in their hotel bar drinking, they watched the TV in shock as news of the attacks on the twin towers in New York filled the TV screens. It is unbelievable how tall, concrete buildings can crumble down to nothing, burying people alive. But no matter how disturbing the event was, life must go on; the world doesn't come to a standstill.

It was nice to be back in the peace and quiet after the hustle and bustle of Bangkok, thought Jon. He wished that he could live here forever. The hotel was surrounded by pine trees. Rays of sunlight filtered through the branches warming the understory. Jon enjoyed sitting on the balcony of his room. He could see the plane landing once a day and hear children shouting and laughing during break time at a school down in the valley, crows crowing now and then, and the occasional car on the road beside the river. At times it was so quiet, he might be able to hear a pin drop.

The next day, they didn't see much of each other. Karma was stuck behind her desk, and Jon was busy working on the aircraft. They came face to face only when Karma offered cups of tea or coffee. Occasionally, he would spot Karma walking across the hangar floor, wiggling her bum and tempting him (so he thought). She was not aware of his gaze, and was minding her own business as she went about her daily rituals at work. If she knew he was watching her every time she went past, she wouldn't have known how to react. Would she take it as a compliment or an insult? While people were working on the aircraft, she hesitated to walk along the hangar floor, but that was the only route to pick up stationery from the stores which were located at the opposite end to her office.

'Hi', 'bye' and 'thank you' was all they said to each other, and they became *hi and bye friends*, as the Bhutanese like to say.

"Will you be able to guide Jon and his colleague for a day, tomorrow, on a hike up to Tiger's Nest, if you are free?" Karma's boss asked.

"I am at work tomorrow," Karma said.

"Don't worry, you can take a day off, and make sure you look after them. But let them know before they leave for the hotel today. I think they are about to leave now," her boss instructed.

She dashed off in a hurry, nearly running into the fly screen door. She could be full of contretemps at times, not looking where she was going. She went bursting outside trying to catch their office bus before they drove off, but to her surprise, they were outside talking with the second boss and some engineers.

Blimey, she is keen the way she came rushing through that door! Jon thought, when he saw Karma hurtling towards them. She felt like a fool and became self-conscious, but she plucked up the courage to speak and approaching them said, "I have been asked to guide you up to Tiger's Nest tomorrow."

"Ok, that would be nice," Jon said. "What time shall we set off?" They agreed to be picked up from their hotel at 9 am and parted their ways.

The next day, at the appointed time, Karma and the driver picked Jon and his colleague up from the hotel. They drove down past the teacher training college, over the bridge, through the hustle and bustle of Paro town towards Satsam Chorten. From there, they took a right-hand turn through the village, and crossed over Pa Chu again. Then, a steep drive to the start of the hike up to Tiger's Nest—local name Takstang. The Tiger's Nest is a monastery built on the side of a 900-meter cliff. It is believed that the second Buddha, Guru Rinpoche, flew on the back of a tigress from Luntshe (Eastern Bhutan) to Paro (Western Bhutan), in the form of one of his manifestations Guru Dorji Dorlo (fiery, fearful and feisty one), to subdue demons and evil spirits. The monastery was built on the site of his tiger's den in later years.

Karma had made a packed lunch of *alu dam*, made from potatoes, chilli, red onion, and turmeric, with chapattis. She didn't know much about the westerner's diet, but she had seen Jon eat Bhutanese and Indian dishes. He seemed to be enjoying them, except when the chilli heat got him. It is common knowledge that *Chilips* don't like chilli. *It is inhuman to make them sweat like that,* she thought. So, with a mild chilli flavoured dish on her back, they set off hiking up to Taktsang Monastery.

Bhutanese don't walk for leisure; they don't understand why westerners are so keen on hiking. Karma liked to hike but only for pilgrimages, and that wasn't often. Her outdoors clothing was very limited. She did not have a rucksack, and ended up carrying lunch in her black shoulder bag. The strap on the bag was digging into her shoulder.

It looks very uncomfortable, but she looks cute with her purple top, black tracksuit bottoms and ill-fitting bra, Jon thought.

Now and then, Karma had to discreetly adjust her bra; she didn't own one of her own and the one she had on was her sister's—two sizes too small. She didn't want to hike up to Taktsang without a bra and make a spectacle of herself, not realising it drew more attention with an ill-fitting one. She tried her best not to be conspicuous, but what she didn't know was that it didn't escape the inquisitive eyes of Jon.

Bras and underwear were not a necessary part of Bhutanese dressing when she was young. She never owned a bra or underwear until she went to boarding school. Karma got the impression that bras were for adults only. Being a shy teenager, she didn't like to show her full bust, and she had tried to hide the fact that she had breasts; instead, she would make her chest as flat as a pancake. Being creative, she invented her own bra. She got hold of some stretchable material, cut it down to her chest size and stitched the ends together, making a flat bra. It looked more like an abs belt than a bra, but she was proud of her innovation. She had that 'bra' for a long time. Now, as a mother of a child, she didn't feel the need to hide her breasts, and ever since, she had been borrowing her sister's bra.

Karma was so used to carrying her load, it took her by surprise when Jon offered to take it. In Bhutan, most of the men expect their womenfolk to carry the load for them, except her dad, who is an exception. She never remembered her dad carrying less of a load than her mum, and he was always the first one to pick up the heaviest bag. Chivalry towards women is the character Karma admired in a man.

Is it a western thing to be so chivalrous? Maybe not, as it didn't even enter his colleague's head to offer, she thought.

The path led up to the cliffside through pine trees with their brown needles settled peacefully on the ground; bare, deciduous oak trees and popular trees were also present. And then a steep descent to a waterfall. The waterfall was not in its usual form; instead of running straight down, it was blown over the path by a zephyr, creating a light shower.

There is nothing more clichéd than a man offering a jacket to a girl and the girl feeling precious. Jon's chivalrous gesture of offering his raincoat took Karma by surprise again. *Is there no end to the goodness of this man? I would love to have this kind of man in my life,* she thought. For the first time in a long time, she felt cared for.

A nice, warm feeling bubbled up inside her. She would give anything to be in this chivalrous world. She didn't know why Jon was being so attentive. She was not too sure how to take it, did he want her or was he just being nice? She preferred the former, but a guy like him and a girl like her have differences like those between the moon and the earth. He may not be remotely interested in her, and she didn't like letting her thoughts run wild. Anyway, she felt blessed to be the receiver of such a thoughtful gesture, even if only for a few seconds.

When they arrived at Taktsang, bundled up in raincoats, she had a hard time trying to get them access into the monastery. She didn't realise that they needed special permission.

"I work for the airline company and these are guests. Surely you can't refuse entry when they have hiked so far? Please, let them in. I will take full responsibility," she requested earnestly. "This is my ID card." It was fortunate that she had her ID card with her.

"You see madam, we can't do that. We have strict instructions not to let any *Chilips* in without a permit," the security man said adamantly.

"Look, I said I work for the company and I have given you proof of my ID, what more do you need? Please, don't let them go without having a glance inside. We will just peek and won't even go right in, just a look around in the courtyard and then we will leave," she said persuasively.

"Don't worry Karma, we can go back," Jon said.

"I agree," said Matthew.

"It would be a shame if we turned back now," Karma added.

"What is this all about?" She heard someone speak behind her.

"*Leybay* (sir)," Karma said, and brought the man who had spoken up to date.

"I am the boss here, let me see your ID card," the security boss said.

"*Kadrinchay, kadrinchay leybay* (sir)." Karma thanked him and handed him her ID.

"OK, you can go in, but no photography," the boss man said, handing back her ID card. "NO PHOTO, OK sirs," he said, glancing at Jon and Matthew with a clicking gesture.

"No photo, no problem," they said, giving a thumbs up.

Some people, Karma thought, rolling her eyes when the guard was not looking.

"You were very persuasive there Karma, thank you," said Jon.

"You are welcome," she said shyly; she was so relieved that she managed to get them in.

The main entrance was not massive but big enough to fit three people side by side. Karma went around spinning the big prayer wheel which stood alongside the entrance. She went around three times and the others followed suit. She didn't know what it was about somewhere like this; it filled her with contentment and happiness. She had always been an eager visitor to these kinds of places. They headed across the courtyard towards a big opening that gave way to a view down into the valley. She dare not look down as it was a sheer drop, with nothing but a wooden railing to lean on. Taktsang is on a cliff edge and surrounded by a big mountain, there was an irenic feel to it. Now and then, a crow would go, "Caw, Caw, Caw," in the distance. The constant burbling of the waterfall could be heard too, rushing down the cliff to join *Pa chu* (Paro River).

"This is serenity," Jon said, taking the words out of her mouth.

"Great minds think alike," she soliloquised

They managed to drag themselves from the view and went into the main temple. Karma started prostrating in front of a big Guru statue, and didn't realise Jon was standing behind her.

Mmmhh...what a view. What I... Jon thought, but he had to stop his thoughts immediately, as there is something intrinsically wrong with having this kind of thought in a temple. He had to tear his eyes away from her derriere. Karma prostrated three times, then a monk dressed in red robes offered her saffron-infused water. She cupped her hand to receive the water, drank it, and wiped her hand dry on her head to complete the blessing. Jon and his colleague did the same. They walked around for half an hour, admiring the beautiful, intricate fine art and the richly decorated statue.

"Are we ok to make a move?" Jon said, and off they went.

They stopped at a cafeteria on the way back down for a cup of tea and the lunch Karma had prepared; she knew that they could get a good view of Taktsang from there. Matthew didn't eat much, but Jon joined in with Karma and polished off the meal.

What a nice gesture preparing lunch, he thought, and said, "Thank you for lunch, Karma. It was lovely." She was self-conscious to acknowledge in words and instead just nodded.

They were gazing at the view of Taktsang, sipping their tea. It was an impressive view. Generally, in September, it can rain a lot, but today they were lucky and it showered lightly every now and then. Taktsang was covered with a light, nebulous mist, creating a hallowed sight to witness. Karma couldn't help but send prayer to Guru Rinpochey. While they were stood there, a zephyr came and started to clear away the mist revealing Taktsang to its full glory. It was glorious, but Karma preferred the earlier view. For Karma, there was always something about mist which brought up piousness in her. They kept on sipping their tea, and now and then, all of them portrayed a strange expression.

"Tea tastes funny," Matthew commented.

"Smoky tea," Karma said, after taking another sip.

"Loveliest smoky tea I ever had in my life," Jon said, with a hint of sarcasm, but he corrected himself saying, "really, it was a very nice lunch and I like this smoky tea. What an experience, thank you."

Karma suspected that the tea was going to taste funny when she saw the girl in the café boiling the water on a smoky, wooden stove. She could have warned them, but she didn't know how to put it, so she chose not to say anything.

"You are welcome," Karma said.

"It was a pleasure spending the day with you, thank you very much. I had a very nice day and a good experience. Do you want to join us for dinner, tonight?" Jon asked courteously.

"Oh, I can't, Mr John."

"Please call me Jon. Not Mr Jon or Sir."

"Come on, we will get you a taxi. Have dinner with us at our hotel; you have got your mother to look after your son, haven't you?" Matthew added.

"I can't stay late."

"Not a problem. We will make sure not to keep you late."

"Ok," Karma said. Jon's colleague was excited but Jon didn't say much. Karma was worried that she had offended him by not accepting his request, but let his colleague talk her into joining them.

To save them from paying for the taxi, she went to see her second boss.

"Sir, I was wondering if you could let me use our office bus?"

"Why?"

"I have been invited to have dinner with Mr Jon. I haven't got a car, and it is difficult to get up to his hotel without one."

"Sure, ask the driver to drop you off, but I don't think he will be able to come and pick you up afterwards," said the second boss.

"No problem getting back. Mr Matthew said they will call a taxi for me. *Kadrin*chay, *leybey*," she said, and hurried to get dressed for dinner.

The dressing was very difficult for her. She did not have much of a wardrobe, but as always she had her sister Dorji's jeans and a loose-fitting shirt. She knew nothing about makeup and usually didn't even bother applying any. She applied a few strokes of eyeliner. One look in her hand mirror and plain Jane stared back at her. She wished that she could cancel her dinner appointment, but again she didn't want to be rude when they were being so thoughtful. So promptly at 6.00 pm, she was entering the hotel. As soon as Jon spotted her, he stood up and met her halfway.

"You look nice," Jon said, not taking his eyes off her. She didn't know how to react, she was a bag of nerves and just smiled. He led her to the table.

It was no wonder Karma felt so nervous; it was her first experience having dinner in a posh hotel restaurant. The restaurant was full of *Chilips* and they were chatting away happily. She felt very alien in that environment. She hoped and prayed that she wouldn't do anything stupid. She could be full of contretemps when she was nervous. She felt like an inept person who fails at everything. *Look, be positive, look at yourself now. You have a good job and you are standing on your own two feet. And you are helping your family whenever they need it, compare yourself to where you were a few months ago,* her conscience told her. She listened to her conscience, and summoning all her courage she followed Jon to be seated.

"Thank you," she said, and lowered herself gingerly into the comfortable chair. She was acting like it was going to scorch her. *Be careful not to get singed by touching such a luxurious item*—Bhutanese humour.

She looked at them and Jon was looking at her with a smile. That calmed her nerves.

"Are you OK?" Jon asked her again. He was making sure she was ok, the last thing he wanted was to make her uncomfortable.

She looks gorgeous in her black top and blue jeans, and with no makeup she still looks gorgeous, he thought. He never liked women who plastered themselves in makeup. He always preferred subtle make-up.

Karma nodded in response to Jon's question, but Jon carried on looking at her. Then it hit her how dumb she might have looked nodding like Philomela. At least Philomela had her tapestry to communicate with, but Karma didn't have such talent, and her tongue was still intact unlike Philomela's; her tongue had been cut off by her brother-in-law.

"I am OK, umm… Sir umm Mr Jon." She was struggling to make a complete sentence. She didn't know how to address him as he specifically asked her not to call him Mr Jon or Sir. In one sentence she managed to squeeze in both words.

"Just Jonathan or J O N for short, please," Jon said, handing her his business card. The card read Mr Jon Francomb.

All the time she thought it was spelt JOHN, not JON. *What a ninny!* She wished now that she had read the nameplate properly at the airport, then she would not be making any mistakes. It was fortunate that Jon and John sounded the same; he wouldn't know that she had made a mistake. Now the spelling of the name was sorted. However, another problem arose: she didn't think she could ever address him by his name, but she didn't know why—she always hesitated to address someone by their name. Was it because she was used to honorific terms, a term of respect? In the end, she addressed him with nothing. Instead, she would try and catch his eye if she wanted to talk. It took her by surprise how beautiful his eyes were: blue with long eyelashes.

It was a luxurious meal with three courses: rich tomato soup, with two croutons floating on the soup as a starter; Chilli chicken, dal, and rice as the main, and vanilla ice cream for dessert. She was worried about how she would manage to use a knife and fork. At home, she uses a spoon if she wants to be elegant, but other times she happily eats with her fingers. She had to keep her eyes peeled, watching them discreetly and ready to follow suit. *Thank God, they didn't notice me watching them,* she thought.

Now and then Jon cast furtive glances at Karma. *She is so dainty the way she holds her knife and fork, and with her neat eating style,* he thought.

They were soon chatting to each other comfortably and the rest of the evening went quickly and smoothly.

Well done me! Karma congratulated herself. *One can learn lots by watching* was another maxim of her mum's. As a child, she used to watch her dad cut the beef into thin strips, polish his boots, chop wood, make bedding for apple trees, so on and so forth. She can now do all these without a second thought. And she used to sit next to her mum while she was cooking. Nobody taught her how to cook, she learned by watching. *Observation is a good skill to acquire*, she thought.

Back at home, she was struggling to go to sleep, as her mind kept wandering off to thoughts of Jon. What a prepossessing and nice man; she wondered if he is married. She didn't remember seeing a wedding ring or a mark on his ring finger. *Chilips* tend to wear a wedding ring if they are married. In Bhutan, wearing rings is not part of the nuptials, and nothing is shown to signify the union of the couple.

She wished that the Bhutanese could have the same traditions for weddings. She would love to wear a white wedding dress, hold a bouquet, have a bridesmaid by her side, and a wedding ring to seal the deal. She didn't know why she always dreamt of having a white wedding. With that thought in her head, she drifted off to sleep.

Karma never shared her dreams and wishes with anyone. She was worried that it would be jinxed if she shared them. *Anyway, it is always nice to have silly and unattainable dreams,* she thought. A white wedding and a life in the west were two of them. *If you want to land on the moon, aim at the sun* was another saying she read somewhere.

Within the last few days, she had developed a feeling for Jon. She didn't know what to call it. *Serendipity?* She felt something for Jon but didn't know what. She was happy to have met him. The trip up to Taktsang had bonded them with an invisible thread. From then onwards, they existed in each other's minds. It could be like the Spanish say, *el hilo roji.* An invisible red thread connects those who are destined to meet, regardless of time, place or circumstance. The thread may stretch or tangle, but will never break.

Chapter 5

The rest of Jon's visit to Bhutan.

Karma had thoroughly enjoyed the meal the previous night, and when she saw Jon the next morning she gave him the biggest smile in the world.

"Would you like a cup of tea, Jon?"

"Yes please, Karma."

They were like old friends now. No hesitation and no awkwardness. Just happy to see each other. Whenever Karma made him tea, the conversation flowed easily, and if there was no work commitment they would go on chatting. One day, Karma was watching Jon working through his X-ray in companionable silence. So engrossed was she, it made her jump when she heard footsteps behind her. She turned around and came face to face with Wangmo, the new store assistant. She had been watching Karma and Jon for a while now. She didn't hesitate to say hello to Jon, and even offered to make cups of tea. Karma would happily have given her the task in the earlier days, but not anymore.

"Hello, Jon," she said in a sing-song voice.

"Hello, Wangmo," Jon said, not even looking up. He then looked up realising that he was being rude. "How are you, you ok?"

"Yes, thank you," said Wangmo grinning.

Wangmo started to flirt brazenly with Jon, flashing her betel nut-stained teeth, offering to make him tea and giggling like a besotted teenager. It was making Karma very uncomfortable, so she bid goodbye to Jon, turned on her heel and left. Karma didn't know how to react to this. She did find it funny, but at the same time, she couldn't help thinking, *how can Wangmo be so impudent? Did she look at herself in the mirror? With those typical Bhutanese village girl looks, betel nut-stained teeth, and kira raised to her ankles. How can she even think that she has got a chance with Jon?* Karma felt guilty as soon as that thought ran through her mind. It was a bit arrogant of her. It was up to Jon how he wanted to react to Wangmo's flirtation.

The place where Karma worked sometimes had a jovial environment. They were like school kids at times. Now and then, female and male colleagues ended up play fighting. One of the store's male personnel was teasing Wangmo. She got hold of an electric water boiler lead, and whacked at him as hard as possible on his back. He bent double with pain and all he said was, "I will catch you later you." It was good of him; if it had been the other colleagues, they might have whacked her back, but he was a very patient man. One time, on the way home, Deki, Karma and he were messing about. Karma picked up a cup and handed it to Deki; Deki whacked him hard and caught his eyebrow and made it bleed. Karma was scared to death and apologised profusely, but Deki didn't have any remorse, and went on babbling about how it was not her fault. That man had the patience of a saint.

However, one day, Karma was on the way to the toilet when she heard a scream.

"*Kuchay, kuchay Aue* (forgive me, forgive me, brother)," Wangmo pleaded and screamed. It was funny to address someone as *Aue* (brother) when it turns out that she was about to be molested.

Karma ran towards the stores where the scream was coming from and peeked through a window. There on the desk, Wangmo was lying flat on her back, screaming the place down. Atop her was the guy who had been whipped by Wangmo a few weeks earlier. So, as good as his word, he caught her and was hell-bent on taking revenge.

"Are you going to whack me like that again?" he asked.

"No, I won't. I won't do it again." said Wangmo.

When the guy saw Karma, he might have loosened his grip. Wangmo pushed him, jumped up and ran towards the door as fast her unsteady legs could carry her. Karma followed suit, forgetting she was on the way to the toilet. When they got to Karma's office, Wangmo looked like she had been catfighting.

Everybody in the office took a lunch break unfailingly. Karma would sometimes bring a packed lunch, and sometimes she would eat in the canteen. But when they have guests in the hangar, like with Jon and his colleague, they were all being fed by outside caterers. After the *Chilips* had had their share, the rest of them would join in. Lunch was over within half an hour and Karma had another half hour to spare. She looked around for Jon, but instead she spotted his colleague with a camera, and he was beckoning Karma. She walked over and spotted Wangmo busy chatting with Jon.

"Can I take a photo of you three together?" said Jon's colleague.

"Sure!" was the reply, and they all stood next to each other; Jon was in the middle.

"Wife number one," Jon said to Karma. Then he turned to Wangmo and said, "Wife number two." All of them smiled as the camera went click.

All too soon, their visit was over. Karma accompanied them to the airport and saw them off. Jon wished he could stay longer, but his colleague wished otherwise. "Back to civilisation!" he announced as they flew into Bangkok. When they got to England his colleague said, "I missed my car. I can't wait to drive it." However, Jon thought, *when can I be back in Bhutan?*

Third visit

At the start of the third visit, Karma met Jon alone at the airport. Karma didn't feel nervous or awkward. They chatted about nothing and everything on the way to the hotel. The hotel was situated above the airport on the hillside. After dropping Jon off, Karma went back to her office. She was so proud of herself for being able to deal with Jon without any apprehension, and she went as far as congratulating herself—*WELL DONE!*

Jon was so glad to be back in Bhutan. He was standing on his hotel room balcony, looking through binoculars at the airport hangar, when a figure caught his attention. It was Karma walking along, dressed in a grey kira and a black tego (outer top worn with a kira). Now and then, high heel trainers would peek from below her *kira*.

What kind of footwear is that? he thought.

Karma was going through her daily duties: tidying her office, sending faxes, printing and receiving calls. She had mastered the phone etiquette: "Hello, how may I help you?" she would say with ease now. Some would compliment her on her salutation, and some would make fun of her. People were forgetting this is good phone etiquette.

She had to get some staples from the stores. She skipped across the hangar floor where people were busy working, some below the aircraft, some on top, and some sweeping the floor. She felt very comfortable in her sister Dorji's white platform heeled sneakers. She was fortunate she could borrow her sister's things whenever she wanted. Dorji didn't mind, as being an archer, she had travelled the world competing, and she had been to South Korea recently where she got the sneakers.

The next day, Jon was in the hanger X-raying the aircraft wings. Throughout the day,

Karma supplied him with cups of tea. They always found time to chat in between. They talked about books. Karma told him she like reading Danielle Steel, Jeffery Archer, and John Grisham; she used to read only romantic books and Mills & Boon were her favourites. She was always shy to admit that she read Mills and Boon. People gave her the impression that Mills and Boon books are all about sex! For her, they are light-hearted books where she could easily immerse herself and get transported to the *Chilips* world. Books were not easy to come by since she left school. To keep up with her reading she registered with a public library. It was in that library that her reading progressed from reading romance to thrillers.

Wangmo seem to be a permanent fixture between them, she would appear from nowhere whenever they were talking.

"Are you married, Mr Jon?" Wangmo asked. Karma winced and thought, *how can she be so bold. I could never ask that question.*

"No, I am not, fortunately," Jon said, looking at Karma. Karma wondered what that meant. "I have a girlfriend and a son," Jon added.

How can he not call her his wife when he already has a child with her? Strange Chilip. I need to stop thinking of him. I don't want to interfere in his life, but I can be his friend, can't I? Hang on there. Men and women can't be friends…" Karma thought. Her wandering mind was brought back to focus when she heard her colleague quizzing Jon some more.

"Do you live together?" Wangmo asked. Karma thought, *is there no end to her inquisition*? Wangmo's questions were making her uncomfortable, and Jon's answers were disappointing her.

"Yes, we live together, and we bought a house together not long ago," Jon added, and that was the final nail in the coffin; Karma told herself that she would never let her feelings show. She can be friends with him and nothing more. She knows how it feels when someone is betrayed.

"I need to buy something for my son. Can you help me, Karma?" Jon said.

"I can!" jumped in Wangmo.

Didn't she hear what Jon said? Some people! Karma said thought.

"Thank you, but no," replied Jon, and Wangmo went quiet.

"What kind of things are you are looking for?" Karma asked.

"I don't know, maybe a *gho*?"

"Ok." Karma and Jon started to decide what Jon could get. They didn't even notice when Wangmo left.

"I am nearly done here for today. I will come and see you when I am finished," Jon said.

Within an hour, they were sat in the staff bus next to each other chatting happily. Karma took Jon to a cloth shop and browsed through *ghos* for boys. Eventually, Jon chose a red *gho* with a white pattern and a *kera* (handwoven belt) and paid five dollars.

"That's the last of my dollars," Jon said.

On the last day before his departure, Jon was outside basking in the sun when he saw Karma walking towards the gate. He ran after her. She looked around when she heard the footsteps behind her.

"Hello," she said, not able to stop grinning.

"Hello, where are you off to?" Jon said, breathlessly.

"I am going home for lunch. I live up there with my son, niece, youngest sister, and Mum," Karma said, pointing up the hill across the river.

"I am walking up to my hotel, do you mind if I walk with you?"

"No," Karma said, and they fell into companionable silence, walking side by side. "Sometimes, I cross this river when I can't be bothered walking up to the bridge," Karma said, when they got to the riverside.

"Do you?"

"Yes, it is cold, but it saves me lots of time."

"Are you crossing today?"

"No, I don't have to be back at the office till two, so I have plenty of time. I will walk with you to the bridge."

They parted at the bridge; Jon wished he could accompany her all the way home.

"Ok then, I will see you at the hanger tomorrow," Karma said.

"Nice and early," replied Jon.

The next day, Jon was flying back home. Karma met him at the hanger and they caught the staff bus to the airport. When he was checking in, they asked Jon to pay the airport tax of $20 and they wouldn't accept any other currency. He took his wallet and went through every partition to check for dollars—there were none.

Karma remembered having some dollars. She opened her purse and there was $20 neatly folded in one side of her purse.

"Here." Karma handed over the $20 and Jon couldn't believe his eyes as he thought, *how can she hand over $20 to someone she just came to know? It could be nearly a month's wages.*

Karma was munificent as she didn't mind helping others. She knew that $20 is a quarter of her monthly salary, but Jon's need was greater than hers at that moment.

"Thank you. You are very kind, I will pay you back," he said gratefully.

"Don't worry, it is ok."

They said goodbye at the final security check. Even as a staff member, Karma was not allowed to go beyond that point.

"Take care, Karma, and thank you for all the help you have given." He wanted to hug her but didn't want to freak her out. So instead, he thrust his hand forward.

Karma was glad that he went for a handshake rather than a hug. She was not a hug person; it had never been a part of the Bhutanese culture.

Fourth Visit

The third visit was the last work visit Jon made. On the fourth visit, he would have liked to have come but he wasn't sent, and his colleague came instead.

Jon was so grateful for all the help and company Karma had given him while he was in Bhutan, and in gratitude, he wanted to send a gift and the $20 he owed her with his colleague. He didn't have the heart to send anything for Wangmo, but he didn't want her to feel left out. So, in the end, he bought a set of small bottles of perfume for each of them. For Karma, he also sent some Danielle Steel books.

Wangmo was over the moon when his colleague handed her the perfume from Jon. Now there was no stopping Wangmo's feelings towards Jon, and she called herself Jon-Wangmo.

Crazy! How can she not know that he is just being polite, and he has a girlfriend back home? Mad! Karma thought. As for Karma, she couldn't stop thinking about Jon in a naughty way, but she didn't let her feeling go beyond friends.

Wangmo was never scared to express her feelings. She came to Karma's office one day to send a fax to Jon. Fax—what an invention! At that time, the internet was very new and was not commonly used in Bhutan, and faxing or using the telephone was the main communication device with the outside world.

When Karma first started working there, she was sat in her office engrossed in her work.

Suddenly, she heard a beep and noises, BRIP BRIP BRIP and a sheet of paper started to print out.

"What was that?" Karma asked Deki, her heart thudding.

"Oh, that, it's a fax machine, all our stores' purchase orders are faxed to the west from here, and that is the reply."

"Is it?" Karma said wide-eyed. She couldn't understand how a document could be sent from the other side of the world, and immediately receive a carbon copy this end. Amazing! She had to have a few practises when she first started using it, but now she could fax with her eyes shut.

"Karma, can you fax this to Jon?" Wangmo said sheepishly, handing her a sheet of A4 size paper face down.

Karma took it but didn't comment as she faxed it. She wasn't the kind to be nosy. A good job it was not Deki, it would be a different matter then. Karma couldn't help mentioning about the fax business of Wangmo to Deki and lo and behold, within a few minutes, she was broadcasting to every single person that entered the office.

From then onwards, people started to call her 'Jon-Wangmo.'

Jon was in his office in the UK when one of the secretaries handed him the fax.

"I haven't read it," she said, but he knew that she probably had a proper read before she gave it to him.

The fax said:

> *Dear Jon,*
>
> *How are you? I am writing to tell you that I am the hardest working and most well behaved girl. I am very good at housework and would be an ideal housewife. I will treat you well and I would suit you better. Be aware of Karma, she will take you to her home, and polish and spoil you with her soft mouth.*
> *With regards,*
> *Wangmo.*

Imagine Karma spoiling me with her soft mouth, he thought. A nice, warm feeling crept up inside him. Funny how things work out sometimes. Wangmo had all the intentions in the world to spoil things between him and Karma, but unconsciously she had made it better. If something is meant to happen there is no stopping it; it will happen no matter what.

Chapter 6

Big wide world and big bad wolves!

In March 2002, I was booked on a computer training course in Singapore for a month. It was the time when the internet was making this a digital world. We had a big, chunky computer and floppy disks in the office, which had less than 1 GB of memory.

The internet was very young then, and I was lucky to be on the training course in Singapore. Thinking back, I was brave in taking this training in my stride as I had never been out of Bhutan. I was born in the capital city of Bhutan, but compared to the rest of the world, Bhutan—with an area of just over thirty-eight thousand square km and a population of less than eight hundred thousand—is nothing.

"Your training is approved and you will start in March, next year," said my boss, sometime in December.

"Thank you very much," I said happily. I couldn't wait, it would be an experience.

November 2001. I can clearly remember the day. I think that this episode in my life made me stronger. Three p.m. and office time was nearly over; I knew that being Friday we would go home early. *Happy hour!* As my boss used to call it. By two-thirty, I would sit there listening, waiting for his footsteps to come down the corridor, and then

I heard him approaching—I knew what was coming.

"You can all go home now, it is three o'clock," came the dozy voice of my boss.

We were preparing to leave when my boss spoke again, "Karma, you must come to my house to sort out some admin stuff. I left it at my place as I can't be bothered bringing it into the office. I won't be seeing you for two days, so I would appreciate it if you could come to my place and sort it out. I will ask our bus driver to give you a lift, and I will drop you off afterwards."

"OK, what time, sir?" I said naively.

"I don't know, maybe at around seven."

"OK, Sir," I said, suddenly feeling uneasy, my sagacity going up a notch.

By seven, I was at my boss's house. I thanked the driver and went inside, and walked straight into an open plan kitchen and sitting room. My boss was sat at the kitchen table with lots of files scattered around.

He let out a big sigh of relief when he saw me. Was there genuinely work for me, or was he just pretending?

"Hello, sir," I said.

"Hello," came the slurred voice of my boss. *Is he drunk?* I thought.

"Come here, you lovely creature," he said.

"How can I help?" I said, closing the gap between us hesitantly.

"I won't bite. Come here," he said, handing me a file.

I took it, placed it on the table, and sat down leaving a chair between us. He got up instantly, and came to stand behind me.

"See this," he said, pointing at a sheet of paper, "can you type it all up?" I could hear him breathe heavily down my ear and neck, and an uneasy shiver ran down my body enticing goosebumps. I didn't know how to react to it, he was making me very uncomfortable.

He did not budge as I did the typing. I hated typing as I typed at a testudinal speed. Deki could touch type, and how I did envy her. I was at an incipient typing speed and took ages to complete a single page.

Just a week after I started my job, my boss was dictating to me as I typed. I kept hitting the wrong keys, and my typing was at a crawling pace. He was stood behind me, sounding exasperated, whilst I was trying my best to type with two forefingers covering more than sixty keys. I felt so incompetent and useless.

"Can I help?" Deki offered, who was sitting at the next desk doing nothing. I did wonder why he didn't ask her to do it in the first place; I didn't understand why he was hassling me.

"No thank you, Deki, Karma needs to learn and we will be finishing soon, not long to go now," he said, sounding a bit more optimistic. TAP…TAP…TAP…TAP…I went, getting agitated as the clock ticked by.

But now my speed has improved, although it's still nowhere as fast as Deki.

At my boss's house, he was easing closer to me inch by inch. He was crowding me with his big frame, and I started to feel claustrophobic.

"Do you want a cup of tea?" he suggested, after a few minutes. His breath stank of alcohol. I shook my head as I thought, *I would rather go home.*

"Suit yourself, you are not going anywhere until you have finished that," he said peremptorily, and disappeared.

"OK, sir," I said, typing furiously, but my fingers were now slow and shaky. How I wish at that moment that I could touch type, but with just a basic computer training, and only a few months' practice, I was typing like a chicken pecking at its feed. I was typing as fast as my two fingers could but to no avail. I felt like I had been typing for ages. I didn't have a watch on me, and there was no clock on the wall, so I lost track of time.

Sometime later, he came back with a bundle of notes in his hand.

"Here, this is for you," he said, and handed me the bundle.

"Thank you," I said, I was so pleased he was very generous. He disappeared again.

I had no clue what I was typing, all I was bothered about was typing as fast as possible and go home. I was so pleased when I was down to the last half page. My boss came back and took up the chair next to me.

Finally, I was done, I didn't bother checking for any mistakes.

"Can I go now?" I said, handing him the paper, but instead of taking the paper he firmly got hold of my hand.

"Sit down, please," he said, pulling me down. "If you do what I ask, I will give you anything."

"NO!" I protested; it came out louder than I intended it to. I knew where this conversation was going. I should have never said I was a single mother. I didn't know that being a single mother can make you easy prey. I regretted not making my reconciliation with my ex known in the office.

"Listen, I won't do anything you don't like. I will give you money and I will buy you an expensive *kira*. You know, the one which is made of silk. You will like that, Gyeden told me."

"Who?" I said, confounded.

"He assured me that if I give you lots of money, you won't hesitate to let me have my wicked way with you," he said salaciously. "I will buy you expensive gifts and I will make sure you go far with your career," he said.

"NO!" I said again. I was ready to burst into a paroxysm of rage, but I had to think twice. If I did that, I might end up losing my job, and then where would I be. Back to square one; unemployed and penniless. I didn't understand what he meant by the *wicked way*, but my womanly instinct was telling me that he wanted to have sex with me. *Slimy bastard*, I thought. I wished I could say that aloud. I didn't know what had got into him. He was old enough to be my grandfather. The thought of having sex with him was making me queasy. *He is too drunk to rape me*, I was thinking, and as soon as that entered my head, I calmed down a bit. I assured myself that he would never be able to force himself upon me. If he wanted it, he would have tried by now. He wanted to entice and tempt me by offering money and material things. My brain was going into full drive to make a quick exit. At that precise moment, he bent over to pick up a pen from the floor. I stood up.

"I need to go now sir," I said, and ran towards the door.

"Wait, I will give you a lift," he said, staggering towards me, but by that time I was outside and in the dark.

I just ran without looking back, my heart in my mouth, down the dirt track and on to the main road.

It didn't hit me until I got to the road that my house was kilometres away. I could walk, but firstly, it could take hours, and secondly, it is not safe for a woman to walk on her own in the dead of night. It was like jumping from the frying pan into the fire, but then I was thinking that I would rather walk and face the consequences than asking that his for help. I half ran, half walked, and stopped when I saw a headlight approaching behind me.

"Please, let it be a taxi," I prayed, and fortunately, my prayer was answered. I waved him down.

"Where to?" asked the taxi driver.
"To Khangku, *leybay*," I said.

"That will be fifty ngultrums," he said, opening the passenger door. I started to panic, as I didn't have my handbag with me, so I hadn't any money. I didn't think I would be able to face walking all the way home in the pitch dark. I furiously patted my jeans pocket and felt a lump, I remembered and was able to relax; it was the money my boss gave me earlier. I am glad I had accepted that money gratefully.

"Ya, OK," I said, and hopped in.

I got home. The house was empty, and a sudden melancholy hit me. I burst into tears. I needed someone to talk to. I knocked at Deki's door at eleven o'clock, hoping for her to still be awake.

"Our boss wanted to have sex with me," I said in tears as soon as she opened her door.

"Oh, I don't know what to say," she said, and gestured me to enter.

"How can I face him in the morning?" I asked.

"The best thing is to go and sleep on it, we will think about it sometime in the morning. It is late now."

"OK," I said, and was preparing to leave.

"You can sleep here on the sofa if you want to. We have a spare blanket."

"Thank you," I said gratefully.

The next morning, I pleaded with Deki to be silent, as I knew what she was like. She and her husband can be very good broadcasters. "*Aue*, please don't tell anybody until I figure out what to do."

"Don't worry. I won't tell anybody," Deki promised.

My boss sauntered in after ten o'clock like nothing had happened. I couldn't face him, so I had to pretend to be busy on my computer until I was sure that he was in his office.

After discussing the episode with one of my colleagues, I decided to go and talk to the manager who was second in command at that time, and who had recently been transferred to our section. I knocked on his door hesitantly.

"Come in," said the voice from inside. "What can I do for you?" he said, sounding very formal, and offered me a seat.

"I need your help, sir," and I narrated the whole sorry episode. He was listening intently and nodding all the time. "Please help me, sir," I said, getting a bit hysterical and teary.

"I will try my best. I am going to see our MD this morning. I will talk with him and will get back to you, but make sure you keep it to yourself."

"Thank you, sir," I said gratefully and left.

That afternoon, my second boss asked me to see him. I went hoping for something positive.

"On my way to see the MD I was confronted by his PA. She was saying that she had heard all about you and your boss." The manager spoke looking disconcerted. I think by that time, my news had travelled far and wide.

"Oh," was all I managed to say.

"I didn't see any reason to bring it up with the MD. Obviously, you haven't kept it quiet as I suggested."

"I haven't told anybody apart from Deki, sir. Oh, and I had discussed it with one of our colleagues too, and he was the one who suggested that I approach you," I said, hoping against hope he would go out of his way to help me.

"Sorry, I can't do anything," was his abrupt answer.

I had never felt so small and alone in my life. It superseded my husband's affair. I went home without telling anyone to wallow in self-pity. I spent the rest of the day in bed crying my eyes out.

The next morning, I got up ready for work. I knew that Deki was the BBS (Bhutan Broadcasting Service) of the company. I didn't even bother to confront her about it. I was a nobody in this world and nobody cared.

It hurts when people gossip and jump to the wrong conclusion. It was hard to be insouciant about all this nonsense. I had to tell myself that what people think is beyond my control, however, I had control over how I dealt with it. I knew the truth and I hadn't done anything wrong, there was nothing to be ashamed about. I carried on with my life like nothing had happened. *The world is round, what goes around comes around*, was my mantra, and it helped me to survive knowing that people like my boss will get their comeuppance.

Chapter 7

Humiliations and sexual harassment.

Nevertheless, I was vilified, and rumours of me sleeping with my boss to get training in Singapore were circulated. Unfortunately, my problems with sexual harassment did not end there.

With my training approved, I was preparing to fly to Singapore via Bangkok; it would be my first time on an aeroplane, and my first time travelling out of Bhutan.

I was so naïve to trust my male colleague and couldn't see how some of them were planning to inveigle me into their snare. Inopportunely, on my flight, the duty engineer was the manager who persuaded my boss to trick me into going to his house; a panjandrum type of person if ever I had seen one in my life before. Just my luck.

"You should ask for help from the flight engineer, he will sort out your hotel and guide you through the airport, so you won't get lost," said one of my colleagues.

"I don't know," I said, "I don't trust him."

"I am sure being a colleague he won't take advantage of you."

"I hope not," I said doubtfully.

The duty engineer was in my office the day before my trip.

"I will help you when you are in Bangkok," he said.

"Thanks," I said. I knew I didn't trust him, but like we Bhutanese say – ***Lha sap lay drey nim dra*** - *A familiar devil is better than a new god.* So, I accepted his offer.

The next day, I took my first ever flight; no apprehensions, nothing, even though it was my first time out of Bhutan alone.

When we landed, the duty engineer was very helpful, helping me to clear customs without any hindrance, and checking in at the airport hotel where the airline crew were staying.

"This is your room," he said, opening the door and showing me in.

"Where is yours?" I inquired naively.

"Here with you."

"OK," I said. I didn't panic when I saw twin beds.

We dropped our bags off and went out for dinner and shopping. I was so overwhelmed by the tall buildings and big shopping malls, and I didn't have time to ponder about sharing a room. It did not hit me until he tried the bathroom door when I was in the bath.

"Can you open the door?" I heard him say, trying the doorknob frantically. I did not know how, but I had managed to lock the door, and I was praying silently, thanking God and dreading to think of the consequences. "Can you let me in?" he said.

"No, I am having a bath," I replied.

"I want to have a bath too."

"I won't be long. Will be done in a second," I said.

I dried myself, dressed and opened the bathroom door. When I came out into the room he was sat on the sofa, smoking with a drink in his hand.

"Come and sit next to me," he said.

"I thought you wanted to have a bath."

"Not anymore, the moment has passed."

"OK," I said, jumped in my bed and wished him, "Good night."

I was dozing off when I heard a dragging noise. I got up and looked in the direction of the noise. He was pulling his bed close to mine.

"What are you doing?" I said, panicking a bit.

"I wanted to sleep next to you," he said.

Just the thought of him breathing heavily on the next bed was giving me the creeps. I didn't know what to do. *How could I be so naive and foolish*, I thought angrily. I was not panicking, that was a good sign. *I am a big girl and I can take care of this like an adult*, I thought. When he did not stop harassing me, I jumped up.

"I think I have had enough of your advances, I want to leave," I said, and started to gather my things to pack.

"Where are you going?" he said.

"I don't know, but I am sure I will sort something out," I said indignantly, and started to unlock the door. Within seconds, he was next to me pleading.

"Don't go. I swear I won't touch you and I promise to leave you alone. I said I will look after you and I will. Sorry," he said. I had to think as I didn't want to end up making a rash decision.

"What are you thinking? I promise I won't touch you, and I will sleep in my own bed," he said again, reviving me from my deep thoughts.

"OK, I will take you at your word." I agreed, as I didn't have any other option. I couldn't walk out; I wouldn't know where to go. The only place I could think of was the airport, and I would have to wait there until check-in time, but that wait would be too long.

True to his word he left me alone and I appreciated that. I hardly slept, worrying and keeping an eye on him. All he did was smoke like a chimney, drink like a fish, and then he dozed off at around midnight. And I followed suit, into a deep slumber.

In the early hours, I was roused from my sleep. "Karma, wake up," I heard him say.

"What time is it?"

"Four. I have to leave now. I will leave the room key here. You don't have to check out until noon. When you leave, drop off the keys at the front desk."

"*Kadrinchay* La," I muttered.

"All the best with your training, and I will see you when you come back. I need to go now. Go back to sleep."

I dozed off again and woke up at ten in the morning. I had a shower, breakfast, and then left for the airport to catch the flight to Singapore.

When I got back from Singapore, he had spread rumours about me having AIDS. I couldn't believe my ears and I confronted him. He denied it and told me it was nothing to do with him.

One day, when I was alone in the office he came to apologise. I was too naïve to understand his crafty nature and forgave him, but I knew I would never forget.

If something does not kill you, it will make you stronger.

Chapter 8

Abroad Alone

I had a great time in Singapore for the first few weeks. Everything went smoothly: one week of work experience and then three weeks of training. By the last week of the training, I found it very hard and I was getting homesick.

There was no chance I would meet any Bhutanese there; Nepalese and Indians were the closest I got to home. On the way back to my apartment on the train, I could sometimes hear people conversing in Nepalese. I used to strain my ears to listen to them. I know it was not my language but I could understand it. I was told eavesdropping was a bad habit, but that was the only way to subdue my homesickness. I felt like joining in sometimes but I didn't dare, I didn't know what their reaction would be.

During the weekends, I went to visit places. The first weekend I went for a walk along the beach and got sunburnt.

The second weekend, I caught a bus to Sentosa. When I got there, I didn't know what to do, so I wandered aimlessly along the seafront past all the shops and restaurants. I was amazed to see so many people wining and dining, and sometimes I sat in the shade just people watching, and wishing I could afford to eat in one of the restaurants.

The third weekend, I went to a theme park. It was very exciting and different. We didn't even have fairground rides in Bhutan. I explored every nook and cranny of the park and ended up on a go-cart ride.

"This is the accelerator to move forward, that is the brake when you want to stop, and you must make sure to put on your seat belt," said an assistant. When we were all strapped into our separate cars, we were ready to rock and roll.

The first part of the course involved the go-kart being dragged up a steep track. This ascending bit was easy, as all I had to do was sit there and the go-kart was dragged slowly to the top of the track. The fun didn't start until I was at the top. I wouldn't call myself totally acrophobic, but I don't like heights. As soon as we hit the top everybody raced downhill. I followed suit, making my heart go from THUMP THUMP to DUB DUB DUB. My go-cart was going extremely fast and I panicked. Instead of hitting the brake, I hit the accelerator and shot off at an alarming speed. I went downhill faster and faster—out of control.

What am I going to do if I have an accident? That was my last thought before I hit the crash barrier made of wagon tyres. The seat belt pulled so hard against my chest, winding me. In a flash, I was at the bottom of the slide, but luckily all the others were safely away from this unfortunate incident.

In agony, I was put on a stretcher and carried to first aid. They did some checks on me God knows what, and I was released saying I was fine to go home. *Home to Bhutan*, I wished. I was staying all alone in a small apartment in

Singapore living on a staple diet of rice, fried chicken wings, and durian fruit drink. During all these times my thoughts kept wandering back to Jon. I could have e-mailed him if it was not very expensive, despite my sensible conscience telling me not to.

The last weekend was hard. I had exhausted all the things I wanted to do, so I decided to stay in the apartment. However, the feeling of homesickness just pounced on me out of nowhere and made me cry. The tears came flooding down my cheeks out of control. I cried and cried and tried to go to sleep, but sleep was hard to come by. The television channel was rubbish; it only showed old Bollywood movies, and I was sick to the core watching the same repeated movies. I decided to go for a stroll hoping to feel better. I felt refreshed but I still wanted to cry.

BRING BRIIING… my apartment telephone rang, making me jump as soon as I entered. "Hello," I said hesitantly.

"Hello." As soon as I heard my ex-husband's voice, I couldn't help but burst into tears again. We had rekindled our relationship before I left for Singapore.

"Hello," I sobbed.

"Are you OK?"

"Yes," I said, tears streaming down my cheek. I was very happy to hear him, and I never thought loneliness could be that exhausting. The first three weeks were very exciting and passed quickly, but the last week dragged on and on; I started to feel like I had been sent to solitary confinement. People in Singapore were not as friendly as people in Bhutan. They didn't smile and they were more like robots than humans; they didn't seem capable of being friendly.

Chapter 9

Keeping in touch.

After her trip to Singapore, her ex moved back in with her, even though the relationship never ran smoothly. Two years later they separated again and he got married, but their relationship didn't end there. Her only solace was thinking about Jon.

The invisible thread was hard to break between them. Even though he made it obvious when he handed Karma his business card at the airport, and asked her to use his office address, not his home address if she wanted to write. She couldn't help feeling hurt, as he made it sound like he only wanted to have a fling with her and that he was committed to his girlfriend. Again she told herself, *what do you expect of a man with a child?* The way to deal with this was to forget that she had a soft spot for him, and think of him as nothing but a friend. It was not easy.

After his third trip to Bhutan, Jon knew he wanted more from Karma, but he was not able to say anything. He was not happy with his relationship, but then he had a son whom he could never abandon.

Their communication was infrequent. The internet only being at its fledging stage, it was difficult to get full access to Jon. She either had to go to the stores' office and use their computer, or to an internet café in the town. All the offices were depending mainly on the store's internet connection. Every time she needed to send an e-mail she had to seek permission, and this was received coldly if she asked too often. The store's manager would be sat there staring at his computer, not uttering a word to her, as if mentally telling her to go away. The store manager's behaviour did not surprise her after she had snatched the house from under his nose. Sure, they had a misunderstanding about the house, but the water was under the bridge now. She no longer lived there and it was high time he grew up, forgave and forgot. Karma could be that way, but she couldn't make him be the same. Due to the store manager's coldness, she had to hold her correspondence with Jon in abeyance for a while, but she took every opportunity when the store manager was not around, which didn't happen often. The internet café being in the town was not feasible for her because of transportation problems —she didn't have a car then.

When she was in Singapore, she managed to write only once, as it was expensive and she had a very limited budget.

By 2006, the company she worked for bought two Airbus A319 aircraft, replacing the older ones, and they moved to new premises. As the demand for the internet had increased, all the new offices had individual connections. That was the game-changer for Karma, and she could write to Jon as much as she wanted to—*as a friend* she warned herself; she only wanted a platonic relationship.

She wanted to write a long-winded e-mail to Jon, but as Shakespeare said, *Brevity is the soul of wit,* therefore, she kept it as brief as possible.

That afternoon, Bhutan time (morning in England), Jon walked into his office and ran upstairs to get milk for his tea.

"E-mail for you Jon, I have printed it out, I haven't read it," the administrator said, and handed him a printout. The e-mail read:

From: karmadenzom@yahoo.com
To: jon@fernilee.co.uk

Subject: Hello from Bhutan

Hi Jon,
This is Karma from Bhutan. I hope you still remember me. I am keeping in touch to see how you are.
Take care and do keep in touch.
Regards,
Karma

Of course, I remember this almond-eyed beauty, how could I forget her? Jon thought. He had to depend on his office secretary to print out his e-mails. but it didn't bother him that much, as there was nothing secretive about their relationship.

He sent a reply:

From: jon@fernilee.co.uk
To: karmadenzom@yahoo.com

Hi Karma,
Nice to hear from you and of course I remember you.
Keep in touch.
Regards,
Jon

Even though the reply was brief, she was happy to hear from him.

After their initial, brief e-mails they never lost touch, in fact, they kept in touch nearly every single day; except during the weekends, when he went away on holiday, or when he was working away from home outside the UK. They wrote to each other about everything and nothing.

During the football season, Jon would always update her with a result. '*Man United won today 1-0 against Liverpool.*'

She was not a fan of football, but she could watch it if somebody with her was watching too. She wouldn't go out of her way to watch it, but she always managed to give him positive feedback.

After a year, they had been in touch almost every day; by this time he was promoted, which meant he had his own desk and computer. He could write what he wanted without a third person reading it.

He wanted to get her reaction with something, and he sent an e-mail:

'I am on holiday tomorrow, helping my neighbour to paint the ceiling,' said the e-mail caption. She wondered where he was off to. When she opened her e-mail, a picture of a girl up a ladder, painting the ceiling, wearing a short skirt, and no underwear filled her screen. It put a smile on her face.

They would e-mail each other daily. Time wise, Bhutan is ahead of the UK—six hours in winter and five hours in the summer—therefore, Karma would have an e-mail waiting for her in the morning. The first thing she did when she got to her desk was to check her e-mails. She knew for sure that there would be one waiting, and she would not waste any time in replying.

Jon always looked forward to reading her e-mails when he got to the office in the morning; they always made his day. He was busy all day and worked long hours. At the end of the day, he would send a reply to her, and Karma would receive it the next morning. This routine carried on for a couple of years.

E-mailing each other over the years brought them closer and formed a bond. They shared everything including their personal problems, but they never misled each other, they never said anything stupid like, "Come to me and I will make you happy," or "leave your girlfriend. I will do anything for you."

For Karma, it was nice to communicate with someone from a different culture and to get a male opinion. For that, she couldn't thank the internet enough.

How far would they go to keep this friendship going? Can a girl and a boy be friends for life?

We can be friends forever, Karma thought.

A boy and girl can never be just friends, Jon thought.

Chapter 10

Beating about the bush.

Life is a book, a written story. Every person's story is mapped by an incorporeal plot. It is difficult to alter the impalpable plot no matter how you try, Karma's credence.

A king had learnt that his son, the prince, would one day be killed by a tiger; this was fate and could not be changed. Nevertheless, the king ordered that all the tigers in his kingdom were to be killed to stop his son from dying. One day, on his way back to the palace, the prince saw a dead tiger by the side of the road.

"You wanted to take my life away from me, and look where you ended up, by the side of the road, rotting, and being eaten by maggots," he said indignantly, and kicked the tiger as hard as possible on the jaw. He accidentally kicked an exposed canine tooth which made his foot bleed. Strangely enough, a few weeks later, he died of an infection.

Nobody knows what fate has in store for them. Karma is a firm believer in fate, and she has lots of reasons why.

If she hadn't got pregnant, she would have completed her education, but that means she wouldn't have a job with the airline company. She would have a good career, but she wouldn't have met Jon.

When Jon told Karma to keep in touch and handed her his work address, she could have backed off and forgotten all about him, but there was something telling her not to. Instead, she suppressed her feelings and decided to be friends. Now and then, her naughty mind kept wondering, *what would it be like to become involved with Jon?* thinking of the unthinkable. When that happened, she would give herself a firm telling off.

But Jon had different ideas. Karma was constantly on his mind, and he wondered what it would be like to go home to her. On his long bike rides, he would wonder what she was doing now. For reasons unknown to him he thought fondly of her, and she was never far from his thoughts.

Since 2006, they had become very comfortable sharing their problems and consoling each other, but Jon wanted more than just swapping e-mails. He didn't want to be too forward, and jeopardise what they shared or scare her off. He had an inkling that she wanted something more out of this friendship, but he was never too sure. That's when Jon started to beat about the bush.

2007: Card number one

One Valentine's Day, Karma was very happy to receive a fascinating envelope. She held it, tore it open, and slowly read the card contained within:

This Valentine's card contains a special message written in magic ink that can only be seen by people who think clean, pure and wholesome thoughts about each other!' announced the front, and then inside the card it added cheekily, *I couldn't see it either! Happy Valentine's Day!*

Below this, Jon had taped his business card facedown and had written 'From ????' on the back of it.

Each sentence brightened Karma's face and made her smile. As she finished reading, she couldn't help grinning. When she saw his writing on his business card, she knew who it was from—it made her very happy. She then discarded the envelope and saved the precious card.

on was disappointed that he had not evoked any reaction from her with the first Valentine card, but he didn't want to be too bold either. Little did he know, if he had been more forward, she would have been all for it.

From: jon@fernilee.co.uk
To: karmadenzom@yahoo.com

Hi Karma,
Nice to hear from you…
Attached are pictures from the lakes. I hope you like them. The Lake District is a beautiful place. If you play your cards right, I may take you there one day…
Jon

From: karmadenzom@yahoo.com
To: jon@fernilee.co.uk

Hi Jon,
Nice to hear from you…
We will see about that.
Regards,
Karma

2008: Card number two – a step further

A year later, Karma was so thrilled to receive an exotic envelope with an airmail stamp. She wasted no time opening it. A Valentine's card! *Who could that be from?* she wondered and read on:

On Valentine's Day, BE MY VALENTINE! said the front. And then on the inside: *Here's a little valentine with lots of love from me. Cos I think you're really special and as gorgeous as can be!*

'*To Karma, Happy Valentine's Day,*' said the handwriting.

Again, a business card was attached face down with ' From????' written on the back.

It was déjà vu. She had a feeling this had happened before, but she could not put her finger on it. Then she flipped the card over and there it was—Jon's name jumping out at her!

In Bhutan, swapping Valentine cards was no big deal, and Karma didn't know much about them, except that they were swapped between lovers. *Could she dare to hope for something meaningful?* she thought. *NO! You can't, you minx! He has a son with his girlfriend, and that's the end of the story,* she soliloquised. She added the card to her collection in her office desk drawer.

Karma missed hearing from Jon when he was away on holiday, and she did wonder why he never phoned her. When Jon was on holiday, he was tempted to call Karma but didn't.

When he didn't get any positive response from his past Valentine cards, he felt like he was not getting anywhere with Karma and he started getting restless. *Was this friendship worth hanging on to?* he wondered:

From: jon@fernilee.co.uk
To: karmadenzom@yahoo.com

Hi Karma,
Nice to hear from you as always and I hope you are doing well.
I would like to invite you to Nepal for a holiday.
Jon

Karma was a bit wary about meeting him alone, so she wrote:

From: karmadenzom@yahoo.com
To: jon@fernilee.co.uk

Hi Jon,
Can I bring my boyfriend?
Karma

At the time of this e-mail, Karma was with another guy. To get rid of her ex, she had gone to extreme measures in getting involved with the first guy who paid any attention to her; this was successful, but it was like jumping from a frying pan into the fire. Her relationship with her new boyfriend was not easy, and this sent her running back to the arms of her ex again. The last thing she wanted was to include Jon into her unstable relationships! However, her previous e-mail to Jon had annoyed him no end:

From: jon@fernilee.co.uk
To: karmadenzom@yahoo.com

Hi Karma,
No, don't bother.

Jon

By 2008, Jon got tired of beating about the bush and hinting without getting any positive responses. Therefore, he decided to visit Bhutan via Nepal with his brother. He could kill three birds with one stone: a trek in Nepal; a trek in Bhutan, and see if his feelings for Karma were still there:

From: jon@fernilee.co.uk
To: karmadenzom@yahoo.com

Dear Karma,
Hope you are ok...
I am planning to visit Bhutan for trekking. Can you recommend a tour agent? Do let me know.

Jon

Karma was very excited to receive this e-mail. She only knew of one travel agent, but she didn't know well enough to recommend his services:

From: karmadenzom@yahoo.com
To: jon@fernilee.co.uk

Hi Jon,
Sorry, I don't know any travel agent to recommend. If you Google it, you will see a long list of travel agents. Let me know how you get along.
Regards,
Karma

From: jon@fernilee.co.uk
To: karmadenzom@yahoo.com

Hi Karma,
All booked and sorted. I will be arriving in Bhutan on 22nd Oct.
Jon

Karma was so excited about Jon's visit. She hadn't seen him for— she had to count on her fingers: 2001, 2002, 2003…2008— *already seven year*s*!* she thought. She couldn't wait to go and meet him at the airport. She wanted to make herself presentable, without going overboard. She put on her favourite blue *kira* printed with white flowers, with matching white *wonju* and blue silk *tego*. At the airport, she took a seat in the waiting area which overlooked the queue in the arrival's hall.

As soon as Jon spotted Karma, he couldn't stop grinning. He gave her the most wonderful smile in the world, and her heart skipped a beat as she thought, *does he have feelings for me?*

"This is my brother, and this is Karma," Jon said.

"Nice to meet you Karma. I have heard lots about you from Jon," his brother said.

That sentence spoke volumes and confirmed any doubt that Jon had feelings for her. Just the thought of being wanted, which had become rare in her life, now made her glow with happiness.

Out of hundreds of hotels, they were staying in a hotel where Karma was renting an apartment on the hotel grounds. Serendipity? If this was not fate, what was it? It was too much of a coincidence. Jon spent two weeks in Bhutan, visiting places and trekking. He had to cut short his trek due to snow. During those two weeks, they saw each other a few times.

They decided to meet up for lunch in a local restaurant after Jon returned from his trek. Jon was already waiting for her in the restaurant when she arrived. They greeted each other and shook hands. The waitress came to get their orders looking flustered and acting very strange. Karma noticed the waitress eyeing Jon surreptitiously time and time again. Jon was trying to make her as comfortable as he could, making small talk, but to no avail. She blushed and disappeared. Karma was thinking, *should I be jealous?* Karma later found out from his brother, that the same waitress was flirting unashamedly with Jon when they (Jon, his brother, and the guide) were having lunch before the trek.

No wonder the poor girl was flustered. She might have thought that I was Jon's girlfriend, Karma thought afterwards.

Karma had Tibetan noodle soup, and Jon had chicken fried rice. They chatted like long lost friends, and the afternoon just disappeared in the blink of an eye. There was no awkwardness and the conversation flowed easily. *It would be nice to spend time together on our own*, they both thought.

"Would you like to come for a drink at my place with your brother, tonight at seven?" Karma asked. She wanted to see more of Jon, but was trying her best not to make it too obvious.

"That would be nice. I look forward to it," Jon said.

After lunch, they caught a taxi back to his hotel and her apartment. Jon was hoping to be invited in for a drink when they got there, but no such luck.

"See you later at seven," Karma said, and Jon had no option but to head back to his room. He didn't want to be too forward and invite himself in. *Baby steps*, he reminded himself.

Karma made a warm liver salad to go with drinks. She was giving the final touches to the salad when she heard the doorbell. She went to check; it was Jon and his brother.

"Come in, come in." She waved them in.

"This is for you Karma," Jon said, handing her a gift in a bag.

"Thank you," Karma said, and didn't know what to do. She felt it would be a bit awkward to dive straight into the bag, but she had a peek and put it on the dresser. She could have a proper look later.

Jon was surprised that Karma didn't even open the bag and have a proper look. She just peeked in the bag and dumped it on the dresser. *That's an expensive perfume. Why did I bother?* He thought, but instead he said, "My pleasure."

"Whisky or beer?" Karma offered.

"Whisky for me," Jon said.

"Beer for me, please," his brother said.

Karma poured out a glass full of whisky, took out a beer from the fridge and took them over.

Jon was surprised the glass was filled to the brim with neat whiskey. He had never had that much whisky in one go in his life before, and for some reason he found it amusing. When she handed him the glass he thought, *I know your trick. You want to get me drunk so I fall asleep on your settee and you can have your wicked way with me!* That was wishful thinking on his part!

Karma had never offered whisky to a westerner before. Her dad was the only man she had seen drinking whisky, and he always filled his glass to the brim. In Bhutan, it is rude to offer only a half-filled glass.

Jon decided to finish the whisky without commenting, as he didn't want Karma to feel ill-informed. He was very lightheaded when they left for dinner!

When they entered the restaurant and were shown to their table, Jon wanted to sit opposite Karma so he could play footsy under the table, but his brother beat Jon to it, and plonked himself down in the opposite chair first. They had a good meal and a pleasant evening, lots of laughter and more drink. Jon was trying his best to look sober, and to create a good impression with Karma. It was midnight by the time they went their separate ways.

The night before they were due to fly out, Jon and his brother were sat in the hotel restaurant ready to eat when Karma walked in.

"Hi," Karma said grinning—she was always happy to see Jon. She hadn't spoken to him since their dinner two days ago. The day before, Karma had spotted Jon outside the bank when she was driving to work, but she didn't have the time to stop and chat.

"Come and join us. There is plenty left as my brother doesn't eat much," Jon said, and he beckoned Karma over.

"Are you sure? I don't want to intrude," she said, but inwardly she was pleased.

They chatted about this and that, and Karma got on well with his brother—he seemed friendly enough. Jon's brother knew that he had a crush on Karma.

"I heard about this night hunting thing," Jon said.

"It is very common in the remote parts of Bhutan, especially in eastern parts of Bhutan," Karma said smiling.

Men are notoriously known for night hunting in Eastern Bhutan. They would visit single women by climbing through their bedroom windows in the dead of night for a night of pleasure.

"Maybe you will have to leave a ladder propped up against one of your windows so Jon can come night hunting," Jon's brother added, and they all laughed. Jon wished that could actually happen; he wouldn't hesitate to take up that opportunity.

"Good night, I need to go now. Hopefully, I will catch you in the morning before you leave," Karma said to Jon.

"Good night," they both said.

The next morning on her way to work, Karma popped into the restaurant, as they were having breakfast to say goodbye and she wanted to wish them a safe journey home. *I would like him to be more than a friend,* Karma thought, as she was getting back into her car. While in the restaurant:

"She'll do for me," Jon said to his brother.

Jon left Bhutan with renewed feelings about Karma, which until then, he thought were fading with time. He was confident now that his feelings were real. He wanted to see more of her.

Chapter 11

Blind and stupid.

Karma's second relationship had started to go downhill too. He was a good man in his own way, but he was not the one she wanted. She had a hard time getting away from him. Like a fool, she ran straight into her ex's arms. There was someone right under her nose who could be perfect for her, but no, she had to rekindle an old flame. Her only solace was to write to Jon:

'From: karmadenzom@yahoo.com
To: jon@fernilee.co.uk

Hi Jon,
I hope you are well.
I have broken up with my boyfriend.
Karma

Jon was glad, but he didn't want to take advantage of her fragile state. So, he replied:

From: karmadenzom@yahoo.com
To: jon@fernilee.co.uk

Hi Karma,
Hope you are ok.
I am sorry to hear that. You take care.
Jon

Karma was always happy to receive Jon's e-mails no matter how short they were. Now and then, she re-read his valentine cards which always managed to put a smile on her face, and in that moment, she would forget her woes.

She would like to be with Jon, but would it be difficult with her being in the east and him being in the west? Whenever her feelings surfaced, she would try to ignore them and took no notice of what her heart was saying.

She wasn't savoir-faire, knowing what to do in this kind of situation. She felt like a fledgling and didn't know how to deal with it; it was a complete mystery to her. She understood courting or flirting and being up close and personal, or did she? She was not sure now.

If Jon had e-mailed: '*You are beautiful and I want you*,' it would be a different matter entirely, but that was never the case. Nevertheless, it was nice for Karma to be lost in her fantasy now and then. It was a pity that she couldn't go on dreaming forever. She needed to return to her real life, whether she liked it or not.

Karma's relationships were going back and forth from her ex to her boyfriend. When one gave her a hard time, she would seek solace in the other. She knew it was not an ideal situation and she needed to make up her mind. So, she ended the relationship with her boyfriend.

Karma revealed her break-up to Jon with gusto, but when it came to breaking the news of her reconciliation with her ex, she hesitated and felt like keeping it a secret from him. But again, it was not fair on Jon, even if he was just her friend. In the end, she sheepishly let him know that she was back with her ex.

When the breakup news was delivered to Jon he was elated, but the reconciliation was not good news for him, and he thought that she was being stupid. However, he was too polite to say that, and always gave the impression that he was rejoicing with her. What he couldn't comprehend was Karma going back to her ex when she damn well knew that he was married and had another child.

Despite her ex's situation, Karma had a small hope that things might work out between them. They got back together for a brief time and forgot their troubles in the past. Isn't it true that *absence makes the heart grow fonder?* She was ready to start afresh with him, but she didn't know what she was thinking. Infatuation had enchanted her weak brain, mind, heart, and soul, making her forget his capricious ways. He inveigled her into having an affair and she succumbed to his blandishments.

"You're not seeing your ex-husband, are you?" said her second sister Dorji, who confronted her one day.

"What makes you say that?" Karma asked, feigning innocence.

"I am telling you, Karma, he is no good for you. The relationship did not work the first time. What makes you think that it will work now? Oh, by the way, he is now married with a child, just in case you have forgotten," she said wisely.

"I don't know," was all Karma could say, and a full-blown lecture from Dorji followed.

"What a cruel thing to do, Karma, I didn't expect that from you. You know what it is like when you are betrayed; you better not get involved with him. If you do, then I won't speak to you ever again," Dorji said.

"Mind your business, I am an adult and I don't need telling what I can and what I can't do," Karma said callously, and Dorji burst into tears.

"See what you have done now making her cry like this. Have pity on her, she is heavily pregnant." Their mum was imploring them and went to console Dorji.

"She has to stop treating me like her little sister then. I am her elder sister not younger," Karma said and stormed out.

Karma did not go to see her sister when she was in labour. Normally, she would have made sure to be with sisters when they were giving birth. Her blind-sighted relationship nearly drove her family apart.

Bja tsa gi awa lam ta lu ya tang lam wo lu ya tang wong - *Men are like Jersey bulls, they can choose to shit wherever they want.* Karma's dad's maxim when talking of infidelity, but when his daughter was in this situation, he wasn't ready to forgive her ex-husband.

"Remember, he has a young child. Your child has got used to not having his father around him, please think of that child, destroying a family is a crime. Anyway, I don't think your ex-husband is the right kind of man for you. If he had loved you, he wouldn't have cheated on you in the first place. Don't ask him to join you when you come to the village," her father said.

"If that is what you want, I will not come to the village either then," Karma said indignantly. A part of her knew that her dad was talking sense, but she was too proud to acknowledge it.

"I don't mean you can't come; you are welcome anytime you want, I want you to come, but not with him," her dad replied.

Karma nodded, and what her dad said made her think. She knew that she was deep into the affair, and the only way to put an end to this was by finding out what her ex-husband wanted. How ironic that she is the *other woman* now: a bitch, a slut, the adjectives she would use to describe the *other women*. How did that happen over a period of a few years? The roles had reversed but with the same consequences—nothing but heartache.

Karma was coming to the end of her tether after a year of the relationship with her ex. She didn't know where she was heading, and sometimes she felt like slapping some sense into herself. She was ready to fall out with her family, and to give his wife and child a hard time. She was going mad with frustration, and she started to hate her complacent ex.

"What do you want from me?" she asked her ex one day, and told him she was sick of just being the other woman.

"I love you and I want to be with you," he said.

"Really? Will you give up your wife for me?"

"Of course, I will. I don't love her as much as I love you. I know that you would be the perfect wife, but I feel insecure with you."

"All right, if you don't want to leave your wife, I want to end this relationship," she said, and could feel tears stinging her eyes. She didn't know why she started to feel emotional about ending the relationship, even though she knew he was not being truthful to her.

"I will leave her one day, but not now. Can we not talk about this? I just want to relax and enjoy the moment," he said, with tears in his eyes.

"OK, just one idea. What if I call your wife pretending to be someone from my office, and break the news that you are having an affair." It was unbelievable what Karma was prepared to do, but she had her reason. He needed to decide what he really wanted.

"If you want," was all he said.

She took that for a yes, and the next day called his wife, "Hi, are you Karchung's wife?"

"Yes," answered a quiet voice.

"I saw your husband's car parked in front of his ex-wife's house," Karma said.

"No, no, that is not possible, he called me an hour ago saying that he is in Phuntsholing and his car is broken down; he won't be home until tomorrow," she said with naivety.

"Are you sure?" Karma said.

"What do you mean? Who are you?" Karma could tell she was getting agitated.

"I am one of the staff from his ex-wife's office. I have seen your husband with her, so be careful or you may end up losing your husband." But as she said this Karma was thinking, *why am I doing this?* She felt very cruel and heartless. What a malicious thing to do, but she needed to be brutal to get the answers she was seeking.

"Who are you? What is your name?"

"Never mind me, call your husband and ask him," Karma said and hung up. After the call, she was remorseful and felt sorry for his wife, but it was too late, she couldn't do anything about it now. She had to wait and see where it went from there.

When Karma got home that evening, her ex-husband was pacing the floor.

"What the hell did you do that for?" he shouted in rage.

"I asked you and you agreed," replied Karma.

"I never agreed! My wife called me in tears! I can't believe you did that. I'm going!"

"Please don't go!" Karma pleaded, but he left her without a second glance. That night, she sobbed herself to sleep. She knew it was pathetic but what was she supposed to do; the love of her life had left her and she was not able to do anything about it. Her heart was broken into pieces. She didn't know how she would get over this.

While all of this was going on, Karma didn't have the guts to reveal any of this to Jon in their daily e-mails. She didn't know how he would react.

Some things are better left unknown. And then disaster struck…

Chapter 12

Death 2007.

It was my mum's dream to build our own house in the village, but due to pecuniary strains, we were not able to until 2008. When we (Dorji and I) managed to sort out some cash, the plan for house building was made. Even Tshering, the least fortunate then, managed to contribute some money towards the building of our village house. Unfortunately, my mum passed away in November 2007, not living long enough to see it finished. Only the foundations were set when she died.

That was the biggest blow in my life. We loved her so much. She was the best mother you could have in your life: caring, loving, and ready to sacrifice everything for her children. She was a woman with love and devotion towards her family. But the trouble was, I didn't appreciate her munificence until she was gone from this world. For now, let not talk about her death just yet.

This world is made up of impermanence, nothing lasts forever. A child is born and grows up to be an adult. Then, old age creeps in, dragging you closer to your death. You were born once, and another time you need to die—fact of life.

We Buddhists believe Buddha was reborn more than a thousand times to attain nirvana. His final birth on earth was to result in him being born as a king, but he chose not to be, as he was wise enough not to go through human suffering again. But I have a different perspective than Buddha. I don't want to be enlightened and attain nirvana. I love my life as a human, even if it is full of ups and downs.

Buddha was a different sort of person. His father tried his best to not let him get involved with any misery, and provided everything he wished for; he waited on him hand and foot. Buddha married his cousin and she bore him a son.

Even though he lived in the lap of luxury, at the back of his mind, he was dissatisfied. Despite his father's efforts to keep him away from misfortunes, Buddha managed to witness four unavoidable sufferings: birth, ageing, sickness, and death.

One day, while riding his glorious, golden chariot in the grounds of his home, he came across a decrepit old man, and was shocked to the core as he had never seen such an age before. Wanting to see more, he went beyond the palace walls and came across a diseased man begging. All of this suffering depressed him, and he left his luxurious life to live the life of an ascetic.

"Karma, get up! We got a call from Dad saying we need to come to the village. Mum is not well." I heard Dorji's distant voice faintly.

"Ok," I muttered groggily, and tried to open my eyes but to no avail; I had dropped off into a deep slumber. It was a nice Sunday afternoon, a day off work and I had felt like drinking.

"Nidup, can you make some scrambled egg mixed with warmed *ara* (distilled alcohol), please?" I had asked my sister, an hour before we got the call from our dad.

"How much do you want?" she asked.

"Just a little," I said, marking a mug with my forefinger and thumb.

However, she brought me a whole mug full of warm *ara* and egg. "That is too much. I can't drink it all," I said. What are we Bhutanese like with our tradition of never offering a half-filled mug!

"Drink it. I know you can," she said and disappeared. I drank it a mouthful at a time, and within a few minutes, I had emptied the mug and I started to feel a bit light-headed. When drunk I can be loud, jovial, and belligerent, or I instantly drop off into a deep slumber. It was obviously the latter when I heard my sister trying to wake me up.

"Mum is dying, Karma, we need to get to the village as soon as possible," I heard Dorji again sounding distressed. In the background, I could hear her shouting at Nidup.

"Why did you give her so much *ara*? None of us can drive, and if something happens to Mum, I will blame you!" She was going mad at Nidup as always. It was not surprising she was called the Hitler of the family. She can be very dominating and forceful, but she does it with a good heart.

"How come this is my fault? She is the one who drank it. I didn't force it down her throat," I heard Nidup protesting.

"What is happening here?" I said, when I finally managed to force my eyes open.

"Mum is dying and look at you, so drunk, you can't even open your eyes properly," Dorji said accusingly.

"Don't forget it is Sunday, and I didn't expect Mum to be sick like this. I dropped her off only a few days ago, after her treatment. I can't drive when I am drunk. You must wait until I am sober," I said thoughtlessly, and went back to sleep. When I think of it, I could slap myself for being so insensitive. That was two o'clock in the afternoon. I finally managed to sober up after a couple of hours.

What have I done? Is Mum OK? Do I have to get drunk like that? A guilty conscience hit me with full force and I started to panic.

"How is she doing? How did it happen? Shall we go now?" I started babbling and threw so many questions at them. I couldn't relax—anxiety was setting in fast and furiously.

"It is all right, you didn't do that on purpose," Dorji said calmly. "If we go now we may get there in time. Dad has called us three to four times now. We have got everything ready: a flask of tea and some snacks in case we get hungry," I think by then she had had time to think and calm down. That helped me to calm down too.

At 5.30 in the evening, we set off to the village: me, Dorji, Nidup, and Thinley (Tshering's husband), driving slowly and making sure we had enough breaks. It is a well-known fact that when a family member is sick, and the family is rushing to be by their side, they tend to meet with an accident and lose their lives. I didn't want anything like that happening to us. We drove in the dark with my car's headlights leading the way: along the winding road ascending to the top of Dochula, then descending to Wangdiphodrang valley, and then following the meandering *Puna Tshangchu* (Puna River). Sometimes, we got as close as a few meters to the river, and then gaining height as far as a few hundred meters above it. Just one mishap and we would go tumbling down the hill into the roaring river.

    There had been an incident where a family of three came off the road and the car went rolling down the hill. A few days later they were found. All of them stone-cold dead: the dad holding on to the grass; the mum headfirst into a bush, and the child sat on a rock with his arms folded, looking up at the sky with eyes full of maggots. There were many ifs and buts about the incident. Some speculated that the dad might have been trying to get up to the road before blackness hit him; the child sat there on the rock calling for help, and the mum going headfirst into the bush and being killed instantly. Just the thought was making my heart go out to them, but that didn't stop me from imagining their spirits wandering and haunting the area.

I drove the car bracing myself, reciting *lamala chasume che…* and we cautiously went down to the village. We got there just before midnight, expecting them to be on the road above the house waiting for us, but there was no sign of anyone.

"Where are they?" I said getting worried. "Can you call Dad, Dorji?"

"Hello, Dad, where are you?" Dorji shouted into her mobile phone.

"We are still here. I don't think Mum will last, and I prefer her to take her last breath on this earth at home," I heard my dad lamenting over the phone.

"What was he thinking? We can't let her die without even trying to get her to the hospital. Tell him we are coming down," I said, looking at Dorji.

"We must hurry then," Thinley said.

We went rushing down to the house, through the orange orchard full of ripened oranges silhouetted against the dark sky. Normally, I would be standing admiring them, but it wasn't the right time, nor had I enough time.

I was afraid to go in, wondering what awaited us, but being the elder sister I couldn't think like that. I went in and saw a few of my relatives gathered around my mum; she was throwing up pools of blood. As soon as the warm blood hit the cold air, it thickened.

"Look, look who's here. Your daughters. You can't die before saying goodbye. Oh, that is terrible. I don't want you to die. Please God, help her. I can't see her dying," Dad lamented and burst into tears. At that precise moment, Mum looked up and gave us a blank stare. I felt my eyes sting with tears, and I wanted to give into my grief, but I couldn't. I had a huge responsibility on my shoulders, and I wanted to be strong for my family. Even now, as I write these words, I can feel myself tearing up.

"They came to see you. Do you see now why you can't leave us?" Dad said.

"I need to go to sleep," she said, after throwing up more blood. It was the last time I looked into her eyes. I never thought she would leave us like this.

"I think we need to take her to the hospital soon before it is too late. We need to make a move now Dad, we can't let her die here," I said, ignoring my dad's protestations.

A temporary stretcher was made and we put my mum on it. In the cool breeze of dawn, four strong relatives carried her up the hill towards the road where my car was parked. Normally, it would take an hour to get to the road, but today was far from normal. It was hard for my relatives to carry my mum up the hill, and they had to go slow and rest a few times. Almost two hours later, we got to my car. I was reclining the passenger seat for my mum when I heard my dad scream:

"She has left us," he wailed, "I said to leave her at home, but you all didn't listen. She is dead outside like a homeless person." He burst into tears cradling my mum's head.

It is better she died outside rather than inside, I thought, not daring to speak out loud. *If she dies at home, then we must follow the stars and see when it will be the best time to take her out of the house. It will drag on*, was my ultimate, selfish thought. I still hate myself for my selfishness.

I know it was egocentric of me, and I regret being such a thoughtless and inconsiderate daughter towards my dad. I should have let my dad have his way. It hits me now and then—does this question my character?

I lost my mum in November 2007, and it left me full of regrets and sorrow. Would we have been able to save her if we had taken her to the hospital on time? But there are people who die in the hospital, even after getting all the medical attention.

My mother was a woman of everlasting loveliness, but that did not stop her from dying. No one has escaped death, except our Divine-Mad lama. It was believed that he managed to escape death and disappeared inside the Jowo Rinpoche—meaning precious one (known as the Jowo Shakyamuni in the west) in Lhasa, Tibet. We believe that he left his dirty boots dangling on Buddha's ear.

It is said that this statue spoke and said, **"*Ma tro ma tro di Drukpa Kunley gi tam ja rey - Don't touch this, it belongs to Drukpa Kunley*,"** and was spoken when a caretaker tried to remove it. Since that day, it has been known as *Sung Jay mi Jho* (speaking statue of Buddha). It is supposed to be the most sacred image in Tibet.

I have heard that when you see it, it fills you with veneration and deep respect. I have always said that I wanted to take my parents for pilgrimage and witness the Jho in its full glory. But before I could fulfil this, my mum's light was extinguished—never to be lit again.

"Life is like a burning lamp amidst strong breezes. One doesn't know when and where the wind is going to blow. One moment it will be alight and another moment it will be extinguished." Buddhist philosophy.

How I wish my mum was still alive, but sometimes I am glad her suffering ended with her passing away. It comforts me to think that her soul exists, as I am a firm believer of life after death, and she will be reborn somewhere in the world. I hope and pray that she will have a better life, health-wise.

Her illness was never-ending. I don't know how she managed to develop gastritis, but she did. By the time we children were adults it had turned into chronic gastritis. Every time she went to the hospital, an endoscopic tube was stuffed down her throat. Afterwards, during evening meals, she would hardly be able to swallow. Poor thing!

All of us sisters took good care of her. I just hope that we made her happy for the last few years of her life. We did our best. When she was not able to eat, we made rice porridge for her, and when she was haemorrhaging, we made sure we cooked something out of pig/cow liver, as the liver is supposed to be a good source of iron.

She was not able to do anything while she was ill, but as soon as she got better she did all the kitchen work for us. Now she is gone, I do wonder, *had we been expecting too much of her, expecting her to do all the work?*

In 2006, she was admitted to hospital after a severe haemorrhage. I was at work in Paro and Dorji was looking after her.

"Karma, you must come as quickly as possible, mother is dying," was the panic call that I received from Dorji. I rushed from Paro. I didn't have a car then and had to catch a taxi; it took around two hours to get to Thimphu. When I arrived, Dorji was as white as a sheet, and as soon as she saw me, she burst into tears.

"Come here, you poor thing," I said, as I hugged her affectionately.

"That was one hell of a nightmare," said Dorji, "she just stopped breathing. I didn't know what to do, so I just wailed. Luckily, the doctor came and managed to resuscitate her. It scared me to death, that was one of the scariest moments in my life," she said between sobs.

"You go and rest, I will take over," I said reassuringly. I could imagine how hard it must have been to go through that alone. She'd had an awful day nearly losing our mum. If it had been me, I would have fainted. The poor girl. I felt sorry for her.

I know it was sad for Mum to leave us like that, but it was comforting to know that her suffering had ended—a blessing in disguise. All we can do now is hope for the best in her next life.

Chapter 13

Affirmation.

If a man sets his heart on a woman he will get her, but not when it is other way around. If both want it there is no stopping fate, Bhutanese saying.

2009: Card Number Three – getting bolder

Jon was confident about his feelings towards Karma. He couldn't stop thinking of that Himalayan beauty. He had an inkling that she was interested in him. If this wasn't so, then why have lunch with him and meet him as much as she could? He decided to send another valentine card that year.

The front of the card read: *BE MY VALENTINE! Some people just sit back and let Valentine's Day pass them by, but not ME! I have a long list of things to do…* And then on the inside: *So, where do you want to start?* The message then continued a long strip of looped paper going around and around, the same words written on both sides: *Kiss you all over, cover you in cream, fulfil your wildest fantasies, get down and dirty, get up close and personal. XXX* and then the concluding greeting: *Happy Valentine's Day!*

To Karma, from your secret admirer, will be thinking of you, was the handwritten message in the card. By now, Karma was very familiar with Jon's bold, handsome handwriting, so she didn't even have to guess. Now she knew more about Jon's feelings and it made her think again; *does he have real feelings for me, or does he just want a fling?* She hung on to the card, re-read it a few times, and then added it to her collection. Three cards so far.

Jon wanted to persuade her to come to Nepal with him, and he couldn't think of a better time than when he knew for sure that she was single:

From: jon@fernilee.co.uk
To: karmadenzom@yahoo.com

Hi Karma.
As always, I'm glad to hear from you and to know you are doing well.
I am planning to go to Nepal soon. Would you be interested in joining me?
Jon

Her heart was beating faster. This is the right time. She knew where she stood with her ex. Why not go to Nepal open-minded and see what happens? She hadn't anything to lose.

Jon had persevered; this was his third invitation to her. He never gave up. Like the Bhutanese Divine-Mad lama once said: **Lap lap mang na Aie gi ya nen wong** - *if you persevere, even your mother will eventually give in*—a well-known quote in Bhutan. The Mad Lama was known for his crazy methods of enlightening other beings, especially women, through sexuality. His mother was said to be a nasty piece of work. He had a presentiment that his mother was going to suffer in hell and it unsettled him. He had to take drastic action, "Can I have sex with you, Mum?" he said one day. His mother told him off with incredulity. Again, the next day he asked and he continued daily until his mum finally gave in. "If you persevere enough, even your mother will eventually give in!" he shouted at the top of his voice, and ran around the village broadcasting the news. It was a very strange way of teaching Buddhism, but this was how he taught it, hence his name, The Divine-Mad Lama came into existence.

His monastery, which was traditionally built with mud bricks made from the earth of the surrounding ground, is still standing small but strong. It is called Chimmi Lhakhang. His stone penis symbol is known as *The Thunderbolt of Flaming Wisdom*. Another name given to this lama is *The Fertility Saint*. Barren women and men go to visit his monastery and carry the symbol of the stone penis. It is believed that if they walk three times around the temple carrying the symbol, they will be blessed with a child. The newborn child must then be named Chimmi after his temple. Karma had read an article that after visiting the temple an American couple had been blessed with a child.

Jon had already visited Nepal a few times on trekking holidays. He was keen on Karma joining him on his next visit:

From: jon@fernilee.co.uk
To: karmadenzom@yahoo.com

Hi Karma,
Glad to hear from you and I am glad that you are doing well.
If you want to come to Nepal the offer still stands.
Regards,
Jon

Karma was really thinking now. She knew that men usually only want one thing, sex, and Jon is a man after all. *What is there to lose?* she thought.

From: karmadenzom@yahoo.com
To: jon@fernilee.co.uk

Hi Jon,
Nice to hear from you.
I will need some time to think. I will get back to you soon.
Regards,
Karma

She knew that she hadn't got anything to lose, but was she brave enough? Those words *nothing to lose* kept popping back into her head. Finally, after a week, she had decided. Both wanted it so much, so why not give it a try?

NOTHING TO LOSE! *If you don't take a risk or come out of your comfort zone, you will never know what could be there for you*, she thought. She checked her calendar and was pleasantly surprised that the Paro *Tshechu* (festival) would be in three weeks' time; it was a government holiday (bank holiday) in the last week of March and the beginning of April.

From: karmadenzom@yahoo.com
To: jon@fernilee.co.uk

Hi Jon,
I hope you are well.
I will meet you in Nepal. Will the last week of March be ok?
Karma

Jon was over the moon when he received that e-mail and he wrote back:

'I normally don't go in March, but if you can make it at that time, I see no reason why not.'

It was becoming very real for Karma now. Her mind was firmly set that she would enjoy herself as much as she could and she wrote:

'In that case, it is done. I will see you in three weeks' time.'

Despite her assurance she couldn't help but be bit apprehensive not knowing what to expect. She thought she would take it one step at a time and go with the flow. It could be a holiday romance and a memory to be cherished. But then…

'*Can I see you?*' Her ex texted her a couple of days later.

'*Why?*' She texted back.

'*I know I was such a dick and I am sorry. I want you, I love you, I can't imagine my life without you. Please tell me you will see me,*' he replied.

He was trying to coerce her as always, thinking that by apologising she would forget the gravity of the heartache he had given her.

Enough is enough, I am not falling for it anymore, she thought. She had been blind in the past but she was not going to let him pull any more wool over her eyes. She needed to be strong for herself and whatever the future held. By now she knew he was like a dog's tail and would never be straight. No matter how much one tries to straighten a dog's tail, as soon as you let it go it returns to its original shape—as crooked as ever.

'*I am not the girl who is besotted with you anymore,*' she texted him.

She felt better and glad that she had finally come to her senses. She had wasted years of her precious life for nothing. Drastic times call for drastic measures, and she changed her mobile phone number.

Jon was happy that she had finally agreed to meet him, but he felt an unease that she would change her mind. For assurance, he wrote to her:

'*I hope you won't get cold feet and change your mind. I have booked my flight and our hotel, no going back now.*'

Upon receiving this message, Karma wrote back:

'I don't give my word easily and when I do I keep it. So, don't worry, and I will see you in two weeks. I am a lady of my word.'

But even as Jon was looking forward to the trip, luck was very much not on his side and he injured his back at work. He was taken to hospital on a stretcher, two weeks before the travel date. *I will not be happy if I have to cancel this trip*, he thought miserably. *Still, two weeks to go, it should be enough time to recover*, he thought consoling himself. He could hardly move and was in agony for three days. Fortunately, after a week, he was back on his feet.

Karma hadn't heard from him for a while and was worried sick. At last, there was an e-mail waiting for her after seven days:

From: jon@fernilee.co.uk
To: karmadenzom@yahoo.com

Hi Karma,
Hope you are well. I am sorry I haven't been in touch for a few days. My back went and I couldn't get into work to write. I am ok now though, well enough for Nepal.
Have a lovely day,
Jon

It was such a relief for Karma. Her unsteady heart started to settle now and she could relax. Their e-mails were back to normal, sometimes being sent two or three times a day:

'We will share a room with a double bed and you can sleep in the bathroom,' Jon e-mailed jokingly.

'No, you can have the bathroom and I will have the bed,' she wrote back.

After that, nothing more was said about sharing a bed. She left it in Jon's capable hands to organise the details. In fact, she was ready for anything; she was going to take it in her stride. She had nothing to lose and she was looking forward to spending time with him; this way, she would have a chance to get to know him personally.

Now the last hurdle, before she embarked on the journey, was to tell her family. She couldn't go blurting out that she was going to Nepal, where she would meet a man whom she had only met for a few days at a time ten years ago, but had kept in touch with ever since. Her family wouldn't know that she felt she had known him forever. Dorji would object if nobody else did. She had to be very wary about what she told them.

"I have to go to Nepal for a conference," she declared nervously. She knew it would evoke a reaction from Dorji, and even though she is four years junior to Karma, she behaved like her big sister.

"Can I come with you, *Ama*?" said her 12-year-old son, Yeshi, shouting excitedly.

"No, you can't. Who will look after you when I am busy attending meetings," Karma replied, but she couldn't help thinking, *meetings! What meetings?*

She felt bad telling a lie, but told herself that as long as they know where she is going, they don't have to know all the ins and outs. It was fortunate that she was involved in an internet business which gave her a good cover story.

"I hope you are not up to anything, Karma," Dorji said as expected.

"I am up to nothing," Karma said, not giving anything away. Maybe she would confess after the trip. *I am an adult and I know what I am doing*, she thought.

The last thing she wanted was to give the game away and let Dorji talk her out of it. It is part of the Bhutanese culture to meddle in the personal affairs of family members. They live in close-knit families and it is expected of each other to meddle. Karma knew that Dorji meant well. It was always nice to have the back of someone that cares about you, but sometimes when it becomes too much she wished Dorji would just leave her alone.

Karma felt that the family meddling was good in one way and bad in another. It's good that her family is there to fall back on if something goes wrong, but in another way, families could influence and cloud your judgement.

In the past, whenever she had a fallout she always ran to her sister, and her sister would always run to her.

"I am leaving him!" Dorji cried, as she went to Karma one day.

"Why?"

"Because he hit me, look," Dorji said, pointing at her bruised eye.

"*Jaydha*, how could he do this to you? *Sharchop Cocktey* (eastern bastard)," Karma shouted in a rage.

"We had a go at each other and he slapped me hard across my face."

"What kind of man is he? A man who hits a woman is not macho but a pussy," Karma said.

Karma's paroxysm of rage was going up a notch every minute. A man hitting a woman was anathema to her.

"Where is he? I will put him in his place," said Karma.

"At home," Dorji said.

"Come on, jump in my car and let's go and confront him." Karma was so fuelled with rage when driving, she didn't notice the journey until she was pulling her car into a driveway.

"Why on earth did you hit my sister?" Karma yelled, as she confronted Dorji's husband. "You think that because she hasn't any brothers you can do what you want, but you are wrong, you have got me to deal with!" Karma was throwing a hissy fit, shouting at the top of her voice. All the neighbours perked up and their ears started to wag, but she didn't care. She wanted to challenge him.

"Sorry, I don't mean to hurt her like that. She was the one who raised a hand first," said Dorji's husband, but he had the grace to look sorry.

"I know, but that does not mean you can hit my sister like that," said Karma. "What kind of man are you hitting your wife in this way?" Karma was ready to pull his hair out, but fortunately, he was being very calm and her rage dissipated. There was no point attacking the repentant.

"I know and I am sorry," he said, apologising profusely and remorsefully. His contrition calmed her down. She was glad he apologised and nothing more was said.

Karma went to Nepal with a clear head and without any presentiments. Sometimes she felt like a fraud for her planned trip, but for the time being this was for the best. If it worked out, she would be happy to share her news with her family, and if not, then they didn't need to know.

She was not sure why she wanted to look nice. Her way of looking nice was to lose weight. She went on a crash diet and brought her weight down from 62 kilos to 55 kilos, and already she had started to feel better. Why did losing weight make her feel better? She didn't know. It was not like she would turn into a beautiful princess after losing weight, but if she was slim her confidence grew, and she would see the world from a different perspective. Looks don't matter, as beauty lies in the eye of the beholder. She knew the saying, but still she starved herself crazy.

Back in England, Jon groomed himself: a neat haircut, shaved everywhere, and he was prepared.

One of Karma's friends e-mailed her with an attachment about an X-ray device; if projected on a fully clothed person, you could see their nakedness underneath. She found it amusing and forwarded the e-mail to Jon. He also found it funny and replied:

'I will be waiting at Kathmandu airport for you with this device. I am excited!' finishing with a wink emoji.

'Go ahead if you could find one in time. Oh, by the way, just to remind you, I am sleeping on the bed and you are taking the bathroom he...he...he...' Karma replied to him jovially.

'No, I am having the bed and you can have the bathroom,' Jon replied.

'OK, you have the bed like a lady, and I will have the bathroom like a gentleman, he...he...he...' Karma e-mailed.

'I was just messing, you can have the bed and I will have the bed too HA...HA...HA,' Jon wrote, testing the waters.

'Never give up, do you?' replied Karma.

'No, I don't, and I am going to stand there with the see-through machine,' said Jon.

'Good, that is what I like to hear. Don't forget, I will dress against such a violation and come dressed in a suit of armour. Here I come Nepal! Not long now!'

A week before they were due to meet, they started the countdown:

'One week to go. Can't wait and I hope you will not change your mind,' wrote Jon.

Six days to go and Karma e-mailed:

'As I said before, I don't give my word easily. When I do I keep it. I have seen some shoes on the internet. Would you be able to buy me a pair?'

Jon thought asking to buy shoes was a bit of a bold move from Karma.

Five days to go and Jon responded to Karma's request:

'Sorry, I won't be able to buy anything for you. If my girlfriend found out she won't be happy.' Karma had a feeling that he didn't want to buy them for her, and that the girlfriend thing was just an excuse. She was not happy with that. *If there is a will there is a way*, Karma thought.

Four days to go and Jon wrote:

'I could buy you some lingerie if you want?' Karma couldn't believe what she was reading. *Seriously, he can't buy shoes, but he can buy lingerie. But what the hell is lingerie?* she wondered. She Googled it and Wikipedia said: *Lingerie is a category of women's clothing including undergarments (mainly brassieres), sleepwear, and lightweight robes. The specific choice of the word is often motivated by an intention to imply the garments are alluring, fashionable or both.'* Karma couldn't believe what she was reading. *How annoying!* she thought. To make doubly sure she checked again and the Oxford dictionary said: *Women's underwear or clothing worn in bed.*

That had really annoyed her. He can't buy shoes but he can buy lingerie, unbelievable. What did he think she was?... No shoes, then no lingerie. *To hell with lingerie!* That was what she felt like saying, but instead she wrote:

'Three days to go now. No thank you, you don't have to buy me anything.'

To which Jon replied:

'Two days to go now. Not a problem. See you in two days. My flight is tonight and I can't wait to see you.'

Only a day to go and Karma packed her things. That day she did nothing but wool-gathering. She was not able to concentrate or pay attention to anything. She took a half-day off work and went home.

The next day at 07.00 hrs, she boarded a flight to Kathmandu, Nepal. *Yahoo!...Nepal here I come. Fingers crossed everything will be as wonderful as I have dreamt,* she thought, as she buckled herself in.

Chapter 14

March 2010: Time in Nepal, Kathmandu.

Jon checked into the hotel a day earlier than Karma's arrival and he was disappointed to be shown into a room with twin beds. He had specifically asked for a double bed. They offered to push them together but it was not up to his satisfaction, so he was offered another room which was no better. However, third time lucky and he was shown a room with a king-size bed. Despite the comfortable bed he couldn't sleep as he was jet-lagged. Nevertheless, he was glad he was finally here waiting for her. The next morning, he was up early and set off to the airport an hour before Karma's flight was due to land.

In less than an hour, Karma would be with her dream man. She was a bit anxious. She didn't know what to expect: sex, love, marriage or it could be something bad. *Shut up!* she told her conscience. *Nothing is going to happen, you are going to be fine. You are a grown woman, you can deal with it. Jon is a good man and I have known him for a while now,* she thought consoling herself.

Despite her apprehension, she was very impatient to get out of the plane as soon as it landed. She was the first one to exit the plane, the first one through immigration control, in fact the first for everything.

Jon waited outside impatiently. Now the moment is here, he couldn't wait to see her. He was watching the arrivals screen when he then spotted Karma running. She looked beautiful in jeans and in a black top. It looked like she couldn't wait to meet him.

Blimey, she has lost some weight, he thought. She had put on a bit of extra weight when he met her in 2008 but he wasn't bothered; he liked her regardless of her weight.

She came out of arrivals and scanned the airport, expecting to see Jon with the X-ray device! She spotted him within a minute, walking towards her with sunglasses on. *Mr Cool,* she thought. It reminded her of an emoji of a cool guy with sunglasses on.

"Hello, Karma, nice to meet you again," Jon said, coming forward to shake her hand.

She was a bit disappointed as she was expecting more than a handshake. A peck on the cheek or something. *Was that too much to expect?* she wondered. *Don't be stupid, amorous gestures are not a Bhutanese thing. You watch too many Hollywood movies,* she thought reprimanding herself.

"Nice to meet you too," Karma said, and shook his hand. She was wondering why he had his sunglasses on. Was he trying to be cool? Was he afraid she would see something in his eyes? Or did he want to feast his eyes on her without her noticing? Whatever the reasons she was going to play along.

"That is not the X-ray device, is it?" Karma asked, jovially pointing at his glasses. She was trying to be witty and hoped it was not too bold on her part.

"I wish," Jon said, with a big grin. She loved his smile and this was the second time she had seen him smiling at her this way.

He was so happy to see her, there was something about her that put a smile on his face; it made him happy and ebullient.

He picked her bag up and showed her to the taxi, coming around to her side and opening the taxi door for her. They chatted happily all the way to the hotel. He was tempted to put his arms around the back of her seat but didn't want to be too forward. Instead, he took his sunglasses off.

"That is better. I can see your eyes when I am talking to you," Karma said. They were beautiful turquoise blue. She didn't remember him having this kind of eye colour, but how would she know, having never been in such proximity with him before. "I feel uncomfortable talking to people when they have sunglasses on," Karma added.

"Sorry," said Jon.

"It is all right."

Jon didn't know how Karma would react when they got to their room and she saw a double bed.

As soon as they entered the hotel room, the double bed caught her attention. Her heart skipped a beat and unnerved her. Despite her inner turmoil, she put on a cool façade.

He was relieved when she didn't react to the bed. He thought she may run a mile, or demand two separate rooms. It would be a bit embarrassing if she had. The last thing he wanted was to put her off. He was not bothered about sex, he wanted to have a nice time with her. To get to know her better was his aim on this holiday.

They dropped off Karma's bag then set off for Boudhanath Temple. It is a dome-shaped stupa with a square tower sat on top. Each side of the tower has a pair of eyes looking in four directions. It is like it is keeping an eye out for an unwanted intruder. A pyramid tops the tower, tapering towards the sky and it was covered in yellow silk.

Boudha (Bhutanese name for Boudhanath) is in the heart of Kathmandu. The stupa is on the ancient trade route between Kathmandu and Tibet. Stupa means heap or mould in Sanskrit. Every twelve years, in the year of the Bird, they host a big festival for Jajima (Ashi Jazam in Bhutanese). Karma had been there once with her family to attend a month-long religious ceremony.

According to mythology, the stupa was built by Ashi Jazam and her four sons, but they had to get special permission to acquire the land first.

So, Ashi Jazam approached the king of Nepal and asked him to grant them a piece of land, the area of a cow's hide. The king granted her wish, thinking that in such a small area she won't be able to construct anything big, but the king had underestimated Ashi Jazma's intelligence. With the help of her sons, she managed to stretch a cow's hide to thirty times the size of the original. King couldn't go back on his words and the land was granted, and there they built Boudha stupa.

"It is believed that if you pray from the bottom of your heart in this temple, your wishes will come true," Karma explained to Jon.

He didn't know anything about praying as a Buddhist. He had been an altar boy when he was young, but that was in a Catholic church. He knew about 'The Hail Mary' but there is something intrinsically wrong about saying a Catholic prayer in a Buddhist temple.

"Please let me have Karma in my life," he prayed instead.

She was apprehensive about wishing for anything. It could be because of her parents' inculcation, *be careful what you wish for*. But again she told herself, if you don't wish you don't get. She prostrated herself three times as she recited, '*Dü sum sangye guru Rinpoche...*' She had wished for a happy life, but she didn't dare to pray for a life with Jon.

"I want to buy some material for my *tegos* and *wonjus*," Karma said, as they wandered around the market afterwards.

"You go in first and ask the price. You know how they are, they tend to charge more when they see a westerner. Maybe the pound sign is written all over my face," Jon said.

"OK, I will come to get you when I have finished haggling," Karma said, and disappeared into the shop. She didn't find anything in the first two shops and went into a third shop.

Jon was losing patience waiting for her. He didn't know how long she was gone, but he had waited long enough. He went looking for her, and when there was no sign of her he called her mobile which went straight to voicemail. He did not know what to do next. He turned around and there she was, coming out of a different store than the one she went in.

"Where were you?" was the first thing he said.

"In the shop haggling," she said. "Are you OK?"

"Yes, I am now. I came to find you. I panicked when I didn't see you in the shop you went to. I was worried, I was trying to call you."

"My mobile does not work here. Roaming charges are very high, so I don't use my mobile phone abroad like you," she said, glancing at his mobile.

"Oh, is that what it is. I thought you can use your mobile all over the world. How am I supposed to know? This modern technology is still a mystery to me," Jon said gormlessly. "Can't you use your mobile at all?" Jon asked again.

"I know I can but that involves expense, I would need to activate it before I leave Bhutan and it would cost me a fortune," she said.

"How am I supposed to know? Technology is a mystery to me," he added again grinning.

"Come on now before they change their mind. Let's go in," and Karma led him to the shop and bought lots of material for her *tegos and wonjus*. Jon paid for them.

Karma was very pleased that he paid for the materials. She found it endearing, drawing her closer to him. She felt guilty for having accusative thoughts of him not wanting to buy her shoes and using his girlfriend as an excuse.

"I will be your yak now," Jon said, offering to carry all her shopping in four plastic carrier bags—enough material for 15 *tegos* and 15 *wonjus*.

"Thank you," Karma said, and handed them to him. *It is nice of him, offering to carry these for me*, she thought.

This kind of gesture, no matter how small, weighs more than anything. She always liked being a recipient of chivalrous gestures which don't come often in Bhutan. It brought her a step closer to him. She was never treated like this before and it warmed her heart. *A good sign*, she thought.

They went to visit Swayambu, known as the Monkey temple. It was said that a lotus was planted by a past Buddha into the lake which covered Kathmandu valley. It blossomed and mysteriously radiated a brilliant light. So, the name Swayambu came into existence, meaning self-created / self-existence.

There were many steps leading up to the temple, in between trees which were littered with monkeys. Now and then, these monkeys would jump into the middle of the path, either to bother pedestrians or to snatch food from children. Sometimes, they would be sat there picking who knows what from each other's backs. Monkeys can be a pain in the backside. In Karma's village, the house, fields, and orchards must be guarded 24 / 7 when the crops are ready to harvest. Monkeys don't just pick and eat but tend to destroy the whole crops. Karma's dad had to make sure they had an adult guard, not just a child. Monkeys take no notice of children. Karma can understand how the phrase 'cheeky monkey' came into existence.

By the time they got to the top of the stairs, Karma was exhausted; it made her think about her lack of fitness. Jon had no problem; it was a piece of cake for him. She envied him and wondered what it would take to get to that level of fitness.

Jon had been running, biking, and visiting the gym quite often since he was in his twenties and he was as fit as a fiddle. It took him by surprise how unfit Karma was being a Himalayan girl, she had to rest a few times before reaching the top. *I could introduce her to hiking*, he thought wistfully.

Once they were on top of the temple, they came face to face with a gilded Vajra, guarded by two lions. Buddhist lions are white with a green mane, mythical and chimerical creatures. Mighty, powerful, and potent are the only common themes between the real and the mythical lions.

The stupa has a pair of eyes on each of its four sides symbolising the perspective that God can see all. In between is a figure representing number one in the Nepali alphabet, signifying that the only way to enlightenment is through the

Buddhist path. A third eye sits above the pair of eyes, signifying the wisdom of looking within.

Karma prostrated three times, while Jon stood trying not to watch her backside but failing. He had been brushing her hands fleetingly as they walked to evoke a reaction, but so far nothing. During three circumambulations, Jon brushed his hand against hers again, a few more times, trying to make it look accidental, and still he didn't get a reaction from her.

They decided to head back. Now and then, Karma had felt Jon's hand brushing against hers. She pretended she hadn't noticed as she wanted to play hard to get (a girl's prerogative!) and had to concentrate on getting back down these stairs. Luckily, it was a gentle descent.

When they got back to the hotel, they dumped everything and went to check out the swimming pool. It was closed and didn't look like it had been cleaned for a while. Disappointed, they headed back. A few more hours to kill before dinner back in the room. Karma sat down at one end of the settee and Jon took the other end, as he didn't want her to feel uncomfortable, and they started to chat.

Karma was very nervous facing the double bed, and was conjuring all sorts of images of her and Jon that night. Chatting non-stop relaxed her and all the images vanished. The settee was by the window and they were able to watch all the activities going on outside.

"Look at that," Jon said, pointing out a motorcycle carrying five people.

She closed the gap between them to peer out through the window. It looked like a family were going shopping, it was a familiar sight for her, but Jon couldn't believe his eyes.

"How crazy is that? No helmets?" Jon was shaking his head.

"We used to get that in Bhutan a lot but not much anymore. My sister Dorji told me that when she was dating her husband they went out for a drink with two other colleagues. After downing a few bottles of beer each, they all jumped on her husband's scooter and rode home," Karma said.

"Seriously, you crazy Bhutanese," he said turning around, and she followed suit. Now they were sat very close to each other. He was happy to be closer to her, and she was enjoying his company so much; it relaxed her, taking away all her reservations which made her feel cosy. They carried on chatting.

Karma's hair started to bother her, getting tangled between her back and the settee. She gathered it up and let it flow behind the settee and left her interlocked hands on her head, her elbows resting on the back of the settee. When Jon spotted her hands he couldn't resist and gave her a feather touch on the tips of her fingers. *A good way to test the water*, he thought.

She felt his fingers touch her fleetingly and it sent a shiver down her spine. It felt so intimate and affectionate. She didn't pull her hand away but looked at him with her lips parted. He couldn't resist himself and leant over and planted a soft kiss on her lips. She liked his kiss, so soft and sure but not demanding. It was like she had never been kissed before. It was nice to be kissed like that.

Hand in hand they went out for dinner. Outside it was still busy, with cars and motorbikes coming from all directions as they crossed the road to make their way to the restaurant. They ordered a curry for dinner and Jon started to play footsy under the table. Finally, his wishes were coming true, he had wanted to play footsy with Karma ever since they had dinner in Bhutan.

He had always had an eye for Asian girls. His infatuation started when he was fourteen and he worked in a Chinese chip shop after school. He thought the owner's wife was pretty with her dark hair, brown eyes, and petite stature. *I want an Asian for a wife,* he thought, even at that age.

That night they fell in bed together without any qualms. It was like they were long lost lovers.

Chapter 15

Chitwan

Karma wanted to go to Pokhara but Jon didn't want to. He once had a fling with a girl who lives there, and he didn't want to run into her in case it upset her. He thought it would be a bit insensitive on his part to explore her domain while with another girl. He thought it would be better if they should explore Chitwan instead. *That's my man*, she thought. She didn't like an inconsiderate man. When she was with her ex, he used to talk about his sex life with another woman, and he always had derogatory comments about his partners. She was pleased Jon was nothing like her ex.

The next day after breakfast, they went to a travel agency to book the trip to Chitwan. Karma was not familiar with Kathmandu so she followed him like a sheep. They came out of the hotel and turned left, then left on to the main road, and then another left down a crowded street. They carried on walking hand in hand and the crowds started to thin out. Then Jon realised they were heading in the wrong direction, so they doubled back on to the main road and headed straight to where the street got busier and dustier. They went into the first travel agent they saw and booked a room in a hotel with a swimming pool.

The next day, they were up early and they caught the bus to Chitwan. They stopped for lunch on the way. It took around six hours to get there, then the hotel minibus picked them up from the bus station. After they checked in, they were shown to their room and dropped off their luggage. A guide was to meet them in the hotel restaurant to give them the itinerary before lunch. Jon went to meet the guide as Karma needed to use the washroom. When she returned, he was sat there nodding enthusiastically in deep conversation with a Nepalese guy; this guy had his sunglasses on because he must have thought it was sunny indoors!

"Hi, I am your guide for the day," the guy in sunglasses said, introducing himself to Karma.

"Hi," she said, and shook his proffered hand. When he left, Karma sat next to Jon to enquire what he had said.

"I've no idea what he said!" Jon admitted. "With his pretend American accent, I couldn't understand a word!"

"Ok, so you have no idea about the plan for today?"

"Nope."

"Shall I go and find out?" she said, and thought, *no point asking Jon to go and ask again. He may come back with the same answer. NO IDEA!*

She found out that the guide would meet them at three that afternoon and take them around the nearby village.

"Shall we go and check the swimming pool while we are waiting? It is two now, we have an hour before the tour," she suggested.

"We can do," he agreed, and then asked, "how long is the tour?"

"About an hour?" Karma presumed. She had forgotten to ask.

They walked hand in hand around the hotel grounds—holding hands had now become second nature. The swimming pool was not hard to find, but it was the dirtiest swimming pool they had ever seen. Both looked at the water in disgust and then at each other. The so-called swimming pool was covered in green algae and looked like it had never been cleaned. It was not even fit for hippos never mind humans. They didn't seem to have any luck with swimming pools in Nepal.

They enjoyed the trip around the village. It took them only half an hour and they made their own way back to the hotel. On the way, they decided to stop under the shade of a big tree. They chatted as Karma sat crossed legged and Jon kicked a pebble around.

When they eventually got back it was too early for dinner. They spotted a hammock near their room, and gingerly they climbed into it and lay there rocking for a while. Karma was enjoying lying very close to Jon with their fingers entwined. But all of a sudden…

"I feel like vomiting!" she said, and rushed off to their room; she suffered from motion sickness, and the rocking of the hammock had made her feel nauseous. When Karma didn't surface, Jon went to check on her and she was lying face down on the bed.

"You poor thing, are you ok?" he asked, and she just shook her head. "Were you sick?"

"I was, and I still feel a bit queasy," she said feebly.

He came around the bed and held her close to him; feeling sorry for her he whispered, "You poor thing. It's too hot in here, I will put the fan on," and he went to switch it on. No such luck—it wouldn't start. "You stay here. I will go and get some help."

She just nodded as she didn't want to move. She had to lie still until the nausea passed. A guy came to fix the fan but to no avail, so they were given a new room in the main building.

The next day, they went on an elephant ride. Karma enjoyed it immensely. There was a funny incident when Jon dropped his camera lens cap and hat; the very helpful elephant decided to pick up the things that Jon had dropped and handed them back to the mahout. As they rode by, they suddenly heard branches rustle and spotted a rhino grazing.

What would happen if I fell off and landed on the rhino. What would it do? Karma thought. It was unnerving to see a rhino in such proximity.

As they went past a hut, they spotted a guy outside chiselling away at a piece of wood held between his bare feet. "If I were him, I would end up losing all my toes and fingers," Jon said facetiously.

"Ha...Ha...Ha..." Karma laughed, imagining Jon without toes and fingers. He found her laughter so infectious that he couldn't help but join in. The other couple riding with them grimaced, but Karma was too caught up in her own happiness.

"Thank God it has come to an end," said Jon after the ride ended. "What was the point of that ride? Stuck with a miserable couple on the back of an elephant in a box! It was the most tedious ride I ever had!" Jon exclaimed.

"I thought it wasn't that bad, I enjoyed it," Karma said.

It was the most wonderful seven days of Karma's life, she was enjoying every bit of it.

Jon enjoyed spending time with Karma, but he was not impressed with Chitwan, or *Shitwan* as he came to call it. He was glad to be heading back to Kathmandu. On that trip they met a couple: a Western woman and an Asian guy.

"Are you going back to England?" the couple asked.

"Yes, I am, but Karma is heading back to Bhutan," Jon said. A look of surprise and astonishment filled the couple's faces. Jon and Karma couldn't comprehend the reason for their shock.

"Is it because we are not married?" Karma said, when they were back in the hotel.

"I don't know, maybe?"

"Come on, this is the twenty-first century and it is a free world," Karma said.

"I know," Jon replied.

On the day of their departure, both Asians were waiting patiently for the bus while the westerners were in the toilet—they both had stomach upset. Asians have stomachs of iron and can withstand anything. They came out of the toilet one after another looking relieved, but Jon's ease didn't last, and Karma insisted that the driver drove via the pharmacy to get some stomach medicine.

They spoke of everything except for their future. They had an unspoken understanding; that only time would tell, and so they focused on the present.

"I love you," Karma whispered into his ear on the fifth night.

Jon didn't know how to respond to that. He knew he liked her a lot, but *love* he was not sure about. He was not going to say the three little words just to keep her happy, so he decided not to say anything.

On getting no response she was hurt, but she had thought, *I better say it before we part and there is no time like the present.* She didn't want to go back wishing or thinking *should I have done this, or should I have done that...* She was a worrier and always a bit anxious about the uncertainty of the future.

She comforted herself by thinking, *I hadn't hoped for anything to come out of it and there was nothing to lose.* But the romanticism in her couldn't stop her heart from desiring a life with him. *Feelings should be mutual and I am not going to spoil things by pestering him. I want him to be with me because he wants to be, not because he must.* She reprimanded herself repeatedly.

They lived on opposite sides of the globe, she in the far east and he in the west. Now she felt stupid blurting it out like that. The only consolation was she knew that she meant it, and she hoped he felt it too.

Suddenly, Karma felt all grown up. She had never really comprehended grown-up feelings, never mind implementing them in the past. It amazed her how she was able to talk herself into not expecting too much from this relationship. She always wondered, how can someone have sex and not talk about feelings and the future. She was so sure of herself that she would never be in this position. However, this was exactly the position that she now found herself in.

You will understand a situation better when you are in it, was one of her mum's maxims.

When they got back to Kathmandu, they were upgraded to a better room after they mentioned the swimming pool. It was a luxury after their time in *Shitwan*. It was nice to sink into fluffy, white, feathery pillows, and a comfortable bed. Comfort is nice, but it was nothing compared to good company.

Their last day in Kathmandu was awful, as they realised they would both be returning to their real lives. They went to *Swapna Bagaicha*, the 'Garden of Dreams' which was famous for its six seasons gardens. The information board said: It was created by Field Marshal Kaiser Sumsher early in the 1920s. The design was inspired by the Edwardian style. Within the Garden walls, Kaiser Sumsher had created an exquisite ensemble of pavilions, fountains, decorative garden furniture, and European inspired features such as verandas, pergolas, balustrades, urns, and birdhouses. He had erected six impressive pavilions, each dedicated to one of the six seasons of Nepal. This was news to Karma as she hadn't known that six seasons existed. These pavilions provided the garden's architectural framework, and lent a cosmopolitan flavour to the formal arrangement of flowers, shrubs and trees. It was a shame that on that day they could only see half of the original garden. They spent half a day walking around the gardens, and at the end Karma laid down on the grass. She always liked to lay on grass, and she never missed the opportunity to do so. Jon found this endearing and carefree.

Early the next morning after breakfast, Jon dropped Karma off at the airport and disappeared. He didn't like long goodbyes. "Lucky that flight is delayed, you would have missed it," the assistant at the check-in counter said, taking her ticket.

"By how many hours?" Karma said relieved. Her first thought was she could have more time to spend with Jon before she went back to Bhutan.

"I don't know, maybe until tomorrow, it depends upon the weather," replied the assistant.

"OK, give me a second," said Karma, and she dashed off to go and find Jon to let him know. She forgot that Kathmandu airport has different rules to Bhutan's airport, and that once in the terminal you were not allowed to go out, and visitors were not allowed to come inside. She dashed to the nearest window but Jon was nowhere in sight. After craning her neck to try and find him without success, she had no option but to go back to the counter with a heavy heart and checked in.

Chapter 16

So near yet so far.

Sometimes, fate plays silly games. After waiting for many tedious hours in the departure hall, Karma's flight had been cancelled and now she was desperately trying to get hold of Jon without success. She didn't know what to do and she didn't have a single penny in her purse. She was stupid enough to stick her American dollars in a bag that had been checked-in. That day she learnt a lesson, and now she never travels anywhere without money in her purse. A lesson learned the hard way.

There is no one who doesn't make a mistake, but learning from mistakes is a great virtue. Another one of her mum's aphorisms rang in her head.

The airline put the passengers up in a hotel for the night. Luckily, she had a twin bedroom on her own; she couldn't face sharing with anyone except Jon but she was finding it hard to get hold of him. She went out to try to get some money with her credit card which didn't work. She tried to call him using the hotel phone, it rang a few times and as soon as he answered the annoying phone went straight to voicemail. It was so frustrating for her. She was spending a night in Kathmandu only a few miles from where he was, and yet with no way of contacting him. They could have had an extra night together. She had never felt so near, yet so far.

Jon kept getting calls on his mobile phone, he presumed it was the guide who had offered to accompany him on a mountain bike tour. He had already found a different guide and couldn't be bothered returning the calls.

It was not in Karma's nature to give up easily. She called her sister and asked her to call Jon and tell him that she was stuck in Kathmandu. Her sister had the same problem, one ring, "Hello" and then straight to voicemail. As a last resort, Karma decided to leave a voice message. Something was better than nothing. *Who knows, he might get this voicemail and call me back?* she guessed.

"Hi darling, my flight was cancelled and I am still here in Kathmandu. Please can you call me back? I am desperate to get hold of you. I am missing you already." She was pleased with how she sounded, she normally hated leaving voice messages.

She knew she was being very bold: not having a single penny, making an overseas phone call and using a term of endearment—darling! Immediately, she felt stupid calling him darling but there was nothing she could do about it. Anyway, she always wanted to use a term of endearment with her loved one, but whenever she had tried to use it in the past it didn't sit well on her lips. She was glad that the word darling came out without thinking.

She showered and went down for dinner. After dinner, she couldn't settle and had a few more tries contacting him using the hotel phone, again to no avail. She was wondering why he didn't try to ring back. She was getting restless now, and even contemplated jumping in a taxi to head to his hotel. The only thing that kept her from going was she was not sure whether he was in the same hotel or not. She had never felt so sad, destitute and forlorn. After exhausting all the tricks up her sleeve, she had no option but to leave it to fate and went to sleep.

Jon was busy the next day. He went for a bike ride and it was as satisfying as always. He wanted to ring Karma, but by the time he got back to his hotel he was exhausted and too tired to call. *I will give her a call tomorrow*, and with that thought he fell into a deep slumber.

As soon as she had landed at Paro, she tried his phone again, but it was the same problem of one ring, "Hello" and straight to voicemail. She was in the mood to hurl her phone across the arrivals lounge but she controlled herself, after all it was not her phone's fault. It was the network's problem; she was sure of it.

Later that day, when she finally got home, her family were excited to know all about her trip and she told them about meeting a *Chilip* in Kathmandu.

"I had an inkling you naughty girl," Dorji said, her eyes glinting with amusement. Karma was glad Dorji was taking it lightly.

Later that day, Karma was awoken from a deep sleep caused by the restless night before. It was her son calling her. "*Ama! Ama!* There is a call for you," Yeshi yelled at the top of his voice.

"Who is it?"

"I don't know," Yeshi said, handing her the phone.

"Hello," Karma said dozily.

"I was trying to call you for ages, what's wrong with your phone?" As soon as she heard Jon's voice, she was wide awake.

"I was sleeping, sorry. I was trying to phone you yesterday every few minutes."

"Was that you?" Jon said, remembering all the persistent calls. "Sorry honey, if I had known it was you, I would have called you."

"It was a nightmare," Karma replied. "I was trying to call you a million times and getting nowhere, and I was worried sick about paying the hotel phone bill. Luckily, when I went for breakfast, I met some Bhutanese. One of them offered to help me and lent me the money to pay the bill," Karma spoke feeling sorry for herself.

"Sorry, I feel bad," said Jon.

"It is OK. It's not your fault, although you should at least have tried to call back once."

"I thought it was a Nepalese guide calling me. As soon as I answered and said hello, the line would go dead. Did you pay back the Bhutanese guy?"

"Yes, I did as soon as we landed at Paro airport. I borrowed some money from a colleague and gave it to him. It was nice of him to help me, but I didn't want to be in debt by leaving it to a later date; this would mean swapping phone numbers and I didn't want to do that," she said. This was very unlike Karma. In the past, she would have given her mobile number without thinking.

"You were lucky then," he said.

"Very lucky," she replied. She had never felt so lucky to have been born a Bhutanese. She didn't think it was possible to get financial help from your fellow citizens when in another country, or was it? She knew that back home, the Bhutanese are generous enough to dish out financial assistance at the drop of a hat. If someone asked to borrow money from her, she wouldn't be able to refuse, especially if she had the cash. But the trouble was, she would get only some of the money back; the rest she would see neither hide nor hair.

In her village, her dad went through the same situation. Whenever he sold his oranges, hordes of relatives would be waiting outside like vultures to borrow money.

"You can't just lend money like that, Dad," Karma said, after he lent all the money made from the first orange harvest. Although, she was a fine one to talk.

"I know, I shouldn't, but it is different in the village. We help each other."

After giving her a lecture about scratching backs, her dad went on lending all his money, but he didn't get it all back and he would chase after the promised arrears. He eventually learned his lesson, and whenever he sells his oranges, he goes straight to Thimphu and deposits the takings in the bank.

Karma was lucky to have run into someone that was very helpful and she paid her hotel telephone bill. She could easily have got away without paying, but she never believed in not paying what she owes—it was against her moral virtues.

After that phone call their relationship went to a whole new level. Karma was certain that they would be together. He called her honey and sweetheart, and she called him darling.

Jon spent three more days in Kathmandu, and instead of e-mailing her, he phoned her every day. However, communicating every day on the phone comes with a price.

Flying back to the UK was a nuisance for Jon. He wished he could extend his stay, but he had to go back to work and he had family commitments.

On arrival at the UK, his mobile phone started to go mad—PING, PING, PING it went. The first thing he picked up was a voicemail from Karma when she was marooned in Kathmandu. His heart went out to her, she sounded so sad and devastated.

The first thing he did when he arrived home was to call her. He couldn't understand, but there was this invisible string pulling him towards her. Every day after that, they would talk on the phone.

"Guess what my mobile phone bill is this month?" Jon asked one day.

"No idea," Karma said.

"Five hundred pounds," he said with incredulity. He couldn't believe his eyes when he saw the bill.

"Five hundred pounds?" she said, wondering why he sounded surprised.

"It's a lot of money to spend on phone calls," he said, as if reading her mind.

She thought five hundred pounds in England was the same as five hundred ngultrums in Bhutan. What she didn't realise was you can't buy much with Nu. 500 but with £500 you certainly can.

"Sorry," she said.

"Why are you saying sorry? It's not your fault."

"You sounded a bit angry about it."

"I'm not angry, honey, it took me by surprise that's all."

Apart from using endearing terms with each other, they still didn't speak about a future.

A few days after his arrival in the UK, Jon and his girlfriend had a big quarrel. That was the wake-up call for him. He knew he had to come to some sort of decision.

Karma was in her office having lunch when her phone went TRING, TRING, and her heart skipped a beat.

After swapping pleasantries, Jon said, "Tonight, I have a big decision to make…"

Chapter 17

Things happen when they are least expected.

I didn't know what to say. I knew I had won him, but I didn't want to be so assured and jinx it. I had a brilliant time with Jon in Nepal, but he never gave me the impression of wanting to leave his girlfriend for me. This was one of the many qualities that I liked about him: no empty words.

The next day, Saturday, I was driving to my village to see my dad with my four sisters, niece, and Yeshi. It was hot and I had to open the car windows to let fresh air in. We were singing along to some Bhutanese pop songs. My car's boot was jam-packed with a gas bottle, kerosene, and spare clothing for seven people. It was lucky that the Bhutan road safety authority had no rules for children having their own car seats. It was amazing how much stuff you could pack into a small car. Travelling light is beyond Bhutanese comprehension.

We had already driven for a few hours along the meandering road, climbing up a mountain pass, dropping down to the valley, and alongside a rushing river. The sky was an empyreal, clear blue, and the sun was blazing when my phone started to ring—it was Jon. I pulled over to the roadside and got out of the car. Luckily, in Bhutan, the traffic is not busy, especially on that kind of road, which looked down at the Sunkosh (golden fish) river flowing gently down the valley. It was believed that a giant, golden fish had been spotted in the river, and that was how it got its name. This stretch of the road would be a stretch that I would either want to forget or remember all my life—it depended on what Jon had to say. We were just a couple of hours from my village.

"Hello, darling, how are you? Is everything OK?" I asked full of anticipation; I could hear my own heartbeat.

"Hello, darling, where are you?" asked Jon in response.

"I am on the way to the village, just a couple of hours to go now, it is so hot."

"I won't keep you any longer if you are driving," he said.

"It is OK. I had pulled over to the side of the road."

"OK, ready for the news? I am leaving her," he said, not giving me time to take it all in. For that short period, I didn't understand what he was saying.

"You are leaving her?" was all I managed to say. I couldn't believe my ears.

"Are you OK?" he asked.

"Yes, not just OK but deliriously happy, this is the best news I've ever had in my adult life," I said, and couldn't stop smiling. When the call was finished, I walked back to the car with a spring in my step. I felt as happy as a bunny in a field. I couldn't wait to share the news with my sisters. They knew that I had gone to Nepal to meet a *Chilip*, apart from that, I did not elaborate much on anything and they hadn't asked. It was only because I didn't want to get too ahead of myself.

"Jon wants to be with me," I announced to my family. I was very happy with Jon's decision, but I felt sorry for his girlfriend.

"OK." That was all they said and gave a nod of approval.

"Who is Jon, *Ama*?" Yeshi asked inquisitively.

"Someone I met in Nepal."

"So, you went to Nepal to meet a guy, not for a conference?"

"Sort of," I said, not wanting to give away too much, as he was too young for a full disclosure, but then I added, "it looks like we are going to the UK."

"YES!" Yeshi said, and he looked as pleased as me.

To this day, I can still picture his cute face full of smiles and happiness. Until then, I didn't realise that he was as desperate as me to get away from this awful mess of a life that I had created. Bless him, my sweet boy.

Chapter 18

A step closer.

Everything comes with a price. If you haven't got anything to offer, be prepared to face rejection, my citation of the day.

"Don't rush into things," my mum used to say.

I knew what my mum meant, but how could I tell if I was rushing into things? Easier said than done, but the saying stuck with me.

"Don't rush into things," I would say to myself, whenever I had an important decision to make. Now I was facing a very important decision.

After our phone call, Jon couldn't wait for me to join him in England. "We have to think about applying for a UK visa now," he mentioned in one of our phone calls, not knowing that I had already been looking into it as soon as I was back in the office.

"I have already looked into it. See what you think. I will e-mail the details over," I said, getting excited as my dream was finally coming true. I didn't know why, but I had always longed for a life in the west.

When I was going through a rough patch with my ex-husband, all I wanted to do was run far away from Bhutan. I even got in touch with a couple of Bhutanese I knew who lived in America, but their replies were not very helpful.

'Hi, will you be able to help me with a visa for the USA? I would like to come if possible.' I e-mailed.

'Sorry, no chance. If I could help anyone, I would like to get my family over here first.' was the reply from an ex-colleague.

'What the f...Who are you?' was a reply from my ex-brother-in-law.

It is very difficult to judge or to know the true nature of a person until you ask a favour of them. Seeking a favour is as bad as being dependent on others. I thought everybody was like me—very complaisant. I was asking, not demanding. I could not understand how someone could use that kind of language. It was hurtful.

I was so desperate. I even sought Jon's help one time and emailed him, *'Do you know anyone in the USA?'*

'I am sorry, I don't know anybody there,' was his reply. I didn't know why, but I was hurt by his short and decisive reply. Was it because of the two rejections in the space of one week that I'd already had, or was I expecting too much? *It would be nice if he could say he would look into it and see if he could help, rather than saying no without thinking,* I thought. *Never mind*, I consoled myself. I knew I had to stop being such a sensitive soul.

And now, a few years later, I was planning to move to the west—my dreamland.

From: karmadenzom@yahoo.com
To: jon@fernilee.co.uk

Hi darling,
Nice to <u>hear from</u> you this morning. This is what I found out.
We can get a six month's visitor visa so I can be there with you, I can't wait.
With lots of love,
Karma

'How soon can you apply?' he replied.

'Sometime this week,' I answered. *But I need financial help,* I thought. I had been independent for so long that I didn't like asking for help. I had enough to live on in Bhutan, but I wouldn't be able to afford to pay for the visa application.

Summoning all of my courage I wrote: '*Hi darling, I need around £200 for visa expenses, do you mind?*' My heart was beating rapidly as I did not know what his reaction would be.

Jon didn't mind helping, he thought it would be unfair on me to let me bear all the expense. '*Don't worry about the expense, I will pay for it. I will send it soon before you leave for Delhi.*' I was so relieved and thanked him.

I gathered as much information as I could. I liked to be prepared. I went to see one of my colleagues at work who had been to England, and enquired about the necessary documents needed for a British visa. I knew that even though the UK was part of Europe, they were not part of the Shenzhen agreement, which was unfortunate as I had a valid Shenzhen visa. I was told it was a simple, straightforward application. My colleague had taken his wife with him when he was on a course in the UK. She didn't even need to go to a visa centre. He went alone first and then his wife applied, and a few weeks later, her visa was approved and she joined him.

"I see. Does that mean I don't have to take my son with me to apply?" I asked, surprised at how simple and hassle-free it sounded.

"No, you don't have to," my colleague said with surety.

With a boost of confidence, I left for Delhi, sometime in April, to apply for the visa. I had read through the visa application form a hundred times, and was thoroughly impressed with my efficiency, but my confidence quickly disappeared as soon as they asked for my son.

"Where is your son, madam?" the visa agent asked me.

"I haven't got my son with me," I replied.

"I can't take his visa application without seeing him, we need to have his fingerprints and photo. I am sorry."

"Can we apply separately?" I asked, having a brainwave. *I will apply for mine today and bring my son here in a few days' time for his*, I thought, after all, something was better than nothing.

"Yes, you can do that." I was so relieved to hear this.

Getting my son over to Delhi was another matter. Being a child, he couldn't travel on his own. After being on the phone for ages, I managed to get hold of one of my colleagues to sort out my son's travel arrangements, and he would find an adult to escort him. It was a good job I had managed to get hold of a Delhi sim card. It was expensive, but nowhere near as much as it would be if I was using a Bhutanese sim card.

I found the pollution in Delhi horrendous after coming from Bhutan, and the heat was hitting over 30 degrees when I jumped into a tuk tuk. I thought it would be better to travel in as it was cheaper than a taxi and had natural air-conditioning, but how wrong I was. By the time I met my son at the airport, I was creating a pool of sweat on the tuk tuk's seat. I was so relieved when I saw my son standing at the airport with a Bhutanese man. We thanked him and left for the hotel.

A day after my son's application, I received a text asking me to come and collect my passport. I was elated and skipped to the visa centre, even though the temperature was now soaring above thirty-five degrees.

I was handed an envelope which contained my passport. As soon as I had my hands on the envelope, I tore it open with exhilaration and went through the letter animatedly.

We are rejecting your application for the reason that you have not applied with your son.

My elation dissipated and I felt like tearing the letter in two and storming back to the hotel. It was disheartening, and the frustrating bit was I had no way of getting in touch with the embassy to explain my situation.

A few days later, my son Yeshi's refusal letter read, *We are rejecting your application for the reason that your mother's application was rejected.* I didn't know how to digest this second rejection and all I wanted to do was throw a fit of rage, but to whom I didn't know and I had to calm down. *The first rejection is the hardest,* I once heard somewhere, and how true it was. I was devastated, and so were Yeshi and Jon.

The second time around I expected to get a more positive response; I had gone through all the possible scenarios with a fine-tooth comb with the help of Jon. Like the French say, savoir-faire, knowing what to do in any situation. I took a bank draft for the visa fee, that was safer than carrying cash.

"Sorry, the fee is too much," said the agent.

"Why? It is for two people," I said confounded.

"Sorry, the fees need to be paid individually. We do not accept joint fees."

"Even if we are applying together?" I said incredulously. I could feel savoir-faire taking leave, and realised that sometimes savoir-faire on its own was not enough. I needed luck.

"Sorry, that is how it works," said the agent apologetically.

"Can we come back to submit the application?"

"Sure, this kind of mishap happens all the time, but don't be long." I was so glad the agent was being very accommodating. I couldn't think of going back to Bhutan without even making the application. How frustrating it would be after all that expense.

"Thanks," I muttered, and we ran as fast as possible to the bank to see if I could cash in the bank draft.

"Sorry, the demand draft is for the concerned beneficiary, you can't get cash," the bank teller told me. I could see another misfortune approaching fast. I had no time to ponder options, and needed to find another way round.

"How about MoneyGram?" I asked, my brain feeding me the question.

"Do you have an account?"

"No."

"Then you can't. You need to have an account with the bank. Have you got any friends in Delhi?"

"Yes, I do, but I haven't got their mobile phone numbers," I said hopelessly.

What could get worse than this and why do things always tend to go wrong, one after another. Is it testing my capability? If so, I think I still have plenty of that. I never leave a job undone and I must finish what I have started. My tenacity surprises me at times, I never give up and I always must find a solution. My thoughts filled me with optimism.

As we came out of the bank, I saw a sign for Western Union money transfer and went to enquire. Even though it was on a busy street, it looked like a place of skulduggery. The entrance was OK, with the glass front and the daylight streaming through. As we entered, a guy was sat in the far corner of the room behind an untidy desk; he looked bored and sleepy. I was nervous to proceed any further, as in normal circumstances, I would not even contemplate using such a place. *But this is not a normal situation and you need to get back to the visa centre before the end of the day*, interjected my conscience.

"Will I be able to get money through Western Union even though I am not an Indian?" I asked, approaching the desk nervously.

"How much?" said the sleepy looking man.

"Fifteen thousand rupees," I said panicking again, and wondering how safe this was. I didn't want us to be murdered for the money and our bodies dumped in a ditch somewhere nearby; our family would have no idea where we were.

"Sure, come back with the unique code and we will pay you in rupees," the sleepy guy said perking up. As soon as he mentioned the unique code, I relaxed considerably.

"Thanks, I will call my sister to send money then," I said calmly.

"Hello, Dorji," I said when I phoned my sister, "will you be able to send me some money? The visa fee I got as a bank draft was a complete failure and…" I was babbling in desperation and praying.

"I don't have any money now but I will ask my husband, hold on for a second… yes, he can do it. Where do you want us to send it? And how much?" she said.

"Can you send it to New Delhi, fifteen thousand rupees, if he has got enough," I said with hesitance, not knowing how much money they had.

"That's fine," replied Dorji.

"Let me know the code and I will get it from the agent. Thanks, Dorji, you are a star. What would I do without you?"

"Return home without applying for the visa, I think," she said jovially.

After sorting out the money, we went back to the agent and re-submitted our application forms. Fingerprints and photos were taken and we went back to the hotel reassured. Then, a few days later, I got another rejection letter.

We hereby refuse your application on account of a submitted piece of paper as supposed evidence of being divorced and a single mother, said the letter. Disheartened, but not as shocked as with the first rejection, I called Jon and explained everything.

"Haven't you got an actual certificate?" asked Jon.

"No, that piece of paper is my single status certificate. And how dare they say it was just a piece of paper? To get this so-called 'piece of paper' I had to present myself in the notary office with my ex-husband, and this was not easy, as he refused to come to the office. It took a catfight with his wife to knock some sense into him," I told Jon with vehemence.

To get the single status certificate, I had waited in the notary office, waiting for my ex to show up to sign over the custody of Yeshi. He had taken no part in bringing up Yeshi. He didn't even pay any maintenance money when we separated. Now, when I wanted to take our son to England, I needed his permission—it was so frustrating. By the end of the day, I managed to get the divorce certificate but not the custody letter, as my ex didn't bother to show up. On the way home, I got a call from my ex-mother-in-law enquiring about the custody.

"I haven't got the custody letter. Can I talk to him please?" I asked politely, even though I was fuming inside.

As soon as my ex was on the phone, I just started yelling. "What are you thinking, refusing to come to the notary office. I have had enough of you; I am going to the UK on my own and you can take care of Yeshi. So far, I have done a good job of looking after him…"

"Listen…" my ex said.

"No, you listen first and then you will get your chance," I screamed again over the phone; I was like a woman possessed.

"You look after Yeshi and I am going on my own. If anything happens to Yeshi, I will never leave you in peace," I shouted in a burst of rage. I had spoken in a rage, but in reality, I wouldn't be able to leave my baby boy behind. My life would never be the same without him close to me.

"Listen to what I have to say, we are coming now," he was now shouting louder than me.

"It is too late now, I am driving back home."

"You bitch, leave my husband alone!" I suddenly heard a woman on the phone. It had taken a second or two for this to sink in, as it was difficult to concentrate on driving and throwing abuse down the phone at the same time. I didn't realise that it was his new wife until she shouted again. "You *rundey* (whore)," she shouted.

"If I am *rundey,* what are you?" I retaliated.

"*Chetom* (bitch)," his wife carried on.

"If I am a bitch, you are a double bitch, not able to control your husband, letting him dangle his dick to whichever woman he pleases," I yelled on the phone. We were not making any sense. Both of us were throwing abuse at each other at the same time and it was a screaming match.

This shouting and screaming went on for a few minutes, then suddenly exhaustion took over and both of us went quiet.

"Hello, listen, I am only asking for him to come and sign the papers. I am not asking him to come and live with me, he is all yours, I don't care about him. I only want to take my son to the UK with me," I said calming down.

"You bitch, *rundey,* blah blah blah," his wife started up again.

Now I had calmed down a bit, I could understand his wife's frustration in one way, after all, I hadn't been pure— I did have an affair with her husband. But, in another way, I couldn't understand why the new wife was being obdurate and impossible to deal with, as the situation was different now. I wanted to take my son, not my ex-husband, and I had made it clear that I didn't want anything to do with my ex.

"You bitch, if you come anywhere near my husband…" The wife carried on and now my patience was wearing thin.

"I am coming up to your place to show you who is a whore and who isn't, you stupid bitch!" I shouted and slammed the phone down. I changed the route I was driving. I wanted to put an end to this. I put my foot down and within no time I was at their house.

"Aie," I called at the door. *Aie* means mother, and this was how I addressed my ex-mother-in-law.

I was so angry, and felt like I could move a mountain with rage pumping blood all around my body. I was so upset that I didn't know what I was thinking of: looking for the mother-in-law when I knew that my ex and his wife were waiting for me.

"You bitch, what do you want?" The wife came charging, pointing a finger at me.

"Why did you think I..." I started but couldn't complete my sentence, as the wife was approaching fast and furious towards me. Before the wife managed to touch me, I pushed her and she went flying backwards.

In an instant, she jumped back at me like a flying tigress and grabbed a handful of my hair. I was caught off guard and nearly lost my balance. High heels and dieting didn't help in this situation; I was feeling feeble. But then the rage in me brought back my strength, and I got hold of the wife's hair—we were like a pair of wild cats.

The irony was laughable. Who would have thought that after more than a decade, I would be in the same position as his previous girlfriends?

Mother and son had a hell of a job separating us. By the end of the fight, the wife disappeared into their bedroom and I sat on a chair in floods of tears. Feeling my sore head, I was surprised when clumps of loose hair came out in my hand. I collected it all and rubbed them into a ball. And then I felt a sharp pain under my right eye, it was bleeding, which made me tear up even more and I wailed.

"Are you all right?" my ex-mother-in-law enquired.

"No, my head is hurting and look, my hair is falling out," I said, running my fingers through my hair and dislodging some more. "Look!" I said, holding out my loose hair.

"It is all his fault, if he had never come back into my life, I would have been OK," I said in tears, looking pointedly at my ex.

"You are the one who is not leaving him alone," his wife shouted from her hiding place.

"I told you that I am not asking you to be with me. All I want is to take our son with me. Is that too much to ask?" I shouted at my ex, ignoring his wife. *I should have attacked him not her, after all, it was his fault for not being able to prioritise things and not explaining the situation properly to his wife. What a deceitful man, nothing but a two-faced individual*, I thought belatedly.

"*Chetom!* (whore) Leave my husband alone," the wife shouted again.

"You can have your husband all to yourself, there are plenty more fish in the sea. Why should I be so hooked on this particular fish?" I retaliated. "I don't give a damn about your husband, I am sick of it." Then turning to my ex I said, "Now, sign Yeshi's custody paper and get out of my life, all I want is to take my son with me to the UK, is that too much to ask?" I felt better but got no response. "Now, I have had enough of this, I am leaving. Come to get Yeshi. I am handing him over to you, I want to see how you will cope with another mouth to feed. And I am warning you, that if something happens to him, I will make you pay," I said this as an empty threat. It was just a big gamble, and I hoped I hadn't got too carried away.

I was relieved to get all of my words out. I started to walk away without a backwards glance.

"Stop, we will go and sort out this letter," I heard him say.

"Really?" I couldn't believe my ears.

"Yes!' I was trying my hardest not to smile. But I couldn't help it. I felt so happy knowing that I could take my son.

"If you had done that before, just like I asked, then we wouldn't be in this situation," I said, getting the last word in. "I will wait in the car," and I walked out looking very happy, even though my hair was dishevelled and my face was bleeding.

That same day, we went back to the notary office and got the custody letter. I bid a final farewell to my ex-husband and prayed never to cross his path again. In the end, the fight was worthwhile. I got what I wanted.

For years after that incident, I felt sorry for the wife, but both of us were the victim. I wished that I had some influence to educate women about men like my ex. *Why do women tend to blame each other rather than looking deeper into their men's character?* I always wondered this. In my case, the main wrongdoer was my ex, who said one thing to me and another to his wife. And what did I do? I ended up fighting with his wife instead. STUPID!

I ended up with a scratch mark just below my right eye close to my nose. For the next few weeks, I could barely move my head; it was sore and my neck remained as stiff as a board.

How dare the UK border agency say it is just a piece of paper when it nearly cost me an eye, I thought.

I explained my tribulations when I spoke to Jon on Skype the next day. Now, instead of e-mailing, we took to skyping every day; this was much easier.

What concerned me with this second rejection was, what if I had to go back to court to get another document, as this would mean involving my ex again. I didn't even want to contemplate it. I was adamant to stay as far away from him as possible.

Living in Thimphu was getting very expensive for me, but I was having difficulty finding an apartment in Paro. I had moved so many times over the years. It looked like every landlord was against me renting their place now. Then the thought struck me. I could ask Jon to help me so I didn't have to move away from Thimphu. I didn't know how to broach the subject, as I always thought of myself as independent and we were not together yet, but I needed help desperately. So, setting my ego aside and vacillating for a few days, I decided to go ahead with my plan, but instead of mentioning it on Skype, I took the cowardly way and e-mailed him.

'I need you to help me financially, could you send me £100 every month…' I said in the e-mail, my heart beating fast. As soon as the e-mail left my mailbox I regretted it, and the whole day I was on edge.

Chapter 19

Cultural difference.

When Jon read the e-mail he was furious. *For crying out loud, what does she think I am*, he thought?

'*Do you see ££££ signs on my forehead,*' Jon replied.

Karma didn't know what to make of this and her eyes started to prick with tears. *The general thought in Bhutan was, if you are involved with a Chilip, you would be showered with lots of cash,* she thought. *But that is not me. I never want to depend on anyone too much, and see what happens when you go beyond your morals.* Just that thought made her cringe, but for some strange reason that didn't stop her from feeling hurt. Maybe if the situation was reversed, she wouldn't hesitate to help Jon.

'*Sorry, I didn't mean it to sound like that. Now we are together, I thought you could help me financially, that is what we do in Bhutan, we help each other,*' she e-mailed back, wishing she had never mentioned money now.

When Jon read this e-mail, his heart went out to her, and he thought he better call and sort this out.

"Forget I even said that. Sorry," he said over the phone.

"No worries," she said.

"Am I forgiven?"

"Yes."

'Sorry for the pound sign thing. I didn't mean to say it. It was sounding like a demand when you asked me to send money,' he later wrote.

'It is all right,' she wrote back but still hurting. All she wanted to do was curl up in bed and wallow in self-pity. What a childish thing to do, but emotions have no age. Some people show them and some don't.

'Seriously, forget what I said, and next time break it to me gently so I can understand better. I am not used to these kinds of things and it took me by surprise when you asked, it is not the kind of thing we do in the UK' Jon said in an e-mail to her the next day.

It could be just a cultural difference, Karma thought, I can't prosecute him for that.

'It is all right, darling, don't worry,' she e-mailed.

'Are you sure? Are you OK? I am sorry for upsetting you like this. I didn't mean to. The way you said it, it made me wonder.'

'It's OK, darling, I am fine now, really.' she wrote. Both were relieved that they were clearing up the misunderstanding.

Karma noticed the difference between her ex and Jon. Jon seemed to know the way to bring her round, and it reminded her of another one of her mum's sayings, *If someone cares for you, they will take your feelings into consideration.*

While all of this was going on, they looked over the UK visa requirements together and realised that they were applying for the wrong visa. With a visitor visa, Karma and her son could stay in England for no more than six months and then they would have to go back. They wouldn't be able to get married on a visitor's visa. What they needed was a 'Fiancé Visa.' They felt stupid now. They thought that they could get a visitor visa, get married, and settle in the UK, as simple as that. How naïve. They were glad that the visa application had been rejected.

"Imagine you and Yeshi were here on a visitor visa and had to go back after six months. How frustrating that would be," Jon said.

"Whatever happen, happens for good now," Karma said. She had always believed in that motto. "We are a clueless pair, aren't we?" she added jovially, trying to bring humour into the conversation

"Imagine if you had to go back after six months and then apply for a fiancée visa," Jon said.

"I know darling. It would be awful, wouldn't it? Being together for six months, then leaving you for an uncertain future and not seeing you for ages."

"I would hate that," he said, "but don't worry, we are in this together. We will sort something out, won't we?"

"Yes, we will. I think applying for a fiancé visa is the only way."

"We will go for that then," Jon added excitedly.

"This man knows how to make this girl happy," Karma added with a eudemonic smile.

He couldn't see her, but he could feel a happy vibe travelling through the ethernet and connecting them.

Chapter 20

Marriage proposal

With a spring in my step, a new mission and full of hope, I started afresh with a fiancé visa application. We filled up all the necessary forms and went to apply, but this time there was no mishap with the visa fee and everything went smoothly.

I went back to court to see if I could get a proper divorce certificate. I was dreading the prospect of getting hold of my ex again. Luckily, this time his presence was not required. The girl in charge made a few changes, tweaking sentences here and there. When I saw it in print, I couldn't see any difference from the original one.

"Sorry to bother you. Is there any chance that you could make it look more official? The visa people said this piece of paper won't work," I requested.

"This is the way we have been doing it for so long. If the visa people are not happy, ask them to get in touch with us. There is a phone number at the bottom," the girl said, handing the paper back and looking at me like I was crazy. I hadn't gone crazy yet, but if things kept on this way, craziness would be just around the corner.

One person says one thing and another person says a different thing, I was stuck in the middle. The visa people were asking for a certificate, and the court could only provide a written letter. I thought that one of the sides didn't want to make it easy for people applying for visas. But which one is it?

The repeated trips to Delhi were getting very expensive. So, we decided to stay in another cheap hotel to save some money, but staying in a cheap hotel without air con was the biggest mistake. It was ok if we stayed under the ceiling fan, but as soon as we moved away from it the heat would get us with a vengeance. It was worse in the bathroom, especially when I went in after Yeshi to have a shower; it was like being in a furnace. If I had expected the bedroom to be any cooler after a shower I was mistaken. The heat was killing me, but Yeshi was sat on his bed under the fan unaffected. I was so glad he was being very compliant; he didn't say much and just followed me. *My lovely boy. He doesn't give me a hard time. I am lucky to have Yeshi for my son*, I thought. *Kadrinchay* for blessing me with a son like *Yeshi*.

I was getting restless in the hotel room but I couldn't go anywhere or do anything; the weather was too hot. I thought that I liked hot weather but now I started to rethink. When it's cold, I can pile on layers and keep warm, but when it's too hot, no matter how many layers I strip off, I am still uncomfortable. *I don't like it hot*, I decided at last.

After our visa appointment, all we did was sit under the fan in our room, waiting for the decision and venturing out only to eat. The only time we would go out was in the morning, as it was cooler. In the morning, there were people with baskets of Tibetan bread to sell. We would have a cup of tea and some freshly baked Tibetan bread for breakfast, and then we'd have a little wander around; this was the best part of the day.

How much I had saved staying in a cheap hotel I didn't know, a few hundred rupees maybe?

Jon knew that I was going through hell in Delhi, staying in a cheap hotel. He tried to talk me into staying in a better hotel, but I wouldn't listen.

The visa decision was taking longer than before, I thought that *no news is good news.* As the heat was getting unbearable, we decided to head home. I told Jon I would ask Raj, one of my friends who was in Delhi, to collect our passports and send them over when the decision was made. We flew home the next day, it was such a relief. We were able to breathe fresh air again, and the peace and quiet after the hustle and bustle of Delhi was like being in heaven.

A couple of days later, my friend called. "Hi, Karma, I got your documents, how shall I send them to you?"

"You know, like as usual. Can you hand it over to one of our aircraft engineers in Delhi? But before that, can you open the letter and read out the decision for me, please?" I asked.

"Let me see," Raj said. After a few seconds of him opening the envelope and reading the letter he announced, "You got your visa."

"Oh, thank you very much," I said. I was so excited and I couldn't wait to tell Jon. I could have called straight away, but it was too early for him, so I waited a few hours before using Skype.

"Hi, darling, the visa application has gone through," I said, after we got connected.

"Finally, I knew it would come through one day. When will you get your passport?" asked Jon.

"My friend is going to send it to me the day after tomorrow. I can't wait to get our passports and then fly to the UK."

"Me neither," Jon said excitedly, "I can't relax till you get your passport back, seeing is believing."

"Now, now, don't jinx it," I added hesitatingly, as I still felt uneasy.

The day I got our passports, I hurriedly opened the envelope. On the covering letter, it said:

Notice of Immigration Decision

Refusal of Entry clearance.
Any documents you have supplied in support of your application have been considered and recorded. It has not been necessary to interview you to reach a decision on your application.

The Decision.
You state that you have been married before and have submitted a poor-quality copy of a document from the Dzongkha Court, Thimphu, on which you have attached a post-it note describing a 'divorce certificate' as evidence of this. You have not presented any documentary evidence to satisfactorily establish that you have undertaken a divorce/dissolution order recognised under

United Kingdom law. I am not satisfied that you intend to live together with your sponsor after marriage.

You propose to travel with Yeshi, who you claim to be your son. You also state that you have sole custody of this child. You have not submitted satisfactory evidence to support this claim. You have no documents from the courts or the child's father confirming you have permission to take him out of the Kingdom of Bhutan.

I could feel my heart plummet. "Please, please don't say it is refused," I said, as I prayed hard with my eyes firmly shut, but when I opened my eyes, the rejection letter was staring back at me mockingly. It was a ludicrous descent from elation to despair, the worst let-down I had ever experienced in my life.

That is ridiculous, I thought.

I was doing all of this hush-hush and couldn't go and chat with my colleagues about it. I felt like screaming. I didn't know how to break the news to Jon but I must. I took a deep breath and dialled his number.

"Hello," he answered, after a few rings.

"Hi darling, guess what?" I said miserably.

"Oh no…you're joking," Jon said, suspecting what was coming.

"It is rejected again," I said.

"How come, your friend said your visa is approved?"

"I think he saw my Shenzhen visa on my passport. He might have assumed that it was a UK visa."

"What a fool! Did you tell him that?" I could hear the frustration in Jon's voice.

"No, I haven't, and I'm not going to. How ungrateful would I sound? He went out of his way to get my documents, and I have nothing but gratitude for him. You can say that to him if you want, I will give you his e-mail address," I said.

"Sorry, that came out wrong. All I am saying is how can someone get it so wrong. Anyway, never mind all that, what are we going to do now?"

"We will have to get married in Bhutan then, won't we?" I said impulsively.

In Bhutan, marriage was marriage, no big deal. People in Bhutan get married without even thinking. Little did I know that it is a different matter in the UK. People don't just get married willy nilly.

In the past, I would romanticise about my guy going down on one knee and dazzling me with a diamond engagement ring. It had come from reading too many romantic novels and watching too many chick flicks.

And yet in real life, what did I do? "We will have to get married then, won't we?" I had said. Should I have gone down on one knee and said, "Jon, will you marry me?" And it was not even Valentine's Day.

I had read that women can only propose to men on a leap year's Valentine's Day. But still, desperate times, desperate measures and all that…

According to a tradition that was believed to have started in the fifth century in Ireland, St. Bridget complained to St. Patrick about women having to wait for so long for a man to propose, so St. Patrick said that women could propose on Valentine's Day, every four years in a leap year.

"All right then, when?" Jon responded instantly to my suggestion. My heart swelled with happiness. *He didn't even have to think. That says a lot about how much he wants me*, I thought happily.

"In June, you will have to apply for your Bhutanese visa. I will e-mail you all the information," I said, not able to stop grinning.

"All right, can't wait for your e-mail."

"Me neither, love you, darling," I said, as amorously as always.

"I love you too, my sweet, what do you think?" Jon replied.

It was so nice to hear him say these words, and my heart skipped a beat every single time; I thought I would never get used to this. *The second time lucky*, I thought happily.

I proudly filled up the visa form, writing that Jon was coming to Bhutan to be married and submitted it. I was told to come to collect it in a week's time.

The week passed very quickly, and with a spring in my step I went to the immigration office. They handed me the envelope. I opened it while my heart went THUD THUD THUD. The letter said smugly:

On the basis that westerners are not allowed to come to Bhutan for marriage, Mr Jon's visa is refused.

Why didn't I do the research before going headlong into something as important as this? I cursed.

My consolation was, even though I had gone through the UK visa application with a fine-tooth comb, and with plenty of research, our visas were still rejected. Maybe this was not meant to happen and it is not part of my written story to be with him? But still, the frustration got the better of me, and I tore the paper into pieces and burnt them; that will teach them.

I didn't like the uneasy feeling of the final door being shut on us. I could see the path of our unity fading away in the distance. It was unbelievable that one time I had seen a big gap open, and yet another time the gap was getting smaller and smaller. So near yet so far.

Chapter 21

Perseverance.

Karma didn't have the guts to call Jon, so instead she e-mailed him:

From: karmadenzom@yahoo.com
To:jon@fernilee.co.uk

Hi darling,
The visa thing does not seem to agree with us. I foolishly said on the visa form that you are coming here to be married and they refused it on that basis. I am so disheartened I don't know what to do.
With lots of love,
Karma.

    She had a little cry in her office after sending the e-mail. At 1.00 pm, the bouncy, smooth ripple sound of Skype filled her computer screen, indicated a call incoming from Jon:

"Hi, darling." Karma said.

"Hello, my sweet. How are you, it's not good news, is it?"

"I am so fed up now. We are not getting anywhere."

"So, what's going to happen now?" Jon asked.

"I don't know darling. I am at the end of my tether. I don't know what else we can do." She was sounding dejected.

"Don't say that, honey. We won't leave a single stone unturned, all right? We will not stop trying until you are here," he said with determination.

"You know how to make me happy, don't you?" Karma said. No one else had made her feel like that, and she was pleased that at last there was someone like Jon who cared for her, and wanted to spend the rest of his life with her. "Love you, darling," she said, and thanked her lucky stars.

"Love you too, my darling. Stop worrying, we are in this together and we will find a way, OK?" Jon said. It made her heart swell with affection, and she knew then that they would win this battle one way or another. It is easier to achieve something when both parties want the same thing.

"I must go now. People are arriving at work," Karma said.

"OK, speak to you tomorrow," Jon replied.

Now, with her confidence boosted, she looked for another solution. A tourist visa, $200 a day for an all-inclusive holiday was all she could find.

By then, Dorji, her sister, was fully aware of her situation and was ever so ready to help her. Dorji hadn't even met Jon yet, but she was trusting that he wanted to make her sister happy. And Karma was happy for her sister's support.

"I can have a chat with my brother-in-law about the visa. I am pretty sure if you pay just the royalty fee the visa will be granted with no qualms," said Dorji, helpful as always. After a few hours and a chat with her brother-in-law, Dorji got back to Karma, true to her word.

"He said he can do it. It will cost $80 a day," Dorji said.

The next day, as soon as Karma got to her office, she e-mailed Jon:

'*We will be able to sort out your visa, but you must pay a daily royalty of $80. I hope that will be all right.*' She wrote feeling apprehensive as she didn't want to upset him by mentioning money again.

"We have no other way. I think we have to do that then," Jon later said on Skype.

"OK, I will look into it seriously then," she replied.

In June, 2010, Karma's soon-to-be bridegroom arrived in Bhutan. She went to pick him up from the airport. She had done this before, but now she was picking him up for herself and nobody else. This time, she didn't have any patience to wait for him at the arrivals hall. Instead, she was waiting through the terminal and past the immigration desks; that's the advantage of being one of the airline staff. She was craning her neck looking for him amongst the arrival passengers, but there was no sign of him. A little voice in her head said, *What if he is not on the plane?*

The plane was full and Jon took his time to disembark as always. It still took him by surprise how calm and peaceful Bhutan was. As he was approaching the arrivals hall, he spotted Karma in a white *kira* and red *tego*. She looked beautiful and she was giving him the biggest smile ever; he smiled back.

As soon as Karma spotted Jon striding towards her, she couldn't help but smile. As he was getting closer, she didn't know how to greet him. She knew a kiss would be too bold a move, as it wouldn't be appropriate to show her affection in public. She wanted to keep this as quiet as possible. In the end, she went for a hug which attracted curious glances from the airport staff and travellers.

Jon hugged her back. It was so nice to feel her in the flesh rather than speaking for many months on Skype. He held her tight and never wanted to let her go, but he had to because of the attention they were attracting.

They left the airport and went for lunch; Jon had fried rice, it was the only dish he felt safe to indulge in. Karma had rice and dried beef chilli. The dried beef seemed to have gone off a bit. She didn't say anything to Jon as she didn't want to put him off. She was used to eating this kind of dish so it didn't really bother her. She always forgot that dry beef is never a good idea to order during summer, as it is hot and humid. The best time to order dry beef is in the dry autumn or winter.

It was a hot and humid summer's day, but they were oblivious to it. They hadn't seen each other for months and couldn't take their eyes off each other.

"So, what is the plan now?" Jon asked after lunch.

"I want to show you my childhood place."

"Sure, that would be lovely, my sweet." Karma's heart filled with joy. It was nice to hear him call her my sweet when face to face.

After they had driven a few kilometres, Jon reached over to touch her. "Oh, it's nice to feel you. I wanted to do that as soon as I saw you but I didn't want to be too bold. I respect the Bhutanese culture."

"It is nice of you to consider that," Karma said, and let Jon run his hand through her hair. It was so nice to be touched so affectionately.

"So, tell me, what you have got planned for our wedding?" asked Jon. Karma loved the word *wedding*—she found it exotic.

"I have arranged a religious ceremony, and after that we will go to court to pursue our marriage certificate," Karma said excitedly.

"I am looking forward to it. Mum and Dad will be here tomorrow."

Jon's mum and dad had decided to attend the marriage ceremony, travelling all the way from Australia.

"It will be nice to have your mum and dad here, but I am a bit nervous about meeting them," Karma said. She had been e-mailing them regarding their visas and accommodation, and felt like she knew them already, but meeting them in person is a different story.

"There is nothing to be nervous about. Mum and Dad know that I chose well," Jon said.

The next day, they went to pick up Jon's parents from the airport. She was nervous, but as soon as Jon's dad hugged her in greeting, her apprehensions disappeared.

"Hello, Mum. How was your flight?" Jon said, and hugged his mother.

"She looks prettier than in the photo," his mum whispered in his ear and added, "can she speak English?"

Of course, she can speak English. What did she think I am playing at? thought Jon. When Jon mentioned this to Karma later, she couldn't understand why his mum had asked that question, especially considering all the e-mails they had exchanged about travel, food and lodgings since they had decided to come for the wedding.

On their wedding day it rained cats and dogs. Luckily, they had the sense to arrange it indoors. Her soon-to-be parents-in-law were staying in the same hotel as the wedding venue. Karma's family got soaked to the skin making their way there. At one point, Karma had to rescue them and in doing so her car nearly got stuck in the mud. The hotel was surrounded by a building site as the whole area was under construction, and the red, slippery mud didn't help. With all the cars going past and the heavy downpour, the mud had churned into a red porridge—sloshy and slippery. With a few hours of rally driving, she managed to get everyone safely to the hotel.

And so, on a wet June 26th, Jon and Karma were married in the presence of Karma's family: Dad, Yeshi, five sisters, nieces and nephews, and Jon's mum and dad. A lama and a few monks helped to perform the religious ceremony.

Karma had on her blue *kira* with a yellow pattern, blue *wonju* and yellow *tego*. Jon was talked into going traditional too. He wore a checked, dark coloured patterned *gho* and *tsho lham* (traditional boots). *He looks ravishing*, Karma thought.

That night, they were booked into the honeymoon suite in the same hotel. Since Jon's arrival, they had been staying with one of Karma's sisters. *It's nice to be on our own for a bit of privacy*, Jon thought.

They met up with Jon's parents the next morning for breakfast. They greeted each other and sat around the table for toast, eggs, and a pot of tea. Karma was being mother and poured the tea. She handed one to his dad and one to his mum. Before handing Jon's over, she thought it would be better if she stirred in some sugar.

"No sugar honey, thank you," Jon said, taking Karma by surprise.

"I thought you take sugar. When did you stop taking it?" Karma asked.

"I never have sugar in my tea," Jon said.

"Remember in Nepal, whenever I asked how many sugars and you always said two."

"No, I didn't."

"Yes, you did."

What will his mum be thinking? He is marrying a girl who doesn't even know whether he has sugar in his tea or not, Karma thought.

On Monday 28th June, Jon and Karma went cheerfully to the high court with their two witnesses at their heels to apply for a marriage certificate. As always, they were filled with certainty, thinking that this time they had done good enough research, that nothing could go wrong, and they would have a marriage certificate within two weeks. They had to queue up for hours before they were seen by the judge. While they were waiting, the registrar approached Jon saying it would be nice if he could wear a *gho* when he comes to the court. Jon was filled with incredulity. *Who does he think he is? A king?* Karma thought.

"What? Has he gone mad? When does any foreigner have to wear a *gho*? I don't remember seeing any westerner having to wear a *gho*, even in the company of our King," Karma said quietly, full of contempt.

"I know," Jon agreed readily.

Karma never liked a panjandrum—a self-important and pretentious official, thinking that they could bully others into doing what they think is right.

The court told them they would hear something within a week. So, they took time to spend time with Jon's parents. They took them to visit Tashicho Dzong, the seat of Bhutan's King and civil government, and the summer residence of monastic bodies.

The next day, they went to Buddha Point, which was still under construction. There were lots of places Karma wanted to show them, but because of their limited time, they were not able to see them all.

A week after submitting their application, there was still no news from the court, so they decided to enquire about it. The staff were being very vague, so they insisted on seeing the judge.

"I am sorry, I cannot make the decision on your marriage certificate," the judge announced.

"Why, do we need to submit additional documents?" Karma asked.

"No, I just can't, it is beyond my power," he said, scratching his head.

"Is there any other authority we can approach?" Jon asked.

"I don't know. Look sorry, I can't make the decision, and I don't want to see you two hanging around the court again," he said dismissively

"We love to hang around the court and we have nothing better to do." Karma felt like saying, but she had to bite her tongue. She wouldn't gain anything out of it except trouble.

Another refusal, but disheartening as it was, they didn't have any option but to go back to the hotel and break the news to his mum and dad. The only good thing that came out of this was Karma meeting Jon's parents.

Jon's parents left a few days before him. They were flying off to see their sons in Thailand en-route to Australia.

Jon's two weeks was over before they knew it.

"I would love to stay longer but I haven't got unlimited holidays," Jon said, hugging Karma tightly at the airport. After spending two weeks together they didn't have any inhibitions hugging in the airport.

Karma found this the hardest valediction. She had never liked goodbyes and couldn't understand why people have to say goodbye. Why can't they be together all the time, never having to say goodbye? The worst bit in seeing Jon off was the uncertainty, and having no definite plans for the future was heart rendering. She couldn't stop crying. Having Yeshi close by kept her from going insane.

Chapter 22

Hindrances and obstacles

Impediments come in all shapes and sizes. Patience and savoir-faire may fight them, but you need a fair amount of luck to beat them, my dictum of the day.

After Jon left, I had to force myself to go to work. It was difficult to concentrate as my heart was not in it. I was reading a piece about Robert the Bruce of Scotland, and the story went like this:

Robert the Bruce was the king of Scotland and he was fighting a war with the King of England. He had been beaten six times and was forced to retreat into the mountains. While he hid in a cave, he noticed a spider weaving its web. The spider didn't manage to weave its web at the first go and had to try again and again; it never gave up until it managed to weave a web. This gave hope to Robert the Bruce, and he went on battling the King of England until he was out of Scotland.

Optimism, that I thought was lost, resurfaced full of vigour.

Jon felt the same way. We might have to try a hundred more times but we were prepared to fight the battle.

So with determination, we decided to apply again. This application was also rejected, but at least something good came out of this attempt. I met two girls in the Bhutan embassy who spoke to me about the British consulate, and they gave me the consulate's e-mail address.

I e-mailed the consulate as soon as I got back to Bhutan.

Dear Sir,
My name is Karma Chhoden.
I have a fiancé in England. I have applied a few times for a visa to visit him in the UK for quite a long time now, each time the applications have been rejected.
I would be grateful if you could help me.
Thanking you,
Yours faithfully,
Karma

I received a response to my e-mail, complete with a telephone number, and this response read:

'Give me a call so we can fix an appointment sometime tomorrow.'

I dialled this number, feeling a bit apprehensive.

"Hello," came a very friendly sounding English voice.

"Hello sir, it is Karma, Jon's fiancée. I got an e-mail from you to give you a call when I am in Thimphu," I said.

"Oh, OK, come to the Namse restaurant. I am going to have my lunch there. Do you know where it is?"

"Yes sir, I do." I knew it was the restaurant where all the westerners gathered.

"OK, see you at one, cheerio," and saying that he hung up. I had never heard the word *cheerio* before. I presumed it was an English word for goodbye.

I didn't know what the consulate looked like, but as soon as I spotted a man sat outside drinking coke, I had a feeling that this was him. He was dressed in a *gho* which was hand-woven locally. The intricate design and beautiful colour of his *gho* made him look like an authentic Bhutanese. He was wearing metal-framed spectacles.

"Hello sir, I am Karma," I said approaching him, and I extended my hand for a handshake.

"Hello Karma, nice to meet you, take a seat," he said gesturing towards the chair opposite him.

"Nice to meet you too," I muttered, not sure whether he had heard me or not.

"We are going to eat now, order something for yourself," he instructed her. He had lived a long time in Bhutan and he knew what the Bhutanese are like. If he had asked me politely whether I wanted to eat or not, no matter how many times, my answer would always be a definite 'no, thank you.' The Bhutanese are full of modesty.

"Can I have a coke, please?" I said, looking at the approaching waiter.

"Are you sure you don't want to eat?" he asked.

"No, sir, thank you." I said, even though I was starving.

"OK, what is the problem with the visa?"

"Like I said in my e-mail, it keeps being rejected, saying that one of the documents I have submitted is only a piece of paper, not an official certificate, they have no idea…" I had to stop myself before I started babbling about the sequence of events.

"Leave that to me. I will see what I can do. SMS or e-mail me your visa reference number," he offered helpfully. I was taken aback by his readiness to help, and I took an instant liking to him.

"Thank you very much. I really appreciate your help," I said, when we left the restaurant.

"No problem, anytime, cheerio," he said, jumped into a waiting Toyota Hi-Lux, and he drove off. He was like a whirlwind.

I couldn't wait to tell Jon all about it. I took out my mobile phone and punched in his number.

"Hello," Jon answered after two rings.

"Darling, I had a chat with the British consulate. He said he will see what he can do about our visas. But don't get your hopes up."

"That is good darling. I won't," Jon said.

"I need to go now. I will Skype you tomorrow."

"Take care, darling, speak to you soon."
A few days later, I received an e-mail from the consulate and it read:

'Sorry, Karma, I got in touch with the Embassy in India and he said it is too late. They have already rejected your application.'

My heart sank. I thought they might have been able to overturn the rejection. *We are stuck again. Why can't anything go in the right direction?* I thought, and so I decided to e-mail the consulate again:

Dear Sir,
Thank you very much for your prompt reply and I really appreciated your help.
We know that our application has been rejected again. I am not sure if we have got the right to appeal. We are looking into it. Can I come to see you again? If you don't mind, I will bring all the documents with me. I don't understand why they keep insisting that the letter from the court is just a piece of paper and not proof.
I would appreciate it if you could go through my documents and see why they are so adamant that my document is just a piece of paper.
Thanking you,
Yours faithfully,
Karma

I received his reply within a few minutes and it read:

'Dear Karma, I am free on Sunday, drop by anytime you want.'

I was getting excited and nervous at the same time. *At least we are not coming to a standstill, we are heading somewhere, hopefully in the right direction,* I thought.

I went to see the consulate. He looked through my documents, and told me that he could not understand why they called my document from the court in Thimphu, 'a piece of paper.' He told me it would be better if he verified all the documents. I was so glad that he did that. I didn't know where I would be without his help. He verified all of my Bhutanese documents.

"There, documents all verified, and now it is dinner time. Tenzing, can you sort out something to eat," he said, turning to his assistant, and then he started to give instructions on what to cook.

It couldn't get better, could it? He does all the work and he feeds me as well, I thought, and I thanked my lucky stars for shining on me at last.

"What are you going to do now. Apply again or appeal?" the consulate asked.

"We are planning to appeal, sir."

"Make sure you send those verified documents. I don't see why they can't overturn the decision."

"Thank you very much for everything, sir. I can't thank you enough," I said, full of gratitude. "Thank you for the nice dinner, *Kota* (younger brother)," I said to the cook.

"I will see you to the door," the consulate gestured. *What a gentleman! This is very rare these days,* I thought.

"Keep me updated with your appeal. Goodnight and take care," he said, and disappeared behind the door.

I had done my bit and now the ball was in Jon's court. Firstly, Jon had to find the right solicitor. There was no shortage of solicitors, but finding the right one was not easy, and solicitors do not come cheap. Jon had spent a small fortune on visa applications, and he was watching every penny. He managed to find a solicitor in Didsbury and what a godsend he was. The solicitor compiled all the documents, reduced his fee by half, and filed for an appeal hearing. He was told the Border Agency needed nineteen weeks to prepare the relevant documents.

"It is beyond my comprehension. Why do they need nineteen weeks to process two applicants?" I asked during a Skype call.

"I can understand it, imagine how many applicants they will be getting in a day," said Jon.

"I would imagine they would have a separate department for this kind of case, especially with the money they charge. I can't believe that we don't get any of our fees back. It is ridiculous," I moaned.

"I know honey, it isn't as simple as that, but we know that we are getting somewhere," Jon reasoned.

"It is annoying how these things work sometimes. It is so frustrating," I said.

"Sorry?" Jon said, struggling to hear me on his computer screen. My voice kept breaking up. "I don't know what you are saying, honey."

PLINK, went the Skype, and Jon lost his connection. It was nice using Skype when the connection was good. It was a pain in the backside when the connection kept breaking, but we were glad we at least had Skype to keep in touch.

Fortunately, we didn't have to wait long for the appeal. We got a hearing date for Friday,

May 13, 2011. I couldn't wait to give the consulate the good news.

"We got our appeal hearing date," I said excitedly, when we met up at the same restaurant for a drink.

"When?" he asked, looking equally excited.

"Friday, 13th of May," I said excitedly.

"Did you know that Friday the 13th is considered as an unlucky day in the west?"

"Is it? I didn't know that," I said, and my excitement went plummeting downhill. Superstitions always unnerved me, and I started to worry; lots of ifs and buts.

"It is supposed to do with the last supper before Jesus' death…anyway that doesn't matter. You are not superstitious, are you? Don't worry, it is just a religious thing," the consulate reassured me.

It was too late. I was worried. I had been born into a culture when important things are not done before consulting astrology. Many Bhutanese believe that oblations solve a problem and bring luck. I didn't want to take this lightly, so I Googled it the next day and my computer screen read:

'It is believed that the superstition may have arisen in the Middle Ages, originating from the story of Jesus' last supper and crucifixion in which there were twelve other people present on Thursday, the night before Jesus' death, on Good Friday.'

I didn't think I would have peace of mind until I did something about it. I discussed with

Jon about the oblations and religious ceremony. Jon was not keen, but I insisted.

Desperate times call for desperate measures.

Chapter 23

Long distance relationship.

Now they had done everything they could and all they needed to do was wait. A year from now, Karma could be in England, or maybe not. Now their priority was to make their long-distance relationship work.

By now, Jon had already left his girlfriend and was living in a rented house. One day, he was driving back home from work; he was in his own world singing along to a tune. He had to brake hard when he realised that he had taken the turning towards his old house. He turned around and headed to his new place. This waiting game was getting too much, but he had no other option but to wait.

The internet was a lifesaver; they didn't know what they would have done without it and being able to Skype every day. The alternative would have been writing letters that would take at least two weeks to deliver. It would have been hard, but something is better than nothing, they would have happily done that.

Luckily, in the 21st century, they didn't have to resort to writing letters. Since Jon moved into his new home he had free reign over his internet; now he didn't have to hide his communication with Karma from his colleagues or his ex. Their daily routine started, thanks to Skype, at Jon's time of 7.00 am and Karma's time of 1.00 pm; this was lunch break for Karma, so she didn't have to worry about her boss telling her off. They would video call for thirty minutes, then break for ten minutes while Jon would shower and Karma ate her lunch. They would resume their video chat while Jon was having his breakfast. They chatted about everything and nothing, and the time would fly.

Every coin has two sides: internet was good for Karma and Jon, but not for those teenagers who picked up bad habits from it, getting into drugs and shouting at their parents like it was the norm. Skype helped Jon and Karma immensely, and it took them safely to the end of the year without any mishaps. Six months had passed, and now they were making plans for Christmas and New Year in Pokhara, Nepal.

Karma had never celebrated Christmas in her life before. The information she gathered from watching Hollywood movies was not enough to get the full picture. She knew for sure that westerners have roast turkey for Christmas dinner, and all the families would come together.

Karma arrived in Kathmandu a few hours before Jon. She was waiting patiently for him at the terminal, but was told not to hover inside and wait outside. Jon was flying via Dubai, and for every passenger that went past her she surreptitiously checked their baggage tags. She knew it was not going to be much longer, his flight had landed twenty minutes ago. She tried her best to stay patient, but impatience was getting the better of her. Suddenly, she spotted him hurrying towards her. She hadn't seen him for six months; the relief of seeing him in the flesh was liberating. She ran towards him as he came striding towards her. They met at the gate and went into a tight embrace.

"My darling, how are you? I have missed you so much," Jon said.

"Me too darling. How was your flight?" Karma said.

"It was ok. Have you been waiting long?"

"Umm…maybe 10 minutes, but it felt like ages."

After giving each other a quick kiss, they walked hand in hand, pulling their suitcases behind them. They left the international airport and headed towards the domestic terminal to catch their flight to Pokhara. They couldn't take their eyes off each other.

Jon had booked everything a month in advance. Within an hour, they were checked in and queuing to board Yeti Airline's ATR 72: a twin-engine turboprop. Karma was a bit nervous about flying in this kind of aeroplane. On a Nepalese domestic flight, a few weeks before, a plane flying from Lamidanda airport to Kathmandu, with eighteen Bhutanese pilgrims on board, crashed killing everyone on board. Karma had a bad habit of having morbid thoughts; they popped up at inopportune moments and she hated it.

As they boarded, they were looking forward to sitting next to each other for the hour long flight, but two selfish women decided they wanted a double seat each. What annoyed Karma the most was how those two women chatted nonstop all the way, not taking advantage of the best views of the Himalayan mountains. *Why don't they sit together if they want to chat to each other?* Karma thought, *selfish or what!*

Jon reached across the aisle for Karma's hand. Holding his hand comforted her no end as she was feeling claustrophobic, cramped up in the small aeroplane; they held hands all the way until the landing at Pokhara airport. They were picked up from the airport by a taxi that had been organised by the apartment they were renting for two weeks.

The apartment was run by a family and was located only a few minutes' walk from Phewa lake. It was a three-story building, surrounded by a few cottages built in the Nepalese style of stone and timber with glass windows. Their apartment was located on the top floor, with an outside seating area which looked out onto open space. There were water taps in one corner for the apartment's laundry.

The day they arrived, they went for a walk along the lakeside. As they were walking down the street hand in hand, they heard a voice call.

"Hello, Jon."

They turned around and came face to face with a Tibetan woman carrying lots of trinkets. She wore a black dress, and her hair was braided into two plaits, each falling over a shoulder. Her arms were covered in bracelets up to her elbow, and she had a black bundle on her back. Karma didn't know who she was, and was surprised to feel the woman's staring gaze on her; it started from her head and went all the way down to her feet. When she had finished checking Karma out, she looked at her resentfully.

"Hi, hello, how are you?" Jon said.

"I am fine, how are you? Are you visiting?" said the woman.

"Yes, for two weeks, we are going for a walk, nice to see you." Jon lifted his right arm to bid farewell.

"Who was that? What was that evil look?" Karma asked.

"That's the mother of the girl I was seeing that lives here."

"Ok, now I know why she was giving me that look," Karma said.

"I know, sorry darling."

"Don't worry, I would do the same if I were in her place. I just hope you didn't lead her daughter on and give the wrong impression."

"No, honey. I made it clear I was not looking for anything out of the relationship. I didn't promise anything."

Poor girl, Karma thought. She felt sorry for the girl as she could easily be in that situation. For women like them, they can easily get carried away thinking they were in for a good future when they go to bed with a *Chilip*.

Each morning, they took turns to make a cup of tea to drink in bed. Jon always ended up making half cups of tea. He was not used to using tea leaves. Back home, he dunks his Twining's English Breakfast teabag in a cup of boiled water and leaves it for a minute to brew. He then takes out the tea bag and adds fresh milk. In contrast, Karma would always get the amount right, she was used to using tea leaves. In Bhutan, they fill the pot with hot water and milk powder, then mix it until all the lumps disappear. Finally, they add tea leaves and boil its head off—perfect Bhutanese tea.

Jon had been to Pokhara a few times now, but the surrounding mountains never ceased to amaze him, and every morning he would climb out of bed and peek through the curtains at Machhapuchhare (Fish Tail Mountain). This always provided Karma with a chance to gaze at his bare, peachy bum in return; she would often give it a playful slap!

Each morning after breakfast, they would see the housekeeping girls doing laundry by hand. Karma joined them once to do theirs. She was used to doing this as the Bhutanese do washing in the same way; Jon found it different, but interesting.

"Where are you from madam?" asked one of the girls in Nepalese.

"I am from Bhutan," Karma replied.

"Oh, I thought you were from Mustang."

"No, I don't know where Mustang is," Karma said.

"It is our neighbouring country, you have a similar look to them," the girl added.

"OK, that is interesting, I would like to visit one day but I don't know when. I need to get to the UK first," Karma said forlornly, wondering how their appeal would go.

"How long have you been married for, madam?" the girl asked inquisitively.

"We got married in June 2010, and I am planning to go to the UK, but I am not having any luck with my visa application now," Karma said.

"I am pretty sure everything will be all right. Some things are worth waiting for, don't get disheartened," the girl added; she might have heard the distress in Karma's voice.

"Thank you, it is nice of you to say that," Karma said, wringing the water out of her washing.

In the meantime, Jon was going CLICK, CLICK, CLICK with his camera.

What is this Chilip like? Karma thought affectionately.

"How did you meet him?" the girl asked looking at Jon, "he seems like a nice guy."

"Oh, to cut a long story short, I met him ten years ago. Our relationship started as friends. Then we decided to meet up in Kathmandu in 2010, and from there our relationship went to a different level. I can't wait to be with him forever," Karma said, looking fondly at him. *If someone had told me that I would be here with Jon, washing his clothes, and planning to spend the rest of our lives together, I would have said stop being crazy. How true it is that you never know where your future will take you.* Karma's thoughts drifted off.

"I hope everything works out for you, madam."

"Thank you, how about you. Married? Any children?"

"Yes, married and one son. I work here and it gives me enough money to look after him," she said looking distressed. Karma could tell that she was finding it difficult to speak, but Karma didn't want to interrupt so she just listened instead.

"How about you, madam?" Karma was asked.

"I have a son from a previous relationship. He is twelve and I am lucky to have him. Children bring happiness to your life, and no matter what, they will help you to get along in life. I don't find it daunting to move to England if I have my son with me," Karma said, thinking of Yeshi who was staying with her sisters now. Lucky that she has a close-knit family who she can trust to look after him. Karma didn't have to worry about leaving him for a week or so. She did miss him, but it was not easy to drag him with her wherever she went. A small part of her died whenever she had to leave him for a while.

"Yes, I know that. My son is my life," the housekeeper said, happiness glittering in her eyes.

Karma hoped that everything would come easy for this woman. She didn't have any money with her. If she had, she would have given it happily.

"I need to go now. We are off for dinner in the town and taking a walk around Lake Phewa later. Isn't the lake beautiful?"

"I know, I am lucky to live in such a beautiful place. I am sure the place you come from is beautiful as well. I have heard about Bhutan but haven't got a clue what it is like," she added quietly.

"It is no different than here; we are all a part of the Himalayas," Karma said. *But it is much cleaner in Bhutan,* she thought.

"How come you speak fluent Nepalese?" asked the housekeeper.

"I wouldn't say fluently but I can communicate," replied Karma.

"I would say that is fluent," the girl added flatteringly.

"I picked it up as a child. We have lots of Nepalese in Bhutan, especially in Southern Bhutan, and my village is half-filled with them," Karma added, fondly thinking about her village. She loved visiting her parents there. "Nepalese is commonly spoken in Bhutan, so as a kid I picked up some phrases here and there. I am good at picking up languages and I can speak four dialects of Bhutan, even if I say so myself," Karma grinned coyly.

Karma was not being boastful. Bragging was not her way, but she was proud of how many dialects she could speak.

"Darling, we need to go now. I am peckish," Jon said from the doorway. *Peckish,* what did that mean, Karma wondered? *It could be something to do with hunger*, she thought.

"OK, darling, coming. OK, *Didi* (sister), I need to go now, bye," Karma said, and hurried towards Jon who was waiting patiently.

Their evening stroll alongside the lake was always nice. The lake is set in a valley. The Peace Pagoda, as white as snow on the mountainside, overlooks the lake, and Sarangkot hill is on the other side. During the daytime, when the sun is high in the sky and the wind was not blowing a gale, the sky around Sarangkot would be full of paragliders; different colours dotted all around in the sky, brightening it up with the empyreal blue sky gracing above the mountain.

We are lucky to be here at this time of the year when it is not packed with tourists and the weather is good enough. I prefer a touch warmer but I can't have everything, Jon thought, happily walking hand in hand with Karma. He had never felt so contented before. He could see his future getting brighter. *Only if the appeal goes through successfully*, he thought wistfully.

One morning, Karma offered to make Jon breakfast in bed: poached egg and toast.

"That would be lovely, sweetheart," Jon said, he was touched by the gesture.

Karma boiled the tea leaves in milk and water and then put the bread slices in the small toaster. She heated the oil in a pan and cooked two eggs. When it was ready, she served it onto two plates and handed one to Jon. He looked at the plate and couldn't see a poached egg.

"Where is my poached egg?"

"What is that then?" she said, pointing at the egg that sat on his toast.

"What's that?" he said incredulously, "you looney, that's not a poached egg, it is a fried egg," he added.

"I call that a Bhutanese poached egg," she said genially. It was news to Karma, she always thought that was how poached eggs were made. Fried in the oil, and leave the egg yolk a bit runny on top.

The next time when Jon was making breakfast, he showed her how to make poached eggs. Boil water in a saucepan, crack the eggs into the water and boil for three minutes; then season with salt and pepper.

"It is lovely," Karma said, enjoying every bit of it. It was such a wonderful way to share the cooking. They had an unsaid agreement between them, and instinctively did their fair share.

Will this breakfast ritual carry on or fade as time passes? they thought.

Chapter 24

First Christmas together

In preparation for their Christmas Day dinner they went shopping. Karma got loads of chillies—she couldn't go without chilli. The vegetable market was no different to the one in Bhutan, smaller than the one Karma used to frequent, but it was in a similar style with open shelters spread out. Vegetables were freshly laid out on a blue, polyester sheet in groups; vendors stood next to them selling their wares. After, they went to buy chicken. When Jon saw the chicken laid out on top of a box covered in flies, he started feeling nauseous.

"Can I have 500 grams of chicken breast?" Karma said. *I hope that's not the one he is going to sell*, Jon thought, looking at the fly covered chicken. He was relieved when the seller took out a fresh-looking chicken from a box underneath.

Karma didn't bring any warm clothes so they decided to go shopping. Their trick was for Karma to go in the shop on her own and find the thing she wanted; she would then set the price without having a westerner by her side, which would always hike the price. Jon would then come in and pay for it. Karma found a red coat that she liked very much.

"How much is it?" Karma asked.

"1500 Nepalese rupees," the shopkeeper said.

"Any discount?" she asked.

"It is a fixed price."

Karma went to call Jon in and explained it to him.

"I wished we had known before, I wouldn't have had to hang about outside," Jon said.

Their first Christmas together was wonderful. They didn't have a traditional dinner with roast turkey, vegetables, and Christmas pudding, but it was Jon's best Christmas. They had a simple Christmas dinner of chicken fried rice, dhal (lentil), and cheesecake from a German patisserie in the town. When they decided to have dinner in the apartment, they would always wander down to buy cakes from the German patisserie to have afterwards.

Sometimes they would go to a restaurant to have a drink. One time, they went into a cosy restaurant with an open fire in the middle. Karma always like sitting close to the fire, but the seats around the fire were all taken; she was a bit disappointed. So, they sat further away. During the daytime it was nice and warm, but in the evening when the sun went down, the temperature would drop drastically. The seat they took gave a good view of those who were sat cosily around the fire.

Jon saw two girls sat on one of the seats, they were not able to keep their hands off each other. Karma noticed them taking off their coats exposing their low-cut tops, their boobs nearly popping out.

She couldn't believe her eyes and thought, *I could never be this brave to wear such a small top.*

At that precise moment, a Nepalese guy sauntered in and plonked himself in the small gap between them.

"I think he wants to sleep with one of them," Karma said.

"I wish him luck, but I don't think he will get anywhere," Jon replied.

"Why?"

"They are lesbians."

"What is that?" Karma had never heard that term before.

"When two girls want to make love to each other."

"Is it? I didn't know that. I know what gay is."

"Gay for guys and lesbian for women," explained Jon.

"You learn new things every day."

"True, true," Jon said.

That was the first and last time they managed to get a seat in that restaurant; it was always full. *Pity!* Karma thought. She liked the cosy atmosphere. *Will this restaurant still be here if we ever come back*? she wondered.

One day, they walked up to the Peace Pagoda and back. The walk up was easy, maybe a couple of hours. When they reached the top, Karma had to sit down to rest and catch her breath, enjoying the panoramic view of Pokhara and the Annapurna range. The Peace Pagoda was constructed by Japanese Buddhist monks, with the help of the locals. The Pagoda reflects four stages of the Buddha's life: Lumbini, the place where he was born; Bodh Gaya, where he was enlightened; Sarnath, where he taught, and Kushinagar, where he reached nirvana.

They sat on the white marble looking down at Lake Phewa, enjoying the view and tranquillity.

"It's nice to get away from the hustle and bustle of Pokhara," they agreed, breathing in the fresh air.

They headed downhill hand in hand. Jon spotted a woman carrying firewood in a bamboo basket, taking all the weight on a strap around her head; he stopped to take a picture.

"Money, money," the woman said aggressively, rubbing her right thumb and forefinger together. There was something about the woman which made Karma uneasy. Her face was all wrinkly, tanned skin from too much sun, and she only had one eye.

"Darling, be careful!" Karma shouted.

"It is all right, ignore her and act nonchalant."

"What do you mean?"

"Act as if nothing happened and walk away," Jon said. All Karma wanted to do was run as fast as she could downhill. After following them for a minute, the old woman lost interest and left them alone.

The main road alongside the lake was closed to traffic for Christmas, another good thing about visiting at this time of the year. They stopped for a bite to eat. Karma had buffalo *momos* (Tibetan dumplings) which were as salty as seawater, and Jon had fried rice for a change.

Karma fancied taking the boat across the lake to the temple, but Jon wasn't keen. Instead, they hired a boat to row around the lake the next day. When Jon was rowing, it looked so easy that Karma wanted to have a go. It was her first time rowing. Instead of going forward, they went around in circles. No matter how hard she tried, the boat refused to go ahead in a straight line. Jon took over and they rowed to the middle of the lake, then they floated around for a few minutes. While floating, they thought it would be interesting to see who could stick a lollypop furthest down the throat.

"BARFED…" went Jon.

"BAR…FED…" Karma followed trying to beat him.

In the end, both were in tears, and they couldn't stop laughing at each other.

The next day, they decided to hike on Sarangot mountain. They caught a taxi to the start of the walk, calling into a chemist on the way to get some painkillers for Karma. When the taxi stopped, Jon jumped out and went around the taxi to open the door for Karma, but before she had time to get out properly, Jon slammed the door shut and strode off towards the chemist. He heard Karma yelp and looked back; she was trapped by her fingers in the car door.

It was so painful. All she could do was squat down then stand up to try to ease the pain. He shot back like an arrow towards her to help, but he couldn't open the door as it was locked. He spotted the driver's side window was open, so he stuck his hand through it to pull up the lock, but at the same time, the taxi driver was tugging on the door handle, which made it impossible for him to unlock it from the inside.

Karma felt like she was stuck there forever, but it could have been less than one minute. Jon and the driver managed to eventually open the door, it was such a relief for her, but her finger was a mess. They rushed her into the pharmacy with blood trailing behind her, and plonked her on a bed while the pharmacist called the doctor. He came, injected local anaesthetic, waited for a few seconds, and then removed the nail from her left middle finger. He then bandaged the finger, put her arm in a sling, and prescribed lots of tablets, probably more than she needed.

"Poor thing, you look like an injured soldier," Jon said, feeling sorry for Karma, but for some reason that tickled Karma and she howled with laughter. Her laughter was so infectious that Jon laughed too, and they went into fits of laughter.

They didn't have the cash to pay the doctor, so Jon disappeared on the back of a motorbike to find a cash machine, while Karma was surrounded by some of the local ladies; they were commiserating her injury and asking all sorts of questions. The ladies made her feel very comfortable and she was engrossed in deep conversation when Jon returned. When Jon came back and saw her surrounded by ladies it tugged at his heartstrings, and he thought, *there is my sweetheart, love of my life, looking so sweet, chatting amongst the ladies.* His heart swelled with pride.

Jon wouldn't have minded if Karma had wanted to go back to the hotel with her injury, but she insisted on carrying on, so they completed their hike over Sarangot. To stop getting sunburned, Jon had to have his cap sat sideways on the right side of his head. He turned to Karma and asked:

"How do I look?" Karma couldn't find a polite answer. With his cap askew he looked very strange and she burst out laughing. "Ok, it is not good," Jon said, and put his cap the right way round. However, Karma couldn't stop laughing, and whenever she tried to stop, the image of Jon's comical face resurfaced, and she carried on laughing for a few minutes, and then Jon joined in too. There was a group of women washing clothes by the river. At first, they looked surprised, but Karma's infectious laughter was irresistible so they joined in too. The area was filled with their peals of laughter. Despite Karma's injury, they had a good day.

As they arrived back at their apartment, the landlord appeared and Jon decided to narrate the whole sorry episode of Karma's trapped fingers. If it was up to him, he would have been there for ages yapping. She had to cut him short as she was feeling queasy and tired, desperate to lie down.

Once they were in the apartment, Jon tucked Karma in a warm blanket near the electric heater, made her a nice cup of tea, and cooked a nice meal. After dinner, they lay next to each other content. *What more do you want than this, a loving husband and a prospective future together*, Karma thought and she dozed off.

The time had just flown by, and in the blink of an eye their holiday was over, and it was time to head back and go their separate ways. Not knowing when they would see each other again was awful.

The last day was a long taxi ride back to Kathmandu, with nice scenery alongside the mountains and meandering river, until they dropped down into the Kathmandu valley; but both couldn't enjoy it.

They checked into their hotel for the last night in Kathmandu and then went out for dinner; an uneasy night for both, not knowing what their future was.

The next morning at the airport, as they were saying their goodbyes, Karma's throat was constricted with emotion. She hated valedictions and wished she never had to do it.

"Take care, honey," Jon said. He knew he had to say something to cheer her up and added, "we will find a way to be together, we are in this together and we will soon see a positive result."

Chapter 25

Waiting game and oblations.

Pray from the bottom of your heart without any misgiving and your wish may be granted - Buddhist ideology.

As my flight was taking off, I glanced through the window and spotted Boudha in the distance. I could never mistake it for anything else with its potent eyes gazing straight at me. Instinctively, I closed my eyes and prayed:

'God, please send us a MANNA and take away our ANATHEMA.'

A few weeks passed since our time together in Pokhara, and now it was a distant but cherished memory.

It was a waiting game now. We had done all that we could, but there was something else that I thought needed doing, and I didn't know how to broach this subject with Jon, so for a while, I said nothing. I knew that he wasn't a firm believer in religious ceremonies, and I also knew that it would involve more expense which would be silly to spend in our circumstances, but I hoped Jon would understand.

A tiny seed was sowed in my mind when our visas were rejected left, right, and centre, and then when we said goodbye at our recent departure. *If I need help from God then I have to offer something*, I thought. I had a firm belief in prayer, and that if you pray from the bottom of your heart, even a dog's tooth will become Buddha's tooth. The story behind this saying goes like this:

A son used to visit Bodh Gaya every year, and every time, his mum asked him to get her a Buddha's tooth so she could worship. Every single time he had forgotten to do this, and on his recent trip, he remembered his mum's wish when he stopped to rest halfway back home. He knew that he couldn't brush his mum's wishes away every single time, so he decided to do something about it. At that precise moment, he happened to look around and saw a dead dog by the side of the road. He plucked a tooth from it and wrapped it in a silk scarf; he then presented it to his mum as Buddha's tooth. She worshipped every day and night, offering prayer and oblations, and one day the dog's tooth turned into Buddha's tooth—shiny and exuding power.

Depa kay ni mang na rochi gi so lay rinchen jung wong- *if you pray from the bottom of your heart, even a dog's tooth can be transformed into Buddha's tooth,* Bhutanese saying.

The Bhutanese have a strong faith in the *manna*—any sudden, unexpected help to aid success. I wanted to offer oblations: divine or spiritual food to God by performing a religious ceremony.

For seven days, I had five monks visiting, praying, and chanting in my home. The day started at five in the morning until seven in the evening. I would collect them each morning. Getting up that early was not my cup of tea, but desperation dictated my actions. By the time we got to my home, my sweet sisters would have breakfast ready for everyone.

The religious ceremony would last the whole day, and consisted of offering divine food and the recitation of intercessory prayer. By the end of seven days, it had overrun my budget and I had to seek financial assistance from Dorji. Now I had to find a way to pay her back, but how was the big question.

'I need a thousand pounds,' I hesitatingly mentioned in an e-mail to Jon after we had spoken on Skype; I didn't have the courage to mention it over the video chat.

TRING, TRING, TRING, went my phone an hour later.

"Hello," I said, my heart thudding when I saw the caller ID.

"Why on earth do you need a thousand pounds?" Jon asked.

"I had to do a religious ceremony."

"I thought religious ceremonies were free."

"Not really."

"Out here, we never pay for religious services. Are you sure they are not ripping you off?" he asked.

"No. I did it of my own accord, and don't say that."

"How come you spent that much for a religious ceremony?"

"Well, it was not just for the religious ceremony. We had to pay and feed the monks daily, and it is not cheap. Four meals a day for everyone, and all the stuff I had to buy for the ceremony, the bills soon piled up."

"Really!"

"It is all right if you don't want to pay. I will find a way to pay Dorji back," I said, running out of patience. I knew that I was sounding petulant, but what could I do? I did it for our benefit and I had worked really hard; I didn't like the way he was interrogating me.

"How?" he asked.

"I don't know. I have to find a way if you don't want to pay," I said, getting agitated. I just wanted to end this conversation and I wished I had never asked him.

Jon was reeling over this. How can she be so stupid spending this kind of money?

"It is not because I don't want to pay, you know that we are a bit tight with money, we have to be careful," he explained.

"I know, darling. I thought that if I did this religious ceremony it would bring us luck. I am desperate, and I don't want to carry on seeing you only every six months. I want more than that and I had to find a way," I said.

"That is a lot of money."

"I am aware of that. I said that you don't have to pay, I will find a way. I understand your qualms about the religious ceremony and I don't blame you, but I know if I pray from the bottom of my heart, my wish will be granted."

If she puts it like that, I have no option but to help her, he thought, and so he said, "Don't worry, I will send you the money. How much did you say it is?"

"One thousand pounds."

"In future, please let me know before you make this kind of decision," Jon said.

"I will darling, thanks." She would have mentioned it to him, but she knew what kind of reaction she would get, and the last thing she wanted was to impede her faith. She was afraid that it wouldn't work if she carried on with a religious ceremony with doubt in her mind.

The Bhutanese go crazy spending money on religious ceremonies; some would spend up to £10,000. At least I didn't go crazy.

I was very hopeful now. With our luck restored, and the appeal hearing date on Friday the 13th, I was ready to face anything.

I was in Southern Bhutan on Friday the 13th having my car repaired. The damage on my car was not of my doing but one of my colleagues. I had left my car in the airport terminal car park on one of my trips to Delhi. To avoid having my car tyres let down by the car park attendant, I asked one of my colleagues to take my car to the office car park the next day. Instead, he used it for his personal use and crashed.

This colleague was the most cunning, sly person I have ever met in my life. He crashed my car, did a half-hearted repair job, and handed it back to me. Without a car, I couldn't commute to work, but I had no option but to accept my car full of dents and a patchy paint job. I had a go at the guy for a rubbish job, and even threatened to take him to court if he didn't repair my car properly. In the end, I resigned and told myself, '*If he thinks he has won and it makes him happy. It won't kill me, after all it is just a car, but the world is round and whatever goes around comes around. Karma will get him one day.*'

Therefore, on the day of the appeal, my car was getting a final coat of paint. I was waiting outside the car workshop agitated with nerves. I was trying to call Jon, but there was no answer and I was getting anxious. The weather being hot and humid didn't help, so I decided to have a cup of tea to soothe my nerves. I was sat under a tree, sipping my sweet tea, when I felt a blob of something warm on my head, and it was starting to run down my shoulder.

"*Jaydha!*" I cursed in Dzongkha, and looked up to see a pigeon sat there having a shit. *This was just what I need, more bad luck,* I thought angrily. I was trying to clean myself furiously, and when it was nearly done my phone went off.

"Hello," I said, still not very happy with the pigeon. If I'd had a gun, I would have blown its head off.

"Hi, darling, are you OK?" came Jon's voice on the phone.

"Sorry, darling, bad timing, a pigeon has just passed faeces on my head and shoulder." I didn't dare use the word 'shit', as I thought it too crude to use in our fledgling relationship. The word "poo" didn't even enter my stressed head.

"Oh, you poor thing," he said.

"I was trying to call you about the appeal," I said.

"Sorry, I left my phone at home. I had to rush all the way home from the court to get my mobile to call you. Good news—the judge has overturned the decision!"

"What does that mean?"

"Our appeal has gone through!" Jon said, sounding very happy.

"Yes!" I said, punching the air and eliminating all the misery. I was so happy, and I didn't care if people thought I had gone mad, and thousands of pigeons had pooped on me. I would receive it without complaint!

"Do you agree now that it is something to do with the religious ceremony?" I said, walking back towards the garage with a spring in my step, not caring if I still had some poo on my head. I could not believe it had finally happened, and that I could be with my husband at last.

"Maybe, whatever it was, we got there finally. We were lucky that the Border Agency representatives were clueless. They came unprepared and asked unnecessary questions."

"What kind of questions?"

"Asking for your English language test certificate."

"It was not needed when I applied," I said indignantly.

"That is exactly what I said, and I told them that your learning medium in Bhutan is in English, and guess what? The judge seemed to know that. He said that he had read it somewhere."

"At last! I can't wait."

"I think they got a telling off from the judge because when I was asked to leave, they were told to stay behind," Jon said.

"Serves them right, they deserve all they get," I replied.

"When I was dismissed from the court with the court usher, she had a look of surprise on her face. She told me that she had never known the judge to overturn the decision there and then, and that it usually took a few weeks," Jon added, clearly delighted.

"Khandenchey la, I thank God for sending us manna," I said.

"Mmm, maybe," Jon replied, neither believing nor disbelieving.

Within the next few days, I received an e-mail informing me to go and collect our visas from Delhi. Then the next step was to resign from my job.

"It is a big, bad world out there and not everybody is lucky. I am not saying you won't be lucky, but be careful," my boss said, when I handed in my resignation. I decided to humour him and thanked him for his advice.

People are strange. Whilst you are among them, they tend to look down on you, and when you are about to leave, they become all nice and good-natured, I soliloquised, and my thoughts wandered back to the times when I was made to feel inadequate.

I could have done with some nice comments during the years I worked for him, but all I usually heard was, "You have got the intelligence, but you are not utilising it."

After I had completed my night classes in secondary education, I wanted to study for a degree and asked for study leave.

"You can go if you want, but don't expect to have your job back when you return," was his curt reply.

Now I was leaving he was trying to talk me out of it, and he even suggested that I extend my notice period. But I was not interested, and adamantly handed in my notice.

In the second week of June, me and my son collected our visas from the embassy in Delhi. Later that day, I called Jon.

"Hello," said Jon, as he answered his phone.

"Hi, darling. I will see you tomorrow at seven am at Manchester airport, terminal one," I said happily.

"WHAAT?" he said, very surprised. He knew we were collecting our visas that day, but he didn't think that we would be able to get a flight straight away.

"See you tomorrow, darling, at seven am."

"So soon," said Jon.

"I know, darling. We have been waiting for this for so long and all of sudden it is happening," I said.

"I know, I can't wait," Jon said. For months he had been thinking of the day he would meet her at the airport.

Me and Yeshi boarded the plane to Manchester, via Brussels, on Tuesday, 14 June, 2011.
"Yahoooo… UK HERE WE COME!!!"

Epilogue

England.

Early morning, 15th June, 2011, Karma and Yeshi were approaching Manchester airport. All Karma could see were fields of lush, green grass spread far and wide, surrounded by hills.

Jon spotted Yeshi first in the arrivals hall and wondered where Karma was. A few seconds later, she appeared dragging two suitcases behind her.

"Hello Yeshi," Jon said, and proffered his hand. Yeshi shook it shyly with a smile.

Karma waited patiently for her turn. She couldn't wait to hug him. It had been six months since they had last seen each other.

"Hello darling," Jon said looking at her, and he handed her a bouquet of flowers.

"Thank you," Karma said, taking the flowers. In the past, she had never understood the gesture of giving flowers. *'What is the point?'* she used to think.

Now here she is in England. Jon buying her flowers made her feel wanted and important. If her life with Jon was going to be as beautiful as those flowers, she couldn't wait.

Let's see what our life together in England has to offer, she thought ecstatically

Printed in Great Britain
by Amazon